Insured Beyond The Grave:

Essays, Interviews & Dispatches
Volume 2

James Calemine

Snake Nation Press
Valdosta, Georgia

Insured Beyond the Grave:
Essays, Interviews & Dispatches, Volume 2
Copyright © 2018. James Calemine.

Printed and bound in the United States of America.

ISBN: 978-0-9979353-3-2 (Paperback)

Table of Contents

Introduction

> *"A man seeks his own destiny and no other, said the judge. Will or nill. Any man who could discover his own fate and elect therefore some opposite course could only come at last to that self-same reckoning at the same appointed time..."*
>
> — Cormac McCarthy

True words. If you're reading this book you'll understand Volume 2 picks up where Volume 1 left off. These works were published in various periodicals from the mid 90s to 2016, and looking back, I'm not surprised they hold up against time. These are strange and dangerous days—for all of us. The portraits of these artists were captured during an era when America existed in a different psychology. People don't buy books, records, or go to the movies like they used to; times have changed. So, if you're holding this book...it's by a grace on your part.

Historically, time proves rough on artists. However, if they complete their work, or some of it, they remain insured beyond the grave. This is also true for everyone else. Think of all the joy your favorite artists have given you. Think of these dark times, and how art serves as a inspirational vehicle to escape from these eerie realities.

Seventy different articles exist between these two volumes. Many artists you know and some you don't. The scope is wide; the shadow long. I believe all these luminaries should be explored and that served as the reason I wrote about them in the first place. It's interesting to see where they are now. Artists—or anyone for that matter—should be appreciated when they are alive. But, no one knows how much time they have on earth.

Death is a great career move for most artists, but that leaves the rest of us with only snapshots, songs, stories or memories. I should know. I'm an expert. As I wrote in Volume 1—which of course holds true here, and bears repeating: "I intended to operate where soul, excellence and timelessness existed as my only standards."

Ghosts run through these books, and if you pay close attention you'll meet their acquaintance. Each article provides a pure glimpse into the artist's soul. And maybe even your own. I hope, dear reader, you will find inspiration in these Volumes. After all, they are true American heroes...

— James Calemine
May 2018

Press

"James Calemine's heart and writing justify him being respected by anybody."

–Stanley Booth (True *Adventures of the Rolling Stones,*
Rythm (sic) Oil, Keith: Til I Roll Over Dead, Red Hot & Blue)

"James Calemine. That's a good name. I'll remember that name..."

— Harry Crews Author of *Florida Frenzy, Feast of Snakes,*
Blood & Grits, The Gospel Singer and others.

"James Calemine digs deep into the soul of rock & roll."

–Snake Nation Press

"*Insured Beyond The Grave* gives incredible insight into the Southern musical landscape. This collection from James Calemine is impressive to say the least."

—Tim Duffy, President of Music Maker Relief Foundation.

" I search to photograph musicians that inspire me—to capture an everlasting image that the artist exudes. Calemine does this with his pen. He seeks what we all seek in life; a deep insight into the inspirational music, film, literature and artists we admire, and find a truthful solace. And his words do just that. He preserves them forever through his own literary lens. Calemine nails these deep insights, soulful stories and resonating truths from the artist on every page of *Insured Beyond The Grave.*"

—Adam Smith, Documentary Photographer

"James Calemine knows his way around the South, around the region's music and musicians and authors and books, its food and its feel. And so much more, and you can feel it on every page of *Insured Beyond The Grave,* which shines light into the dark corners of famous musicians like the Black Crowes and Steve Cropper as well as underappreciated genius writers like Harry Crews and Stanley Booth. Great stuff on every page."

—Alan Paul, *New York Times* best-selling author of
One Way Out: The Inside History of the Allman Brothers Band.

"Insured Beyond The Grave is an endlessly fascinating collection of conversations with some of my all-time favorite writers and musicians. I felt I was right there on the barstool eavesdropping."

—Ace Atkins, *New York Times* Best-selling author of *The Fallen*

"Insured Beyond The Grave Volume One is one of the best books of 2017."

—Michael "Buffalo" Smith, Author of
Capricorn Rising, My Kind of Country and *Rebel Yell.*

"James Calemine's writing executes a perfect balance of soul to science, flourish to frankness, and imagery to movement. His writing reveals awareness of intracacies of life-the human experience with a 'lifted experience'."

—Eleanor Underhill (Underhill Rose)

"James Calemine is one of my favorite writers."

—Todd Nance (Widespread Panic, Interstellar Boys)

"It's certainly not inappropriate to describe James Calemine as a rare poet, even when he's working in prose...but ultimately the categories don't matter. All that matters are the words themselves, and James' words are high octane, electric, signigicant. I'll go ahead and say it: He's one of our great living American writers, and that's a sure bet."

—Daniel Hutchens (Bloodkin)

"James Calemine is a seeker of truth...which makes him a good friend of mine."

—Marc Ford (The Black Crowes, Ben Harper, Magpie Salute)

Bob Dylan's *Renaldo and Clara:*
Asleep In The Tomb

In 2016, Bob Dylan won the Nobel Prize for literature. Dylan's buried film, Renaldo and Clara still remains unreleased. The film hit theatres at the same time as Martin Scorsese's documentary about The Band called The Last Waltz, where Dylan made an appearance. I obtained a bootleg copy of Renaldo and Clara in a video store in Atlanta's Little Five Points during 1997. I wrote this article for Hittin' The Note the following year. One can only hope this film classic will see the light of day.

"I've been double-crossed for the very last time And now I'm finally free."

—*"Idiot Wind"* Bob Dylan

IN AN AGE OF DVD, reissued classics emerge every so often. For those aficionados seeking obscure music cinema, Bob Dylan's *Renaldo & Clara,* a film he wrote, directed, and produced, remains an unburied treasure. *Renaldo & Clara* contains threads of traditional southern music throughout this film. Dylan's cinematic epic, originally released in theatres in 1978, unfortunately exists only as a rare bootleg in the mainstream world of rock and roll films. *Renaldo & Clara* remains Bob Dylan's classic subterranean film. Dylan intended the four-hour movie to be twice as long, considering the filming process for *Renaldo & Clara* began with Dylan's Rolling Thunder Revue tour in 1975, and continued for nearly two years. This enigmatic motion picture features an all-star cast, including Ronnie Hawkins, Harry Dean

Stanton, Roger McGuinn, Allen Ginsberg, Sam Shepard, Ronee Blakley, David Blue, Sara Dylan, Joan Baez, Arlo Guthrie, Ramblin' Jack Elliott, Bobby Neuwirth, Scarlet Rivera, Mel Howard, Rob Stoner, T-Bone Burnett, Helena Kallianiotes, Mick Ronson, Steven Soles, Luther Rix, and David Mansfield. It's a wonder such an obscure gem remains buried in a vault.

Renaldo & Clara operates deeps beneath the surface compared to other films involving Dylan, such as *Don't Look Back, Eat the Document, The Concert for Bangladesh, Sam Peckinpah's Pat Garrett & Billy the Kid*, and the disastrous *Hearts of Fire*. The film's narrative weaves a mysterious musical and visual chronicle of Dylan's traveling medicine show during a time when America celebrated its bicentennial anniversary. Dylan biographer, Robert Shelton, wrote about the movie: "The finished film, running nearly four hours, became a candidate for commercial suicide. It was a complex, often non-communicative film that was triumph musically but a dramatic failure."

In 1978, *Renaldo & Clara* confused critics, and most gave the film low marks. Somewhat disturbed by the criticism, Dylan said, "Reading the reviews of the movie, I sensed a feeling of them wanting to crush things. Those reviews weren't about the movie. They were just an excuse to get at me for one reason or another. I was disappointed that the critics couldn't get beyond the superficial elements. They thought the movie was all about Bob Dylan, Joan Baez, Sara Dylan…and it wasn't."

In the movie's opening concert footage, Dylan wears a clear rubber mask while leading the Rolling Thunder Revue through a swirling version of "When I Paint My Masterpiece." This masked stage appearance seems strange, even for Dylan. Filmed in an atmosphere of improvisation, the movie alternates between scenes of intense live performances and abstruse vignettes providing an interesting collection of images. Perhaps while playing "Alias" in Sam Peckinpah's great 1973 western *Pat Garrett & Billy the Kid*, Dylan (who wrote the film's soundtrack) absorbed certain cinematic techniques from the legendary maverick filmmaker. Some of the grainy film's best shots capture austere landscapes, railroads, churches, graveyards, and rivers, accompanied by an undeniable soundtrack. An early scene filmed from a train window reveals a desolate winter landscape covered with snow at sunset, echoed by a lonesome fiddle and piano version of Dylan singing Hank Williams' "Kawliga."

Another interesting live performance scene shows Dylan wearing eerie white face paint during an intense, theatrical version of "Isis." Dylan plays harmonica and roves the stage without his guitar like a medicine man orchestrating a band of musical gypsies. The Rolling Thunder musicians, mostly from New York, served as Dylan's band for the studio albums *Desire* and *Street Legal*. The musicians included Rob Stoner, bass; Steven Soles, rhythm guitar; Bobby Neuwirth, rhythm guitar; Roger McGuinn, twelve-string guitar; Mick Ronson, lead guitar; David Mansfield, violin, dobro, and pedal steel; T-Bone Burnett, rhythm guitar; Howie Wyeth, drums; Luther Rix, percussion; and Scarlet Rivera, electric violin. Dylan discovered Rivera walking the streets of New York and asked her to join his band on the spot. Dylan released a live album, *Hard Rain*, involving the Rolling Thunder Revue musicians. After completing *Renaldo & Clara*, the next underrated studio album, *Street Legal*, foreshadowed Dylan's Christian albums that were mostly recorded in Muscle Shoals, Alabama.

Sara Dylan, Bob's ex-wife, appears throughout the movie. From the time filming began in 1975 to its release in 1978, the Dylans suffered a bitter divorce, soaking the film with irony, considering Sara Dylan's paradoxical role as "Clara" in the film as Joan Baez's rival. The movie operates on a delicate balance between fiction and nonfiction. In a 1977 interview, Dylan spoke about *Renaldo & Clara*: "Let's say that in real life Bob Dylan fixes his name on the public. He can retrieve that name at will. Anything else the public made of it is its own business. The film is no puzzle, it's A-B-C-D, but the compositions are like a game – the red flower; the hat, the red and blue themes. The interest is not in literal plot but in the associated texture—colors, images, sounds.

Ronnie Hawkins and Ronee Blakley portray Mr. & Mrs. Dylan in the film. In a kitsch motel lobby press attack, a clueless reporter asks Hawkins, "Who is the real Bob Dylan?" and Hawkins replies, "A hero of the highest order." Connections from Dylan's past represent another cultural and personal layer in the film. Dylan stole The Band (then the Hawks) from Ronnie Hawkins years earlier. At most of the venues where the Rolling Thunder Revue played to a sold out house, Dylan and the Hawks had endured booing crowds a decade before.

Later, the film progresses onto a scene involving a contemporary Iroquois Indian town hall gathering. To Native Americans, Rolling Thunder translates into "speaking truth." At one point, Dylan walks through the crowd shaking men's hands, kissing an old woman on the cheek, and smiling at the children during a Thanksgiving celebration. The soundtrack transmits a soulful piano rendition of Dylan singing Curtis Mayfield's "People Get Ready."

The songs hold this dense film together. At least forty tracks performed in rehearsed, unreleased, and live arrangements bend the listener's ear during the uncut film version. At one point, a two-hour version of the movie circulated for television consisting mostly of live footage. Some of the Dylan compositions include "A Hard Rain's Gonna Fall", "I Want You," "It Ain't Me Babe," "Catfish," "Knockin' On Heaven's Door," "She Belongs Me," "Sara," "It Takes a Lot to Laugh, It Takes a Train to Cry," "If You See Her Say Hello," "Just Like a Woman," "Romance in Durango," "One Too Many Mornings," "One More Cup of Coffee," and "Sad Eyed Lady of the Lowlands," as well as songs by Baez, McGuinn, Elliot, and Blakely.

Dylan informed playwright Sam Shepard he wanted to create a film with an atmosphere resembling the French films *Children of Paradise* or *Shoot the Piano Player*. Shepard later published a book about the tour called *The Rolling Thunder Logbook*, but much of his work was discarded for *Renaldo & Clara*. Shepard later collaborated with Dylan in 1985 when they wrote "Brownsville Girl," an eleven-minute epic on Dylan's *Knocked Out Loaded* album. In a 1978 interview Dylan elaborated on the script situation: "*Renaldo & Clara* was originally intended as a more structured film, I hired playwright Sam Shepard to provide dialogue, but we didn't use much of his stuff because of a conflict of ideas."

Even though Shepard felt somewhat frustrated on the tour, he never doubted Dylan's musical talents. In his *Rolling Thunder Logbook*, Shepard described Dylan's power in a quiet hotel bar on that tour: "Dylan moves up on the platform to the rickety old upright piano used for years for the sole purpose of producing middle class pabulum Big Band sounds of the '30s and '40s. He sits, stabs his bony fingers into the ivories, and begins a pounding version of "Simple Twist of Fate." Here's where it's at. The Master Arsonist. The place is smoking within five minutes. The ladies are twitching deep within their corsets. The whole piano is shaking and seems on the verge of jumping right off the wooden platforms. Dylan's cowboy heel is driving a hole through the floor. Roger McGuinn appears with the guitar, then Neuwirth, and the whole band joins in until every molecule of air in the place is bursting. This is Dylan's true magic. Leave aside his lyrical genius for a second and just watch this transformation of energy which he carries…"

Dylan's grueling tour schedule added a complexity to the filming. Dylan edited some one hundred hours for *Renaldo & Clara*. In 1978 he said, "I knew it was not going to be a short movie because we couldn't tell that story in an hour. Originally I couldn't see how we could do it under seven or eight hours. But we subtracted songs and scenes and dialogue until we couldn't subtract anymore. There was a lot of chaos while we were making the film. A lot of good scenes didn't happen because we had already finished improvising by the time the cameras were ready to film. You can't recapture stuff like that. There was a lot of conflict during filming. We had people who didn't understand what we were doing because we didn't have a script. Some who didn't understand were willing to go along with us anyway. Others weren't and that hurt us. It hurt the film."

On another occasion Dylan told *Maclean's* magazine: "There's no way I should or could explain the movie…but I can't explain "Desolation Row" either…Sara (Dylan) and Joan Baez were the same woman…it's like a cubist painting. Maybe there are only two or three people in the universe who are going to understand what the movie's about."

In one scene, Sam Shepard and Sara Dylan portray a married couple in a transparent domestic setting, discussing staying together, having babies, and earthly strains between a man and a woman while Dylan's beagle dog sits next to Shepard on the couch. Subtle conflicts arise between man and woman throughout the film. After the Rolling Thunder tour, Shepard wrote a play called *Suicide In B Flat*. The play deals with an artist's death of his own self, a concept Dylan had in mind for *Renaldo & Clara*. "It's about the essence of a man being alienated from himself and how in order to free himself, to be reborn, he has to go outside himself. You can almost say that he dies in order to look at time and by strength of the will return to the same body…"

David Mansfield wrote soundtracks for the movies *Heaven's Gate* and *The Apostle*, and at seventeen years old played violin, pedal steel, and dobro in Dylan's Rolling Thunder Revue. Recently, Mansfield told *On the Tracks* magazine about *Renaldo & Clara*: "Bob owns it lock, stock, and barrel. He distributed it himself, I think with his brother's help. It played on the BBC and some other places, so there are tapes floating around, like check air tapes. To a certain degree the film, as a dramatic piece, was sort of conceptualized after the fact. Bob asked Sam Shepard to come along to be the writer of the film. Sam got out on the road and was thoroughly confused and bewildered because it was unlike any other gig he had before as a writer. He became a participant like everybody else. As I gathered—and I think I'm right about this—it seemed somebody would come up with an idea and say, 'Okay, let's grab the crew and go do it!' It was all extemporaneous, and consequently, on the technical level, there were never any reverses or reverse angles, because it was just one handheld camera for the dramatic sequences. I mean really for me, more than anything else, it's like a very surreal home movie documentary, an extemporaneous psychodrama."

Joni Mitchell appears briefly in the film. Although she played a more prominent role on the Rolling Thunder Tour than *Renaldo & Clara* revealed, Mitchell really shined in Martin Scorsese's *The Last Waltz*, which eventually coincided with the release of Dylan's film. In Levon Helm's book, *This Wheel's On Fire*, he mentioned Dylan's reluctance to be filmed the night The Band recorded *The Last Waltz*: "I wasn't that surprised, Howard Alk had been saying all week it wasn't going to work because Bob didn't want to compete with himself having *The Last Waltz* and *Renaldo & Clara* go head to head…"

A sad mood guides *Renaldo & Clara* like an undercurrent, evident in a desolate silent shot of a marble angel located in a graveyard under bare winter trees outlined against the pale blue sky scattered with pink and gray clouds as a distant piano version of Dylan singing "In the Pines" lingers over the screen. Dylan's epic overloads the viewer with mysterious images, scenes, characters, and songs throughout this dense film. In one moment, a shot pans quickly from a mad preacher shouting his sermon at a crowd gathered on the street to a live-shot of the Rolling Thunder's swirling and reckless sound sending Dylan out on a desperate fringe in white face paint, singing, "Where have you been, my blue-eyed son?"

A certain vaudeville intensity masks *Renaldo & Clara*. Cinematic qualities of the film's theatrical dynamic resemble Ingmar Bergman's *The Magician*, or the silent frames call to mind Federico Fellini's *8 ½*. Yet, even in its glorious self-indulgence, the film operates on a humble appreciation for beauty in the ordinary.

An interlude of *Renaldo & Clara* concentrates on actual footage of boxer Rubin "Hurricane" Carter bidding for a new trial for release from prison, inspiring Dylan's song "Hurricane," Carter tells the story of Dylan coming to visit him in prison on a special trip from France after receiving Carter's book, *The Sixteenth Round*. Dylan then organized a concert for Carter at Madison Square Garden. Shepard wrote in his *Logbook*, "It is billed as a benefit, and it's for sure that the public interest generated by the presence of Muhammad Ali and Dylan in the same space is going to leak down to the New Jersey jailhouse and work its own kind of leverage on the law. Already the papers are talking about reprieves and retrials, and there's no doubt that this event will add some muscle to the whole cause."

Harry Dean Stanton (an old Peckinpah actor-friend) surfaces out of nowhere in the film, strolling down an anonymous street in a conspicuous manner. Soon, he's singing and kissing Baez in a scene where Renaldo trades his woman for a horse. Beat poet Allen Ginsberg also appears throughout the film. Ginsberg traveled with the Rolling Thunder Revue, and the beat writer serves as another dimension in *Renaldo & Clara*, saluting that American literary tradition Dylan admired. In one unforgettable scene, Dylan and Ginsberg read from Jack Kerouac's work while standing over his grave. For faithful fans and scholars, this one scene redeems years spent searching for this rare film. Ginsberg points down and asks Dylan: "Is that what's gonna happen to you?"

"No, I want to be in an unmarked grave." Dylan responded.

In such scenes, a stark clarity impresses upon the viewer a rare glimpse into Dylan's soulful cinematic intention, especially when he sings:

> *Tell me what will you do when Jesus comes?*
> *Tell me what will you do when Jesus comes?*
> *Will you kick him out in the street?*
> *Will you drive him out in the heat?*
> *Tell me what will you do when Jesus comes?*

A final confrontational scene culminates between the Dylan, Baez, and Sara Dylan characters, reminding the viewer of a thin line between an artist's life and his work. Possibly the most viewed clip from *Renaldo & Clara* remains the last live performance scene in the film, with Dylan playing "Tangled Up in Blue" solo on an acoustic guitar. The infamous close shot reveals Dylan's painted white face, and every once in awhile his wild blue eyes peer out from under the gray hat with a red flower in the brim, projecting direct intensity.

Perhaps one day Dylan will decide to release *Renaldo & Clara*, especially in this golden age of DVD, but it's doubtful. Unheard versions of old Dylan songs and his choice of cover tunes render the film a classic. After searching for a copy of Dylan's buried film, for ten years (conjuring a certain thrill searching for something so elusive all those years). I obtained a mid-grade full-length version in 1997 in Atlanta. Perhaps this obscure movie satisfies only avid collectors, bootleg freaks, film aficionados, and Dylan fanatics. If you ever get your hands on a copy of *Renaldo & Clara*, you'll scratch your head wondering how long this mysterious musical vaudeville must remain asleep in the tomb.

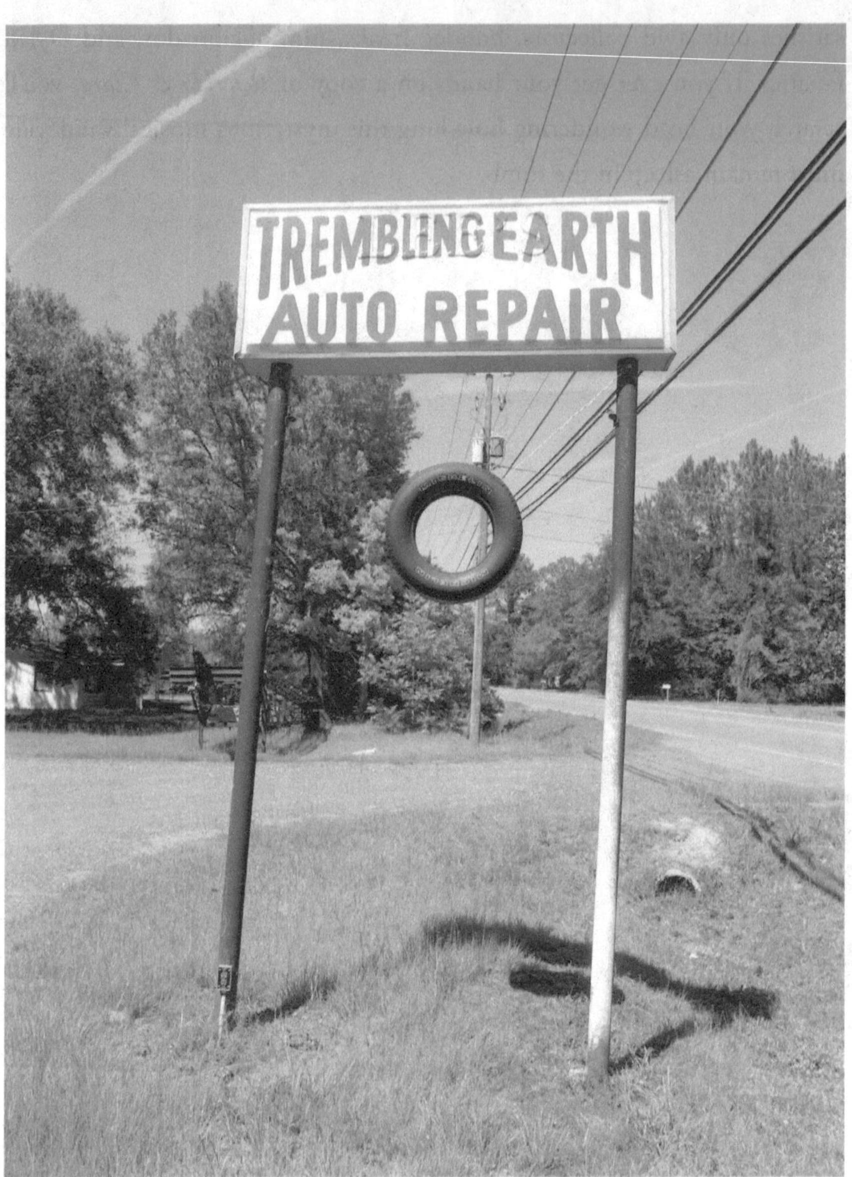

Trembling Earth Auto Sign

The Chuck Leavell Interview:
A Rolling Stone & Tree Farmer

*In 2008, the Athens, Georgia, band, Widespread Panic, was in-
ducted into The Georgia Music Hall of Fame. I was commissioned
to write Panic's official induction into The Hall of Fame Almanac
that year Mr. Leavell and I talked about the ceremony at first. Then
we decided later to go on the record regarding Chuck's latest ongo-
ings. At the time, Chuck was on his tree farm outside of Macon
and I was calling from my home in Atlanta. At presstime, Leavell
is rehearsing with the Rolling Stones for their Europe 2018 tour.*

*"The cultivation of trees is the cultivation of the good, the beautiful
and the ennobling in man."*

— J. Sterling Morton

James Calemine: Hey Chuck.

Chuck Leavell: Hey man. Howya doin? Your timing is good, you want to
talk? (Chuck tells his dogs to load up). I'm just running my dogs here—I'm
piddlin' and riding around on my place.

Getting any rain down there?

CL: Well, we've been getting fair rain. None in the recent days. I don't
think it's gonna affect us. They say 50 percent tomorrow, but I think that's
optimistic. Thursday we might have a better chance.

Tell me about your new website.

CL: It is *The Mother Nature Network*. Eventually we'll be known as MNN. com, that's what we're pushing for the website. It's the brainchild of my partner Joel Babbit—I guess you read that AJC article. Basically, Joel came to me. Joel and I met through a mutual friend, Dan Beason. We had a nice lunch about five years ago. We liked each other's company. We stayed in touch and then one day I called him because I was looking to get some advice on a project I have called, *Love of the Land,* which will eventually be a television program. Joel helped me with that and we became closer. Then he calls me one day and he told me he wanted me to look at something. He had a powerpoint presentation covering all the Green websites out there. Then he said he represented too many different companies, and all of them want this image and they all do truly want to do better for their companies and their employees to be Greener and more eco-friendly, and more energy conscience, but there's a lack of somewhere to go to get good information. He took me through all the existing sites, and he felt like there was a void where we could provide a valuable service to the general public as well as allowing these companies to have a place to go and tell their story. So, it looked incredible to me when he gave me the presentation. Then I said I think you're right. I'm out there giving speeches and interacting with politicians on forest policy. I'm sitting on a couple of boards.

(President) Bush recognized your work.

CL: That's nice. Actually, that particular situation had to do with the Healthy Forest Restoration Bill, which I'm glad was passed. It was a positive thing for forestry. Anyway, I realized Joel was right. He said he'd really like me in on this, and I said you got it. We've started this thing. As you know, we've had some very strong backing—some very smart, powerful, intelligent and caring investors on our team. We have good content people – we're building the company. We have Glick International helping us build the site. Everything is getting closer and closer. We don't have an exact launch date yet, but we will soon. Certainly we want to do quite a push to let people know about this by the fi rst of the year.

I have to say your *Forever Green* book is a definitive book about trees, wood—it should be in schools.

CL: Well, I appreciate that, James. The book has been out for quite some time now. I worked very hard on that project. I wanted it to be accurate, thoughtful and hopefully entertaining pictures of forestry in America—where we've been—where we are now—where we're going. It's probably time for an update on that thing. It's continued to do well. It's been translated into German, and released in Germany and Austria. That really ties into my new CD—*Live In Germany*—Because the tour was designed not only to place music but to discuss these issues in a public forum in Germany, and we did that—it was very successful.

The musicians were all German, right?

CL: That's right, all of them. Tim, the Stones' horn guy, helped me find the band. Tim played with me on the *Southscape* record, but he was not on the Germany record—it's a German sax player. Anyways, it was a marvelous experience—both musically and helping to address the environmental issues and concerns. We made more friends and met more interesting people. I'm sure this relationship will continue and I'll be going back to Germany and doing other things in the future. Now, it's catching on here in the States and I've been able to do some shows to promote the CD and I've enjoyed that. I've tried to be clever about the outreach and do radio programs and TV interviews and also in print—like yourself—and let the people know that I've got something out there. I've been able to do some shows connected to it and have fun with that. Now, I do want to mention I have a Christmas CD you're probably aware of...

I am....

CL: This is the tenth anniversary of *What's In That Bag*. So, we're going to be celebrating that. We have the tenth anniversary re-release of *What's In That Bag*, and I'm hoping to maybe do some shows to help promote both CDs through November and December. Keep your fingers crossed. Talk to your friends and support live music (laughs)!

The packaging on the new CD is killer. Talk about that a little bit—it's all recyclable.

CL: Thanks for that very much. The last several CDs that I've done—being the environmentalist and trying to maintain that angle—they've all been as eco-friendly as possible. They're using paper products, recyclable materials, trying to keep a low foot-print carbon in the making of each CD.

It is more difficult to produce these CDs? Is it more of a pain?

CL: It requires…I wouldn't call it a pain because it's a labor of love, but I would say it requires some extra effort to do it, I enjoy it. To put together a nice little story of what that experience was all about. I think it's important for the public to get a better feel for what it was. I appreciate your comment man, because we worked hard to make it good.

The music is very complex music.

CL: Well, I hope it has a sophisticated feel. I appreciate that thought as well, James, because these guys were very talented and they are very stud-ied musicians that worked hard to get where they are. To be able to bring them on board—it just put such an interesting twist on my music and on the rock and boogie playing that I normally do. As far as the set list is concerned it's a retrospective of my career. That's who I am. I've been fortunate to work with these people—The Stones, George Harrison and Clapton—it's been a joy, an honor to work with such high caliber artists. To be able to do my version of some of their music that I've been privileged to play and be on and then mix it up with things I more personally attached to like *Sea Level*—those songs and my own more recent music. Then also a couple things for fun like the "Wee Wee Hour" song that was a classic Professor Longhair. Compared to what was an important record for me with Les McCann and Eddie Harris from the Swiss Movement album *Live at Montreux*. So, that's what it's all about. It's being grateful for the career that I've had, and bring it all together and having some fun.

Your book, *Between Rock and a Home Place*, is really one of the best books written by a musician.

CL: I appreciate it. I wrote that book when I was turning 50 thinking that was an interesting time to reflect back and look at some of the things I've done. I'd been fairly good about keeping some kind of journal, or speaking into the tape recorder and written diary. I had the resource there which was very important and then my good friend I have to compliment Jeff Craig, my co-writer, J. Marshall Craig, Jeff's friend. I felt like I needed an outside perspective to help tell the story so he worked very hard and I thought did a good job to help me verbalize and really tell the story in a way that would be interesting. We talked about doing it in just chronological order, that's the easy way out. We figured well why not start at the last big event, which was the last show of the Stones tour. Then coming off the Stones tour and getting back home. Then typing all that stuff in and then going back and looking at it. So, I appreciate the kind words on that. It was a lot of work…

Indelible facts. The *Forever Green* contains great facts--like wood is an ingredient in toothpaste.

CL: (Laughs) Well, you know cellulose is used in so many different products in one form or another. It's a coagulant. People don't think about that but it's true. That's a good thing. It's a natural organic product. It's a good thing that cellulose! It's the preferred filler in coagulant in some of these materials—that's good. You don't want synthetic or chemically enhanced products. It surprises a lot of people all the things that trees are used for. Another category that is often neglected or overlooked is the mineral cleaning agents that come from the saps of trees. Now we're talking about using trees for energy. There's a lot of cellulosic….there's a lot of discussion about cellulosic material to be used to make ethanol and other liquid energy products to help reduce the petroleum dependents. There's also a lot of talk about woody biomass to be used for making natural gas and even making electricity. I'm very happy to see this because quite frankly those of us that are family forest landowners need markets for our wood. These are new markets and this helps us to pay the taxes on our land and helps us to keep these lands in our families. Right now, quite frankly, it's a depressed time for forestry. You've seen the loss of a great deal of paper pulp and paper mills across the country in the past ten years. A lot of that business-like many other businesses—have move offshore. That has created a lack of market for those of us that are growing these trees. So we need a market especially for that young wood. What we call juvenile wood.

Is the forestry situation as desperate as it seems to the general person in the street who might have a moderate interest in the subject?

CL: Look, quite honestly, it's remarkable that we have what we do have. The fact is that right now in America we have as much forest cover now as we had 100 years ago. How incredible is that given the fact that the population has tripled in that time, too. That says number one we are doing a good job now managing resources. The thing to point out there is that they majority of the forests in our country are owned privately as opposed to shall we say Canada that 95% of the lands there are owned by what they call the crown—the government. It's a totally different system. We believe that private ownership is essential for the best management of the forests. So we like talking about family forestry. We like talking about keeping lands intact. We like keeping families on the land. So that's the good news. But—are there pressures in that situation. I like to talk about the unusable forest health crisis; when I mean by that is we're losing in the Southeast from Virginia down to east Texas approximately a million acres a year to growth and development—strip malls, residential sections…all the above. Therefore, that's the reason for the impetus of me new book that I am just now beginning and will probably take six months or so to wrap up and hopefully get out in that time. I will be working on those issues. That's a great concern. Now look James, we're gonna have this growth. It's not like we can press a button and make it stop. What you got to go is grow in the right way. You have to really be sensitive to what's out there. That's why we put these efforts forth so the public better understands. That was the reason for *Forever Green*. That will be the reason for the new one. It's the same thing for the children's book. It starts with young people and as they grow they need to be learning about these issues. Your question is is it being done that's my concern. In some places people, governments and communities and developers have been sensitive to the issues but in to many cases they have not been sensitive. That's why I want to beat this thing home. I want to drill it into people's heads that we have to growing in the right way.

You wife's family has owned that land you're living on before Sherman burned through Georgia.

CL: The land that we live on goes back to the 1930s. Some of the land that Rose Lane's family touches goes back to the King George III land grant. There's a heritage of ownership—a stewardship of the land. There's a lot of history and it's interesting. My wife is very knowledgeable that means she pays attention to what's going on now. It's really because of her that I'm doing this.

So we got this Widespread Panic induction coming up Saturday. I wrote their bio for the book and you're inducting them.

CL: I have the utmost respect for these guys. Of course, I became aware of them I guess around the time they signed with Capricorn. Phillip Walden— that was his pet project and he believed in them so strongly fand he brought them to the label. They became an integral part of the label. They were one of the most important artists there. I remember seeing the guys up in Johnny Sandlin's studio in Alabama. We began to know each other a little bit. They would play a show here and a show there and they'd write to come and I'd go and sit in. And this went on for a number of years and still goes on. Then, of course, also in that process my best friend Buck Williams becomes their agent rep-resentative as well as a co-manager for the band. That brought us a little closer I suppose. The relationship just goes on. I have such an admiration for these guys. To me, I would compare it something similar to the Rolling Stones, and that is their work ethic. The guys are constantly working with their nose to the grindstone—writing songs, doing shows, touring, interacting, coming up with new ideas—innovation, using a horn section – they have Randall in there. The personnel has changed. They've also—like the Stones and other bands—face tragedy, the loss of Mikey was a horrible thing for them. I'm sure there's been other trials and tribulations they've overcome, but the main thing has always been the music—moving forward.

They never really sold out to the record companies.

CL: Absolutely true. They have integrity. They've remained true to themselves. They've proven that they have a special brand and blend that people like—and I like it. The other thing I would point out that's been remarkable in their career is the appreciation from the younger crowd—the college students and the way that has continued. Even college students of today—and college students 15 years ago loved the band. Every year they appeal to that crowd. I think that's a very important part of their success.

Give folks a sense of the website, Mother Nature Network's mission statement.

CL: There are a lot of environmental websites out there—over 6200. My partner, Joel Babbit, and I did quite a lot of research about this back when we were exploring the idea of MNN, some two years ago, but we could not find a site that we felt 1) spoke in a voice that the average person could really understand, 2) was comprehensive and covered all aspects of environmental issues, and 3) was well designed, easy to navigate and didn't have all those distracting flash ads, pop up banners and such. So we decided to build what we felt people were searching for. Our mission was to build an environmental site that would be accurate and well vetted; have content that people were yearning for so they could make changes in their lives that would reduce the impact on our planet; present the content in a classy and easily digestible format, and in general be a pleasant experience for the visitor.

Talk about working with The University of Georgia's Agriculture Department. Any experiences you'd like to share regarding the good folks of UGA?

CL: Well, I've been involved with UGA for some three decades or so. My wife, Rose Lane, and I sponsor a scholarship at the Warnell School of Forest and Natural Resources, and have many friends up in Athens that work at UGA. The Agriculture Department is top notch and has been a source of innovation and research here in the south and beyond as has the Warnell School. Georgians should be very proud of what UGA has to offer in these fields. We have many friends up in Athens that work at UGA. They have some of the most talented folks in the world working there in all aspects of the outdoors.

Any latest tree farming developments? Legislation? Good news?

CL: Good news and challenges. Our markets have fallen sharply in recent years, which is disturbing. Family forest landowners like me and Rose Lane... as well as industrial and institutional tree farmers need a good reason to keep our lands in trees...and if we can't get a reasonable price for our natural, organic product, the sad truth is that much of it will be converted to de-velopment. There is a saying among us tree farmers that "asphalt is the last rotation." I don't think any of us want to see us lose these forests....but they are indeed at risk. I call this the "invisible forest health crisis". Here in the south, we've been losing about a million acres a year to growth and develop-ment. That is a tremendous number and very disturbing. On the upside... there has been quite a lot of research and discussion about possible new markets. Carbon sequestration, biomass for energy, ecosystem services like clean water, clean air, recreation, home and shelter for wildlife, etc. Congress will likely be taking up some of these issues soon, and if they do it right, there is hope for keeping forests in forests. But if they miss the mark....then we'll continue to see this "crisis of conversion" continue. So I guess I would say that we are hopeful for good news.

Any plans for writing any other books? Music or children's?

CL: Yes, I'm in the process of writing a new book called *Smart, Strong and Sustainable* that will be about these above men-tioned growth issues. My writing partner, Jeff Craig, and I have gone out and looked for some positive models for the growth we will experience. We've been researching ways that we can deal with growth that will have the lowest possible impact on the environment. We're about halfway through our first draft...so it will be a while before it's published...perhaps by late spring or early summer. As for music, my next project will be a tribute to pioneering piano players...mostly pre-WWII blues players...but reaching a bit beyond that.

Will you play any holiday shows for the 11th year release of your Christmas CD?

CL: I have only a couple. One is a homecoming show in Tuscaloosa, Alabama, where I grew up. It will be at the recently renovated BAMA Theater, and I'll be backed up by the Randall Bramblett Band. That is on Nov. 20. The other is a solo show in Stuart, FL. at the Lyric Theater...that's on Nov 28. Both should be lots of fun, and I look forward to them.

Any upcoming Stones plans? Solo plans?

CL: The Stones have been idle for over two years now...so while I can't say definitively, I have to believe the band would want to work in 2010. But of course that is totally up to them. I think they have been wise to sit on the sidelines for a while, but I can say that I am personally getting anxious to get back together... and I hope they feel the same. We'll just have to wait and see. As for me doing further solo shows into 2010, that will largely depend on

Stone's plans. I am considering doing some things in the spring of next year. Again, a wait and see.

Give some of the latest news and pertinent information on Charlane Plantation.

CL: We continue to manage our forest and wildlife...but because of the down market, are not harvesting anything now. We do have some areas that are prime for a first time thinning, and I would like to get to that next year if possible. It's like weeding the garden....when you do a first thinning,you open up the forest stand so that the remaining trees grow stronger and better..and the wildlife tends to use it more. We did do some thinning a little over a year ago, and those stands look fantastic now. We've had great rain this year...and at present (Nov of 2009) we have about a 10-inch surplus. That is really good news. The wildlife population is in great shape here...lots of black bear, white tail deer, wild turkey, quail, waterfowl, songbirds and such. So all in all, we are blessed.

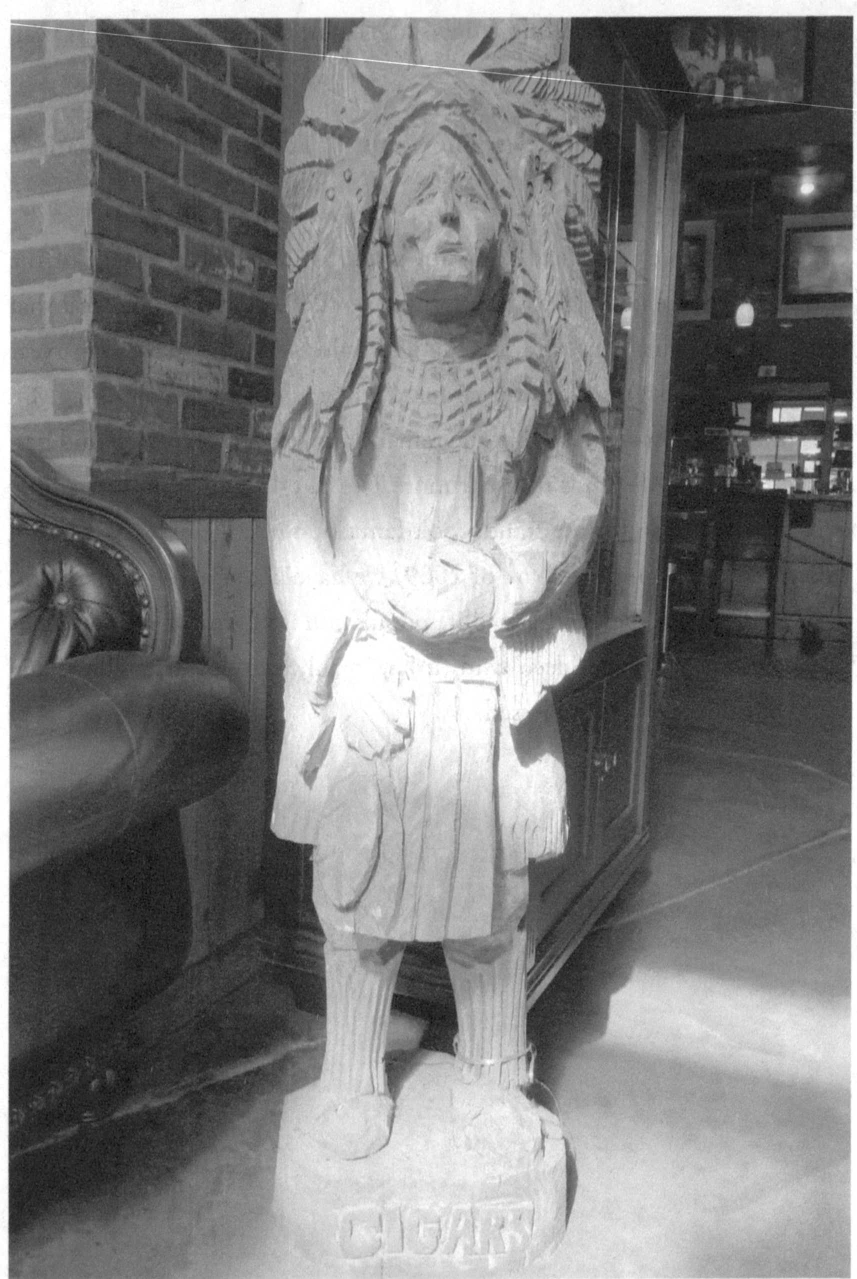

Wooden Indian

Zora Neale Hurston: *Tell My Horse*

ALABAMA BORN AUTHOR ZORA Neale Hurston wrote, *Tell My Horse: Voodoo And Life In Haiti and Jamaica*, in 1938. The vivid stories reveal how voodoo is interwoven within the cultures. It's a strange tale. *Tell My Horse* exists as a first hand guide—Hurston experienced most of the stories she wrote to the power voodoo wields in these countries as well as unforgettable photos, drawings and illustrations. Also included in this book are political outlines, song lyrics and even an eerie recipe for poisoning an enemy by using lizards, spiders, dust of bamboo, black sage and other unsettling ingredients.

Her family moved to Florida when she was a young girl. Hurston wrote short stories, novels and folklore. In her story "Black Death" she wrote of a "hoodoo doctor" in Eatonville, FL. Her novels included *Jonah's Gourd Vine, Mules & Men, Tell My Horse* and *Their Eyes Were Watching God.* Hurston, a dedicated folklorist and anthropologist, called folklore "the boiled down juice of human living." All her works represent folklore, and especially the mythological rural South. Hurston was also a singer, her best known rendition—"Crow Dance"—which is a 'story' of the sacred African buzzard swooping to eat and flying away. She ranks as a great American storyteller.

Chapter titles of *Tell My Horse* reveal the fertile soil of where Hurston participated in the studies of voodoo's weird mysteries: "The Rooster's Nest.", "Curry Goat", "Hunting the Wild Hog", "Night Song After Death", "Women in the Caribbean", "Rebirth of a Nation", "The Next Hundred Years", "The Black Joan of Arc", "Death of Leconte", "Voodoo and Voodoo Gods", "Isle de la Gonave", "Arcahaie and What It Means", "Zombies", "Sect Rouge", "Parlay Cheval Ou *(Tell My Horse)*", "Graveyard Dirt and

Other Poisons", "Doctor Reser" and "God and the Pintards". The book also contains songs of worship to Voodoo gods…

Ishmael Reed wrote in the book's introduction: "…But *Tell My Horse*, the result of Hurston's travels to Jamaica and Haiti, is more than a Voodoo work. She writes intelligently about the botany, sociology, anthropology, geology and politics of these nations in a style that is devoid of pompous jargon and accessible to the general reader. It is an entertaining book."

If you want a firsthand, authentic account of real voodoo… then pick up a copy of *Tell My Horse*.

Charlie Musselwhite Interview:
The Master of Smokestack Lightning

John Lee Hooker served as best man at Charlie Musselwhite's wedding. That speaks volumes regarding Musselwhite. Musselwhite continues recording in this day and age even though his career began with some of the country's seminal bluesman. This Master of Smokestack Lightning interview documents the musical odyssey of a true American bluesman.

During his career, Musselwhite has earned 11 Grammy nomi-nations. In 2014, Musselwhite won a Grammy with Ben Harper for their album Get Up! His resume is an impressive and long read. His latest record, No Mercy In This Land, another collaboration with Ben Harper, hit stores March 30, 2018.

"I'm ready as anybody could be..."

—Muddy Waters

MISSISSIPPI NATIVE, CHARLIE MUSSELWHITE, has been called "the greatest living harmonica player". Musselwhite would never say such a thing, but it seems true. Musselwhite grew up in Kosciusko, Mississippi. His family moved to Memphis, Tennessee, when he was ten. At an early age, Musselwhite learned to play harmonica and guitar. He kicked around Memphis for years lis-tening to all sorts of blues, country and gospel music.

In the early sixties Musselwhite moved to Chicago where he met and played with blues greats such as Muddy Waters, Little Walter, Robert Nighthawk and many others. Musselwhite played an instrumental role in the Chicago blues scene where he met Mike Bloomfield, Big Joe Turner and Sonny Boy Williamson in local clubs.

In 1967, Musselwhite played his first gig on the West Coast at the veritable San Francisco theatre, The Fillmore. Here Musselwhite learned the blues was a strange animal to California, and that one could make a living playing music up and down the coast of The Golden State. Musselwhite even persuaded the great John Lee Hooker to move to California. Hooker and Musselwhite became friends in Chicago. They recorded on the others' albums, and John Lee Hooker served as best man at Charlie Musselwhite's wedding. Musselwhite is a great storyteller. His latest album contains a spoken word ditty called "Black Water" concerning the Hurricane Katrina disaster.

Musselwhite will also appear in a film later this year called *The Pig Hunt*, a modern day horror film. We conducted this interview a few days before he went out on the road. He talked about growing up in Memphis, Memphis radio, hanging out with Elvis, the early days of rockabilly, jamming with Muddy Waters and his entire career up to this point. Charlie Musselwhite is one of the last players linked to those purveying blues masters. He's also played with Ben Harper, The Blind Boys of Alabama, Luther Dickinson and Tom Waits in recent years as he continues bringing his singular music mojo to many folks.

You grew up in Kosciusko, Mississippi.

CM: I was born there in 1944. We moved to Memphis in 1947. I moved to Memphis in 1947, but I continued spending many of my summers in Kosciusko and other parts of Mississippi staying with different relatives. So, there's always that strong connection. I still have relatives there.

You still own property in Mississippi.

CM: I have a building in Clarksdale right on the Sunflower River. Right outside Kosciusko is the old Musselwhite cemetery—back when that was the West.

Indians still owned the land.

CM: See, Kosciusko was right on the Natchez Trace. The Natchez Trace was really the first highway. It went from Nashville down to Natchez, Mississippi. People would go down that and back up the river. It was an old, old trail. The first settlers learned from the Indians. That's why Kosciusko is there. It's right on the Natchez Trace.

Talk about your early musical paths. I know you got your first guitar at 13, but what are some of your earliest musical memories?

CM: Well, there were always harmonicas around. My dad played guitar and mandolin. My mother played piano in church. There was an uncle that had a one man band. There were a lot of people that played music, but not professionally. I run into Musselwhite's all over the place in Europe, Canada—wherever they settled and most all of them I run into are musical. So, I guess it's genetic.

Indeed. So, of course instruments are always around and music is being played so it's natural.

CM: Yes, when I was 13 my dad gave me his guitar. I was already playing the harmonica. I never remember not having a harmonica. They were always around. But anyway, at the beginning I was just a little kid making up kids tunes. I wasn't thinking about anything. I'd take it out in the woods with me and make up stuff.

What were you hearing at the time? Memphis radio—from what I understand—was a powerful medium.

CM; Memphis radio was great. Still today—it's the best gospel music you'll find on the radio. They play church services. Back then—I guess still—tent meetings were held in the summertime. I didn't go in them, but I liked to hang around outside where you could drink beer and listen to the music. They would roll up the sides of the tent because it was too hot to keep them down. You could watch and listen and you could be part of it without having to actually go inside. Memphis radio was really cool. You had Dewey Phillips, Rufus Thomas—you had black radio, white radio, rockabilly was just getting started around there. Johnny Dorsey Burnette lived across the street from me. There were garage bands all over the place. There was music all around. There were a lot of street singers in Memphis. Downtown you'd see guys playing on the corner for tips—blues singers. There was no end to the music.

You were in a good place to see the Memphis music scene unfold. Sun Records...

CM: Yeah and it was all over the radio. Rockabilly was the deal. You could hear a band playing and just follow the sound. You'd come to some drug store or maybe a used car lot and they'd have a band playing. Often it would be in that style of rockabilly.

There was another guy that lived in the neighborhood named Slim Rhodes and he'd set up in his yard and have a barbecue and all the neighbors could come over and eat and listen to him play. And I was aware—I liked everything—of jazz, country, blues, rockabilly music. Today when I hear country music—or what they call country music just sounds like pop music to me. I like the old country and hillbilly stuff. It was some tough music. The rockabilly was really happening which is home was a mixture of country and blues. All of it was happening at once and I liked it all.

You were right in the middle of it.

CM: Yeah, I wasn't thinking about being a professional musician or nothing like that. I just liked the music. I liked listening to it. It felt so good to listen to it. I figured it felt even better to play it. Once I decided to play it, it was just for me without any ambition to do anything with it on a professional level. I just loved the music. If nothing ever happened where I had gotten a job playing music and I ended up doing something else I'd still be somewhere playing music even if it wasn't for anybody except me.

You even ran moonshine back in those days.

CM: Yeah, I did a little bit of that—construction work—factory work.

When did you really start playing with other musicians?

CM: Well, around Memphis there was a lot of jamming going on in people's homes. We'd get a bunch of beer and get together and just have fun. As soon as I got out of high school I knew—I felt like there wasn't anything for me to do around Memphis as far as work or trying to make a living. To me it seemed like it was economically depressed. I heard about all these big good paying factory jobs up north. I didn't know a thing about Chicago except that it was a big city. I went up there to get a job. The first job I got was as a driver. I drove an exterminator all around Chicago, so I got to know the city real fast. I'd see signs and posters on telephone poles and windows of bars advertising the blues. I remember driving by Pepper's Lounge—they had a big painting of Muddy Waters. I'd write down the addresses and at night I'd go back and hear these bands playing. I didn't know all those guys were happening in Chicago. I'd seen Jimmy Reed and Muddy in Memphis. I had their records—I knew the music, I just didn't know where they were. I didn't know there was this scene in Chicago with all these blues clubs. In fact, it didn't occur to me to even wonder about it because I didn't think myself as having a career in music. I just liked it. I played a little bit and I learned a little bit but it was not a goal in mind to become a professional musician.

So, there I was hanging out in all these little blues clubs. I wasn't promoting myself, or asking to sit in or anything. I didn't even tell anybody I played. I was happy to be there hanging out and have some drinks and listen to the music—that was enough for me. It was interesting because at this time blues was just adult music. There was nobody my age hanging around these blues clubs. There wasn't any young people black or white hanging out in these clubs—sometimes I'd be sitting there and there'd be a bunch of kids from The University of Chicago. They'd park as close as they could to the door and they'd all get out and run in (laughs)!

I'm sure those joints could be mean and dangerous.

CM: Oh yeah. I was kind of crazy myself. I felt right at home. I wasn't intimidated at all. I was too dumb to be afraid I guess. I was just hanging out. I was just part of the crowd. I was accepted. Like I was saying before, this was adult music. You didn't see people my age there so when I'd request tunes or something guys like Muddy were flattered that I knew who they were and that I came to these clubs, drink and hang out with them. I knew the names of their songs and their records—so this was flattering to them. There was nobody my age hanging out there. One night, a waitress I'd gotten to know really well—she told Muddy, 'You should hear that boy play the harmonica. That changed everything. From that point Muddy had me sit in which wasn't unusual because people sat in all the time. Pepper's Lounge went until 4 AM. So, that's a lot of time to fill up. If there were musicians who weren't working that night they'd hang out or sit in. Even some lady—or housewife—would get up and sing a tune. Some guy who just came in from the factory, maybe he played some guitar, he might get up and play a number. So sitting in wasn't unusual, but for somebody that young it was unusual. Especially for somebody young and white it was very unusual.

That's amazing. The first time you were on stage was jamming with Muddy Waters.

CM: I remember thinking it was quite a thrill to be onstage standing next to Muddy Waters playing harmonica. It was like Wow. It wasn't even a dream come true—I had never even had this dream—it was just something put on me. The blues over-took me.

I guess through Muddy you met all sorts of great musicians.

CM: Well, what happened from that night was—I went to Pepper's a lot— I went to a lot of other clubs too, but I liked Pepper's because they had a restaurant at that time. You could get a whole meal there—like a meat and three—home cooking. I was used to that from the South. It was hard to find food like you could in the South, but you could in Chicago. You'd get a home cooked meal. You could drink and hear great music. When you hang out any place you get to know people. Muddy always had me sit in. From that moment on, long as Muddy lived—when I'd show up to see him, he'd always let me sit in.

Sitting in with Muddy, other musicians would see and hear me playing and invite me to someplace where they were playing at some club. Word started to get around and I started being offered gigs. That was amazing to me that I was going to get paid to play—that got me a little more focused (laughs). It was just a hobby up until that point.

Any insight gained by suddenly playing with blues legends in a world that only heard of bluesman through Dylan, The Beatles or the Stones?

CM: Well, I thought it was great music, but I was also aware this wasn't the Top 40. It was obvious it was on its way out because it wasn't being carried on by younger people. Here's an example of what I'm talking about. I was working in the factories during the week and on Monday mornings you'd be on break time talking about what you did over the weekend. I'd say, 'I went to hear Muddy Waters and these black guys my age would say, 'Man, what's wrong with you? You ain't up with the times.' I'd say, well I like Muddy Waters—and I like Howlin' Wolf—and they'd say, 'That's old folks' music. What's wrong with you? You crazy?' I'd say well I like it. I think it's great music. To them it was just old folks music. They didn't want anything to do with it. They just thought I was out of my mind. Well, I mean that shows you they thought the blues was over with as far as they were concerned. There was nobody taking it up. Obviously, that's not the way it turned out, but at that point that's what it was.

You're one of the last links as far as players who actually played with all these blues legends. When you met Muddy, he probably in his forties, right?

CM: Yeah, I think he was in his forties when we met. He'd put on a show back then. He'd be running around onstage—I mean it was wild. I've seen him do shows for white audiences and they were really different from his usual show.

He'd tone things down a bit.

CM: Oh yeah. Muddy would do things like, he'd been playing "I'm A Man" and Muddy would step back—James Cotton would come to the front of the stage taking a solo while Muddy would shake up a beer bottle, put it in his pants, then he'd come back singing "I'm A Man"—unzip his pants, pull out the beer bottle—pop the cap off of it and foam would go all over the audience. Women would be swinging their purses saying 'Sing it Muddy Sing it!' This isn't the show you'd see at a folk festival.

Who did you meet in those days?

CM: Well, I met everybody just by hanging out. I remember one night seeing Walter Horton. Walter saw me sitting at the bar and he made his way through the crowd to where I was sitting and he said, 'Charlie, I want you to meet my friend Robert Nighthawk. That's how I met Robert Nighthawk. Then I played with Nighthawk for a while. That's how things would happen. I was just partying. I was just going with the flow. Just name the key (Laughs). There was no rehearsing going on.

Let's go back for a second. Talk about hanging out with Elvis back in Memphis.

CM: Oh yeah. I had Elvis' phone number. I'd call up and find out where the party was…this was when I was in high school back in Memphis. I knew several people that were close to him that worked security who went to highschool with me. I'd show up. There'd be a line of these guys who waved you through the gates if they knew you. At some point—I don't remember the occasion—somebody just gave me the phone number so I could call his house. See, Elvis would rent a theatre where he'd have movies like all the latest movies and a whole bunch of Road Runner cartoons (Laughs). Or he'd rent the Fairgrounds and you'd go there and all the rides would be free—hot dogs—everything was free. It was always from midnight until 8 AM—an all night party. Usually, these places would be closed and that's when he would rent them because those were his hours. He was up all night—he was a night owl. Or he'd rent the skating rink. I was going there because all these pretty girls were there. I wasn't taking it all very seriously. It's like when they say the grass is always greener on the other side. You don't really realize that when you're right in the middle of it. It's like the whole thing with Chicago—as the years have gone by I have a perspective on how great those days were and I wished I'd paid more attention, but when you're right in the middle of it, you're just living it. When you're at that age you don't think about how one day all of this is going to be gone. You feel so invincible yourself. I really didn't get to play harmonica around Elvis. Even when I first got to Chicago I wasn't telling people anybody I could play. I never even thought about promoting myself like that.

Talk about running across harmonica great Sonny Boy Williamson.

CM: He was another guy I was a big fan of so when I had a chance to go see him I was right there. He used to play at a club called Curly's Twist City. I remember seeing him there. There was another place—I remember there was one day I was with Louis Myers and Louis had a gig that night—he was a guitar player. Sonny Boy would call him up and ask him to come play with him at this club. Louis said, 'Well I already got this other gig. As it turned out, Louis gig fell through so he said, 'let's go see Sonny boy'. We got there and Sonny boy was playing by himself. He had nobody—no bass, no drums, no guitar—nothing. He was just playing harmonica and singing. Louis said, 'Hey Sonny Boy, I got my guitar in the trunk of my car, you want me to go get it?' Sonny Boy just looked at him and said, "Nah, I got it myself (Laughs).

You even knew another harmonica legend, Little Walter.

CM: He used to play at different clubs. In fact, one was called The Red Onion. Hernando's Hideaway was another. Big Johns and I can't remember where else, but he liked me for some reason. I'd be sitting there listening to him, hanging out like I liked to do, and he'd just walk up and hand me his microphone and harmonica, and say, 'Play boy,' And he would leave to go talk to some woman at the bar. Or he'd give me a ride home. He knew I liked his music because I was always coming to see him. He'd buy me drinks and stuff. He'd keep an eye on me to make sure I didn't get into too much trouble.

How did things progress when you were in Chicago?

CM: Well, I also got a gig working at the Jazz Record Bar. Big Joe Williams lived there in the basement. They had folding cots down there. Joe and I would sit up all night just drinking beer and playing music or him telling me stories about Charlie Patton, Robert Johnson or whatever he felt like talking about. He'd take me around to the guys even before Muddy's time. So, I was meeting a lot of old time blues guys while they were still around. I was playing with Joe. He'd get these gigs in these coffee houses where they had folk music and they thought of Joe as some old folk singer. They didn't know what they were getting into. So we had fun. At one point, I got a job in another record store in a part of Chicago called Old Town. There was a record store in the front and there were rooms behind it. The guy that owned the record store drove a cab in the daytime. I'd gotten into a fi ght with the guy who owned the Jazz Record Club. Joe was out of town at the time. When he got back to town, and found out I moved—he moved in with me (Laughs). We'd just hang out in the record store all day, people would come by—Homesick James would come by. Different musicians. We'd sit around and drink beer. We'd talk about one thing or another—the ball game or something.

I was playing in these little clubs with Joe then Mike Bloomfield— who lived a few blocks away—was coming over and hanging out. There was a little neighborhood bar down the street called Big John's. Big John's usually didn't have music, but they decided they'd like to have Joe—they knew he lived down the street—they asked him to come play for some holiday—I can't remember, maybe the Fourth of July. So, Joe had this gig and he asked me to play harmonica with him. The place was packed. They sold a lot of drinks that night so they told Joe 'Hey come back tomorrow night. Just keep playing.' We did great business. We were playing there—Mike Bloomfield decided since there was an upright piano there that he'd like to join in playing on the piano. So, Joe played guitar, I'm playing harmonica and Bloomfield is playing piano.

Joe would never stay any place long—he always had to go. There came a time when Joe said, 'I gotta leave town. I gotta go see somebody.' I think he went to Omaha, or some place. So while he was gone, Mike switched to guitar and we got a drummer and a bass player and we just kept the gig going. This place—Big John's—on the nights we weren't working we told the people that ran the club—how they should hire blues bands like Otis Rush, Little Walter, Muddy Waters, Howlin Wolf. They started hiring these blues bands from the south side to come up and play in their club. Then these other clubs on the northside saw the great business and what the other guys were doing and they wanted to have blues bands too. So, that's how the whole scene switched over to the north side.

You were the catalyst for the whole scene.

CM: Yeah, well it's all sort of a fluke really. If the guys at Big Johns didn't know big Joe lived down the street, they hadn't hired him and Mike hadn't showed up to keep the ball rolling, who knows what would have happened.

That was around 1963. During that time, did you notice The Rolling Stones somewhat brought Americans' interest back into the blues?

CM: Well, I really wasn't paying attention to that. People were getting turned onto the blues that would ordinarily not go to the south side. Now they were able to hear it on the north side and it was becoming a pretty big deal.

When did you first begin studio session work?

CM: I think the first thing I remember doing was for a folk singer. I don't even remember the name now. I remember they only had a few tracks. These days they have 64 tracks. Back then it was two or four. Four was about it. If you what they call over-dub now—they would combine tracks so it would free up another track. Maybe the guitar player would play rhythm the first time around. They would combine his rhythm with the bass. Then they'd open up a new track so he could play lead.

I don't even remember what label it was—we were backing up some singer—Tracy Nelson's first album. I played on her second album too. Paul Butterfield's album came out and Sam Charters knew me the Tracy Nelson album and he was with Vanguard. So Vanguard was kind of on the level with Electra—that's where Paul was, so they thought maybe we'll do something with this guy Musselwhite (laughs). So Sam Charters asked me if I wanted to make a record, and I said yeah. Sure—why not? To me, it was kind of a lark. I didn't expect much to come from it one way or another. I thought it would at least be fun…maybe make a little money, but as it turned out it gave me a whole career. That album came out and put me on the road.

You're talking about your *Stand Back* album, right?

CM: Yeah.

What was your perspective about songwriting then?

CM: I always experimented with writing tunes for fun, but I wasn't thinking of myself as a songwriter. It was always easier to remember a song you made up yourself than to remember someone else's. I wasn't thinking of songwriting in a professional sense. To me, it was still all about having a good time. I didn't know where it was gonna go because I was so young. I had no responsibilities. I just wanted to have a good time.

Your discography is formidable (I read a list).

CM: Oh yeah, I forgot about all that stuff. *The Chicago Blues* series had me and Walter Horton playing harmonica. There were three volumes. It had three different tunes by different guys like J.B. Hutto, I can't remember everybody. Johnny Shines played guitar.

How long did you stay in Chicago?

CM: Well, it was five years, but I did about fifteen years of living in those five years. In August or September of 67 I was out in California doing my first gig, which was at the Fillmore and it was me, Butterfield and Cream. It was Cream's first U.S. gig. That was my introduction to the west coast. I thought I was gonna go out to California and do a few gigs and then come back to Chicago. When I got out to California, I found out all up and down the West coast were tons of great gigs that paid good money. I'd been working in these little blues bars for not much money and in California it was easy to see that you could make a living. Out here on the West Coast blues music was something exotic. They didn't really know about the blues—it was something new to them. It was the underground radio that really did it because they weren't playing me on the radio in Chicago. So that underground radio on the West Coast, and that first album gave me a career. That was my ticket out of the factory…I was twenty-two or twenty-three.

In San Francisco you played with everyone from members of the Grateful Dead to John Lee Hooker.

CM: They had all these big jams in the Golden Gate Park—they called them Be-Ins. There was jamming going on all the time. You'd go to these clubs and you could sit in with just about any-body…The Avalon, the Fillmore, The Matrix—man there were clubs all over the place. Live music every night of the week.

Heaven for a musician.

CM: And you met a lot of connections and met a lot of people that way. Things were happening.

I interviewed Jim Dickinson a few months ago.

CM: Oh, I know Jim.

He's a big fan of yours and that y'all were in Memphis together at the same time, but he was out in the sub-urbs and you were down in the city. But Dickinson loves Champion Jack Dupree and you ran across him also. I love his *Blues From the Gutter* album.

CM: Yeah, in Germany I met him. We played a show together with a famous horn player—whose name I can't remember—yeah I had that record.

What's been the hardest thing for you to learn after all these years?

CM: Well, in the beginning for me, going from these little clubs to suddenly thrown into the deep end of the pool, then it was supposed to be more professional…like signing contracts, being on time, having a band and rehearsing. Then it was a whole new ball game and I didn't have a booking agency. I really didn't know anything about the business. From that angle I was just used to playing on the streets for tips. I was playing in these rough little bars for a few bucks. There was nothing about it that was professional. So suddenly it was sink or swim—figure it out. I guess I figured it out enough to survive. I know I made a lot of mistakes too. I wouldn't if I'd had a manager.

Talk about your relationship with John Lee Hooker. He was the best man at your wedding.

CM: He lived in Detroit, but he would come through Chicago fairly regularly to play. I was a big fan of his music so if I wasn't doing anything I'd go to where he was playing, and we just became immediate friends. We just stayed in touch. We both moved out to California. I came out a little ahead of him, but I remember telling him, 'Man you gotta come out here it's really nice. I don't know if that's what did it, but he did move out here. We were always real good friends. I often stayed at his house. He was the best man at my wedding. I recorded on his album. He recorded on mine. He was a good friend. I spoke at his funeral—that was really hard.

I'm going to skip around here a bit Charlie. I've got many questions to ask. Time's always an issue—but I just thought to ask you about your music appearing in Craig Brewer's *Black Snake Moan*—another Memphis connection.

CM: I'd done some other stuff, but I think that was my first major film.

You also played with James Burton.

CM: Oh yeah, we were on a bill together. He was playing with The Killer.

Jerry Lee Lewis…

CM: Yeah. James and I were talking backstage…just kind of hanging out. I was around him a lot in Memphis and didn't know it—just like Jim Dickinson. We may have brushed shoulders and never knew it.

Since I'm throwing out different artists—talk about recording with Tom Waits. I somehow see you too getting along very well.

CM: (Laughs) Heh Heh Heh. He's a great guy. Anybody who should know anything about music should know about Tom Waits. Anyone that has any depth to them.

You guys live pretty close together. How did you meet him?

CM: Well, we met years ago when we were both still drinking—there are stories about us having these big conversations with huge laughs, but neither of us remembered (laughs). We know each other from those foggy days. Now, we're relatively neighbors. He's about a half-hour drive from here to get from his house to my house. I met him back in the late 70s. I'm on about three of his albums. We see a lot of things in the same way. Tom and I enjoy talking to each other. We get together now and then for dinner. We entertain ourselves pretty easily (Collective laughter). We get some good laughs in…at some else's expense (laughs).

Your album *Sanctuary* was great. And *Delta Hardware* contains some real gems. On your last record you recorded a sort of spoken word piece about The Hurricane Katrina disaster. You usually refrain from making any sort of political statement.

CM: You're right. I've never made any statements that could be considered political or socially heavy. I felt like it was time to say something. I just thought what a terrible mess the way the whole thing was handled. Me and the producer of that album wrote that together. My bass player at the time wrote that other tune called "The Invisible One's", it's a companion piece to "Black Water".

You're taking a little break, but you'll be hitting the road again soon.

CM: Yeah, that's what I do.

We should try and eat some barbecue together when you come to Savannah in November.

CM: Yeah, we're playing a festival there.

It's on a Saturday—the 8th—The Roadhouse Blues and Barbecue festival.

CM: It sounds like fun. I fly to England the next day.

So tell me about this new horror film—*The Pig Hunt*—you're in. The trailer looks interesting. You seem to be a kind of menacing character.

CM: (Laughs) Well you could put in that way. I play a guy named Charlie who owns a little country store. These guys come in looking for directions and I send them on their way to mayhem! (Laughs) It's got bikers, hippies, cults, naked women, and dope dealers. For a joke I sometimes tell people it's a documentary on daily life in backwoods Arkansas (collective laughter).

Who is the writer?

CM: Well, I know the writers—Robert Anderson and Zach Anderson. They're from northern California. Robert Anderson had a bestseller novel called *Booneville*. *Booneville* has its own language called Boon Boot-ling. And I have to speak some Boot-ling in the movie. I think it's the first Boot-ling ever spoken in a movie.

Give me an example.

CM: There's a word, timmy—I can't remember what it means. I don't even remember the lines now—you'll hear 'em when you see the movie. It's supposed to be out this year, but they haven't given me a date yet. But they also have three more movies lined up that they have me in mind for—it should be fun.

It will be cool to see you up on the silver screen. Well Charlie, I appreciate you talking to me.

CM: Thank you man. I'm flattered. This was great fun. Feel free to stay in touch.-

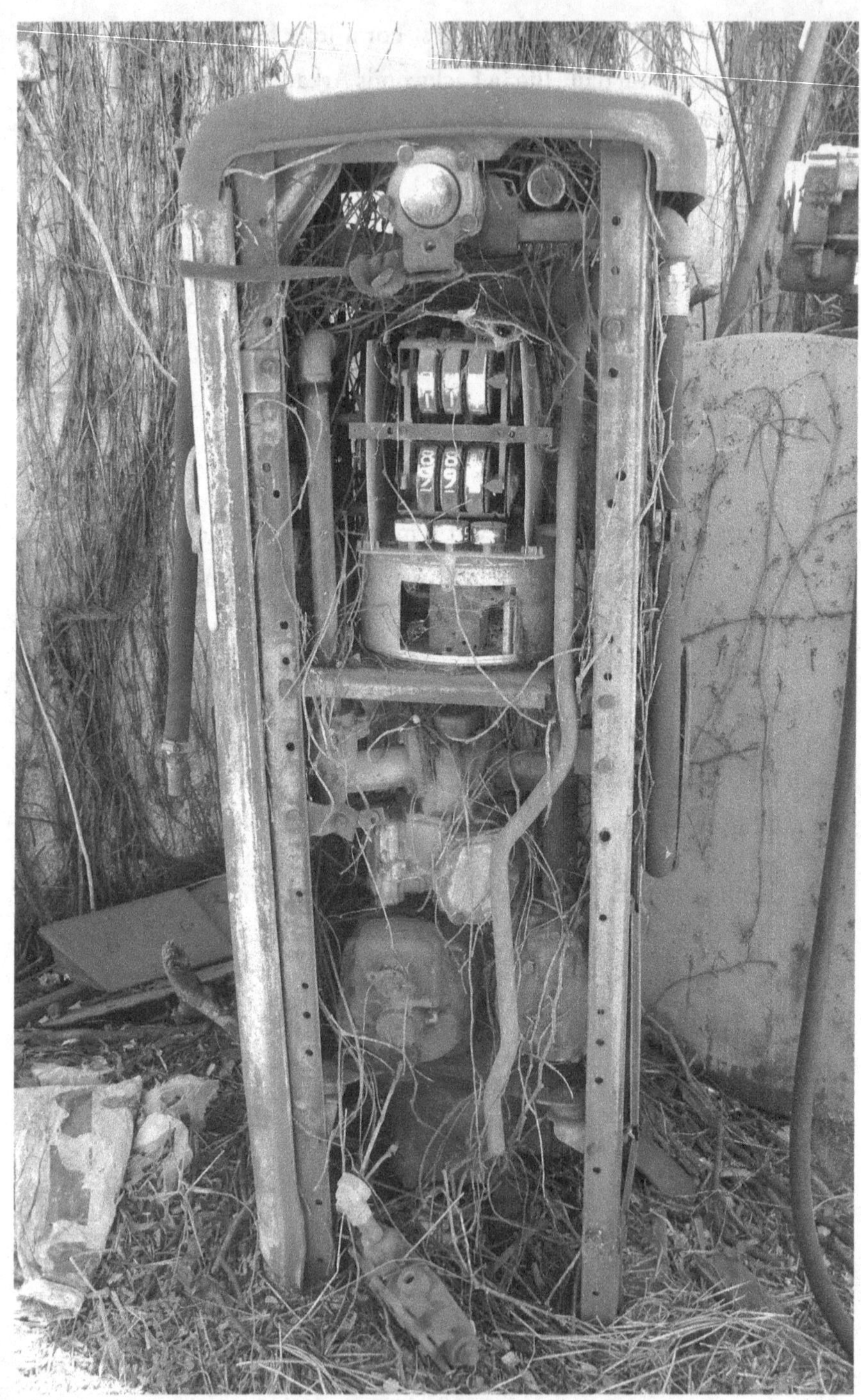

Old Gas Pump

On the Road: *Email Dispatches from Charleston, South Carolina*

From: James Calemine
To: Paste Travel
Date: Jan 30, 2015 at 6:07 PM
Subject: The High Road To Charleston, South Carolina …

We hit I-95 early, driving north from the Georgia coast to Charleston. With me are Griffin Bufkin, proprietor of St. Simons Island's Southern Soul Barbeque, and my friend Comer Smith. Griffin needed to drop off some sauces at High Wire Distilling Co., and that was our excuse to get out of town. The three of us are hard-boiled nomads who know the face of decadence, and Charleston always serves as a good place to let loose.

When we arrived, the fresh sea breeze smelled sweet. Maybe it's the Revolutionary and Civil War history that springs from the cobblestone streets. Or maybe it's because there's something like seven women to every man here. Regardless, this town always stirs the poet in me. The salt air awakens the technicolor realization that Charleston provides a port city-meets-high Southern confluence of the finest elements in American culture.

Before we checked into our rooms at the hotel on King Street, we dropped off the barbecue sauce at High Wire. From the barrels of bourbon I smelled that familiar fragrance: the rising energy of the weekend and a high fever of impending the-boys-are-back craziness. Drinking the rare contents from those barrels might have contributed to that sensation.

From: James Calemine
To: Paste Travel
Date: Jan 30, 2015 at 8:12 PM
Subject: Out The Door And Down The Street …

You might be jealous after this email. I make no apologies. When in Charleston, you just do it. I told you you should have come—your loss.

After cleaning up, we hit the streets. Charleston always reminds me of a cross-pollination of Savannah and New Orleans. There's a beauty to the seediness. I love that laid-back, rustic atmosphere mixed with aristocracy.

At Edmund's Oast we ordered numerous dishes: tuna, cow pea & spicy squid salad, lamb meatballs, rare beef jerky, fresh ricotta. I sipped a high-gravity raspberry beer. The Oast cast a comforting golden light over Charleston's business people, purveyors, movers and shakers.

Then we devoured raw oysters at Leon's. A funky, low-to-the ground, no-nonsense, aesthetic here with a wide beer selection. Can't beat the seafood in this town. Leon's drives with a rock & roll edge. No pretentious bullshit. Next, we grabbed (with both hands) the tail of the dragon at The Royal American, which emits a dirty subterranean neon vibe and it's where bands like Lee Bains III & The Glory Fires perform. We drank two beers, but gathered no moss …

We ate bacon-laced oysters and swilled raw oyster shots (with cocktail sauce & vodka) at the Rarebit. This sleek joint is a straight-up, high-class saloon with a long bar and low-hanging lights. Many pretty women dining here. You feel like you're in a Robert Altman film standing in that place. A smell of flowers and seafood filled the room.

Husk served as the last stop of the evening. The upscale Husk is for the sophisticated, the believer, the cultured and Southern gourmand. The chef, Sean Brock, a James Beard winner, is a culinary artist of the highest order. At Husk's lo-fi lit bar, Comer and Griffin enjoyed pork tails. I drank several Moscow Mules (Tito's vodka, Ginger Beer and a lime) in a freezing brass cup.

Walking back to the hotel, Griffin experienced a moment of clarity: "Charleston, in my opinion, contains the highest per capita collection of classic history, first-rate restaurants, Southern artists, brewers and distillers—it is a wellspring of talent. I will have to die here before I die."

From: James Calemine
To: Paste Travel
Date: Jan 31, 2015 at 7:17 PM
Subject: To The Heart of Charleston's Bohemia …

We visited Martha Lou's Kitchen to start the day. We ate fried chicken, collard greens with mac & cheese for a long journey ahead. This is where tourists come to get their authentic vittles in a small, quiet place. Then we walked through a rough part of town to Hannibal's Soul Food. This, amigo, is where real people act real. You just know when the sun goes down, these checker-board floors transform into hotspot. I ate cheese & grits, shrimp and lima bean soup.

That night The Drive By Truckers played in town. Earlier in the day, I chatted with Patterson Hood about my new book in the courtyard outside of Kudu Coffee & Craft Beer. At Kudu, the owner continued to bring Comer and me the latest brews on tap; some aged in whiskey-soaked oak barrels for three years. The beers would be tasted by the public for the first time the following day. For an early dinner, we ate at an upscale Mexican restaurant, Minero, which served mezcal that was $30 for one shot. Minero served the best chicken tacos I've eaten in a long time. Comer ordered beef tongue.

Later, my friend Heather Renee—one of the most beautiful women in the Low Country—met us at King Dusko. This hip locale has coffee shop, a bar and a clothing store, and great photos lining the walls. Heather Renee invited me down to see the historic Palm Fountain, and enjoy a drink with her at the Griffon Bar. The brick walls inside the Griffon are at least 100 years old. True grit at The Griffon. We traveled by horse and carriage through the streets like ghosts. As the sunset, the briny scents mixed with seafood, bourbon, lavender and distant wood smoke drifted the air.

From: James Calemine

To: Paste Travel

Date: Feb 1, 2015 at 6:07 PM Subject: The Last Day…

Sunday morning was a rude awakening. Exhausted. I hate to leave Charleston … and get back to the grind. I already miss the cemeteries, mysterious plantations, rare shops, unforgettable restaurants, coastline and even the 400 churches.

It was then that I thought of the passage from James Caskey's book, *Charleston's Ghosts: Hauntings in the Holy City.*

"But like any great seductress, Charleston presents a careful veneer of half-truths and outright fabrications, and lets you, the intended conquest, fill in many of the blanks. Seduction, after all, is not true love, nor is it a gentle act. She whispers stories spun from sugar about pirates and patriots and rebels, about plantations and traditions and manners and yes, even ghosts; but the entire time she is guarded about the real story. Few tourists ever hear the truth, because at the dark heart of Charleston is a winding tale of violence, tragedy and, most of all, sin."

Amy LaVere Interview: *The Majestic and Graceful Music of Amy LaVere*

I met Amy LaVere in Atlanta during 2007 when she performed at the Variety Playhouse with the North Mississippi Allstars. This interview coincided with the release of her album, produced by Jim Dickinson, titled Anchors and Anvils. That day in Atlanta I gave her a copy of a Cormac McCarthy novel. I liked that she was from Memphis, acted in Walk The Line, recorded with Jim Dickinson, sounded great and wrote sultry tunes. Amy's still out there recording and touring...

"You hold the key to my melody"

—Amy LaVere

AMY LAVERE RANKS AS one *of the most talented musicians on the rise. Born in Shreveport, Louisiana, LaVere was raised in a musical family where she began honing her musical talents. The humble Amy LaVere's voice evokes true emotion. She portrayed Wanda Jackson in Walk The Line as well as appearing in Craig Brewer's Black Snake Moan, which will surely lead her to larger roles in film.*

LaVere's two albums, This World Is Not My Home and Anchors & Anvils, encapsulates her depth, aptitude and power regarding her musical ethos. As a Memphis resident, LaVere soon fell in with the nucleus of Memphis musical company when she began working with Jim Dickinson, The North Mississippi All-stars and the wide network of musicians located in those environs. LaVere is now out on the road opening for the North Mississippi Allstars. She intends to tour until it's time for her to record this fall.

In this interview, LaVere discusses her musical upbringing, musical infl uences, the Memphis music scene, literary preferences, Jim Dickinson, Anchors & Anvils, Bob Dylan and various other avenues of interest. Her inspirational voice and talent behooves one to seek out her soulful work.

Congratulations, *Anchors & Anvils* sounds great.

AL: Ah, thank you.

You recorded it last year.

AL: Yeah, it's been a little longer than a year at this point. We released it last May a year ago.

You were born in Louisiana.

AL: Yeah, Shreveport.

And your parents were pretty musical, right?

AL: Right. My dad was a drummer. My Mom was a songwriter and guitar player. They really didn't play in a band together. My dad played in a band and my mom was a folk singer. I saw my Mom playing a lot more music than my dad. She would play at home all the time.

Did you get an instrument at Christmas one year and that's how it started?

AL: No, nothing like that. Just one old Alvarez guitar that was beaten around the house…I never got great at it, but enough to play country chords.

From what I've read you family moved like 13 times before you settled in Detroit. Did you decide early, music was going to be your ticket out of town?

AL: Yeah, it was always music. My parents were real social. There were always parties at the house with people coming and going. Mom would entertain everybody. I guess I just wanted to be her. I wanted to light up the room like she did.

When you were in Detroit, was that when you played in your first band?

AL: My very first band was called Blatant Death Mongers, which was a group of 13-year-old kids who started a band in a garage. I played drums. The kid lost his drumsticks and I played with wooden spoons. We had two shows at school. That was my first band. After that I was invited to sing for a band that had already been around for a about a year—they were called Last Minute. It was two brothers—a drummer and a bass player…we had a few different guitar players over the years. They asked me if I wanted to sing for them. We were together in an on and off again way for about six years. Then we'd go through spells where we'd go into Detroit and Flint and play shows. Then we would hole up in the basement. We rehearsed every single week—it was more of a party than anything else. It was a blast. I want to clarify—initially, I think I wrongfully said it was a punk band, where I was probably selling short my interviewers short because it was so much more aggressive than what I do now…it was an alternative-teen angst thing.

What instruments can you play?

AL: I won't pretend I can play anything with any real virtuosity. The upright bass—not to sell short any other upright bass players, but the way I play it—it's more percussive—holding down the big notes. It's something to hide behind. I enjoy playing and singing at the same time—having to do something besides just sing on stage. Like any other hack, I can play a little piano, drums, guitar, bass—the only lessons I really ever took formally was mountain dulcimer from David Schaffner who I wrote one of the songs on the record with who passed away before he could play on it.

What song?

AL: He wrote "Tennessee Valentine". It's pretty far removed from some-thing that I would write, but it always struck such a sweet chord with me. I always loved it. When we got ready to do this record I asked him if I could record it and he said I could. Of course, I insisted he play on the song, but he passed away just a few weeks before we got to do it.

I'm sorry.

AL: It was awful. I loved him so much. He was my neighbor. That was the only thing I took lessons for…

Eventually you moved to Nashville.

AL: Yeah, Nashville was the second place I ever moved to on my own—outside of my family moving around all the time. I tried to move back to Louisiana because I felt like I didn't know my extended family. We'd go back for Christmas, but I never really had that big family feeling. It was always the four of us against the world. So, I wanted to get to know my cousins, aunts and uncles so at the last minute I went down there and it only took me three months to realize I didn't like it at all. The only reason I moved to Nashville was because I had an offer for a job to work in a management office. I thought, 'Well, I've got a job waiting on me there if I want it and I'm not quite 21', so I decided to go try it out. I lasted almost two years in Nashville.

Let's talk about your appearances in a couple of films.

AL: Well, I didn't do any acting until last year when I did a little indie film project. I'm not sure what happened to it.

Well, you played Wanda Jackson in *Walk The Line*.

AL: Yes, I did. That was totally surreal. I'm a total fan of Wanda's work. I really admire her. It was very strange how it came about. I was playing at this little club called Murphy's In Memphis. I had a regular gig there and the assistant casting director happened to be in the room unbeknownst to me. Every now and then I'd cover a Wanda Jackson song, and that night I happened to do one. He told me I should audition. So I did and somehow I got the part. I even went in there with a guitar. They had a handful of girls in there that had some semblance of likeness to Wanda Jackson with their acoustic guitars and I just thought I was awful, but somehow I got the gig. It was a real honor. It led to getting to meet her. I opened some shows for her. I think she's really amazing.

The next movie was Craig Brewer's film, *Black Snake Moan*.

AL: Yeah, Craig Brewer is the first person who gave me a true acting opportunity. The Wanda Jackson role was nothing more than just having the appearance of Wanda Jackson in one particular scene. Then there was a duet with the other actor—Waylon Payne—who was playing Jay Lee—who finished the duet, but it didn't make it into the scene. You could just hear us in the background, but they cut to Johnny Cash trashing his dressing room—so that scene got cut out, but it wasn't an acting role, it was just…I was an extra that got to portray a famous singer. Craig Brewer really gave me my fi rst role. He—I guess you could say he was a fan of mine. Craig would come see us play. He liked my band and he just basically said there was a role that looked like me, and he thought I could do the role.

You were Christina Ricci's friend, right?

AL: Yeah, but it's a real brief role. It's hardly a role. I'm just in a scene, but that was—aside from being both Dorothy and Cinderella in the school plays (Laughs) I'd never done any acting. Do you remember those Fisher-Price little black and white video cameras?

I think so…yes.

AL: That looks like a toy? My sister and I made a ton of film when she had that, but…nothing…

Significant.

AL: Yeah, so that was really my first role. Since then, I've had a few other indie film projects with much more meatier roles where I got to explore the craft of acting.

Where you actually had to remember some lines?

AL: (laughs) Yeah, I really enjoyed it. But at this point in my life I haven't spent my life honing the craft of acting. At this point I feel like I do have an actual ability to do it, but it would be very assumptive to say I could step into some great acting career. I hope I get another opportunity to work on a major set at some point because it was really fun.

Well, nonetheless, those two films look really good on paper.

AL: I guess so because I see it a lot (laughs). I'm so thankful for the opportunity—it is making mountains out of mole hills. I hope one day I get to make a mountain out of it.

Well, a great voice like yours leads to other opportunities. So, you moved to Memphis in 1999. How did you meet the great Jim Dickinson?

AL: Well, I actually had become aware of Jim—living in Memphis I rented a room from this girl named Misty White. Her and her sister and some other girls have a pretty popular rock and roll band called the Hellcats. Misty was really wrapped up in the music community. She's a great storyteller. I just got a lot of the history of Memphis music living in that house because she was all about it. I was already in love with Big Star, the Replacements—and to find out he had something to do with that I just couldn't wait to meet him. I had brushes with him—we were aware of each other but it wasn't until I started to play with Paul Taylor—my drummer now—who grew up with the Allstars. He was in a band for years with Luther and Cody called D-D-T, which was Dickinson-Dickinson and Taylor. Paul even lived out at their house some when he was a teenager. They're family to him. It was Paul who truly made the connection. I actually got to back up Jim Dickinson on a couple shows before I ever got the nerve up to ask him to produce my first record *(This World Is Not My Home)*. Without Paul playing in the band I don't know if I would've had the nerve. He's a huge presence—intimidating in his own right, but getting to know him—he's so…

…Imposing…

AL: …Yes, imposing—that's a good word for him. He's imposing, and he deserves every bit of credit he gets. I'd been playing around Memphis a while—doing my own thing by playing corporate and private parties. I've got that natural flap ability of the upright bass, and I could stand in on any country, blues or rockabilly outfit to make a living on. I had my own band too—so I'd get hired for all kinds of random events. It was a helluva lot more profitable than what I'm doing now, but this is more rewarding. It was Ward Archer—Archer Records—is a huge music lover who made things happen. I think the first band he signed was the Gamble Brothers. It was kinda like he loved music and he saw the need. They were really taking off in some ways but they just didn't have any support or label help. Ward had a little bit of money to put a label together and he decided to do it. So, he signed them and he signed Sid Selvidge—who is actually my guitar player's dad, and then he signed Lily Ashar—an Iranian classical guitarist—just a totally eclectic mix of bands and he also had a girl named Kelly Heard—this beautiful black jazz singer. So, he had this really weird mix of people that he was helping. There was no discrimination—if he loved it and thought it was quality—he helped.

When I met Jim I was actually playing one of those private parties. I had been hired by the Arts Commission for some sort of fundraiser and it was the first amalgamation of my original band called Amy & the Tramps. It was Scott Bomar on guitar who is the guy who did the music for *Hustle & Flow* and *Black Snake Moan*. Paul Buchignani, who played with the Afghan Wigs was there. Scott Bomar was really helpful when I started out because I had my smattering of original material, but he was bringing things to the table. It was so long ago, but he was the one that bought me the Carla Thomas tune "That Beat" that I recorded on *Anchors & Anvils*. I guess that was four or five years ago that he brought that song to me. So, ward of Archer records approached me and it was probably a few months before that he called and invited me to lunch. I had actually…Young Avenue Studio was trying to start a new label, but I actually had a contract in my hand from Young Avenue, but I just got a feeling from Ward that really seemed much more homespun. It was a strange deal and I felt more comfortable with Ward. I'm so thankful that I did because he's so much more of a friend than a label. I wouldn't call him a benefactor—he was totally artist friendly and it felt more like a collaboration—as far as creating the way we're going to do…it's so loose and open-minded. It's great working with Ward. He's continually helped me me not to fail as far as being able to go on the road.

It's just not as easy as people think.

AL: Oh, man. Especially now that I'm at this very strange level where it's not like go to the club and make what you can. It's getting to the point where I'm getting invited to open shows for people like the Allstars. We had wonderful fun with this guy Langhorne Slim. I hadn't heard of him before being invited on that tour, but they're amazing.

You still live in Memphis?

AL: Oh yeah.

But you're in California today.

AL: Yeah, I'm in Santa Cruz in the middle of these fires. It's really unbelievable.

What's your approach to songwriting? Is that your main focus? I know you're an Emmylou Harris fan—I also love her because Gram Parsons discovered her—she's not necessarily a great songwriter, but she sure does convey an emotion with any material.

AL: Oh, I love Gram Parsons. I'm a huge fan of his. I labor over songwriting. I beat myself up over it. Songwriting is something that I feel like I have to do. There is a reward when you fi nally do something that is clever, meaningful or worthwhile—they're just too few and far between for me. I'm totally critical. I know a good song when I hear one, but they're not necessarily mine. I really don't have any shame in that. I write constantly, but I make no apologies for playing someone else's song. Paul is a wonderful songwriter. He's more prolifi c than I am. I have a really close friend named Kristy Whitt—she's not a performer—she's got a whole other creative outlet, but songwriting is something she loves to do. It's something she relaxes with and she's always bringing me songs. I love that. Her songs deserve to be heard. I like being able to be a vehicle for other songwriters' material. It's always indicative of an artist's depth by what material—other than their own—they choose to cover. I'm very impressed with your rendition of Bob Dylan's "I'll Remember You".

AL: Yeah? Well, thanks.

Through Luther and Paul you met Jimbo Mathus.

AL: Yeah, that was another Paul connection because Paul had been on the road with Jimbo. Actually it was Paul. I admired Jimbo, but it was Paul who said Jimbo would be good, and Jimbo just out of the blue brought me a song called "Nightingale" he wrote and he thought I'd be great on it. I just loved it, that's one of my favorites on the road. I love Jimbo—we've become really good friends.

So, once again, we're back recording *Anchors & Anvils* with Jim Dickinson.

AL: Oh yeah. I really hope I make the next one with Jim. We're going into the studio during the fall. I'm so excited. It feels like forever since I've recorded. They're releasing *Anvils & Anchors* in the UK like it's new. They didn't want me to release anything else until the first of the year so I had to wait, which is probably for the best because every day you discover something new about yourself or a different song you want to record. It's always a process. I guess it's only right to do it when you do it. But I'm excited to do record again…

There's a cohesive mood on *Anchors & Anvils*—it's sequenced great. The opener, "Killing Him" is a spooky kind of song. By the way, how long did it take to record *Anchors & Anvils*?

AL: We paid for the studio for 20 days. It wasn't a full 20 days. It was a lot of fitting in musicians schedules—there's a large cast of people on this record. Nobody came all at once. It was a scheduling nightmare. Some days it would be going down and just goofing off. Other days it might be someone just putting this or that on there. The bulk of it was all recorded live in two or three days. The meat and bulk of the record was just recorded with me, Jason Freeman—my longest running guitarist—who doesn't play with me any more because he doesn't like to tour, and Paul cut the record within the first three days. Then everything else was built upon from there.

Jim doesn't fool around in the studio with unnecessary takes.

AL: You're right. He doesn't. Probably being the least experienced of anybody that was in the studio I defi nitely demanded more takes than necessary. I guess because I felt insecure and I wanted to do it better. But Jim was always right. Always.

"Pointless Drinking" is another favorite of mine.

AL: That's a Paul Taylor song—my brilliant songwriting drummer. He just played it for me and apparently it was an old one from a couple of years ago. He didn't want me to record it. He's got a record out and then he's got another one in the can that he hasn't found the right home for. He's really a genius. He's got boxes around the house with all these projects around that he hasn't done anything with but they're just brilliant. But I heard that song and I felt it was very moving. It's a funny song, but it's so true. I just wanted it so bad—it took a couple of weeks before he agreed to let me record it because I think he was saving it for himself. I hope he still releases it. I don't do it justice.

Well, tell me about recording the Bob Dylan song, "I'll Remember You" from his *Empire Burlesque* album. Interesting choice.

AL: There was this concert of his and I can't remember what it was, but it was an old Betamax concert that I loved of Dylan's. I just loved it. I didn't know it was on his *Empire Burlesque* record. It wasn't until I went to record it on the first record when we tried to cut it. In my opinion that was the worst Bob Dylan record.

Yeah, but even at his worst, songs like "Seeing The Real You At Last", "Something Is Burning", "Dark Eyes" and "I'll Remember You" are classic songs for anyone else.

AL: It's a gem of a tune. Every time I sing it, it makes me think of somebody else. I'll be singing it in my head to the person I met the night before or some old loves, or whatever—I can never go wrong performing that one. I can always think of someone to sing it to. It's quite a pop song for Bob Dylan to sing isn't it?

Certainly when you hear your version of it.

AL: The production on that album is so bad.

The sonic production in the mid-80s was not a good time for the older rock and rollers.

AL: (Laughs) No, I guess not.

I intend to make your show here in Atlanta next Friday. I'll bring you some 1940's produced songs.

AL: Please do. Hey, before you go I'd really like to mention my band I'm touring with. We've talked a little about Paul on the drums. Steve Selvidge—he's a longtime friend of Luther and Cody. Steve's band was Big Ass Truck. This band that I have right now is definitely the closest thing to having a real band together on the road that I've ever had.

It's a nice rock and roll trio.

AL: Yeah, at first it was economics—I couldn't afford to bring along anyone else. We don't even have a tour manager—I do all of that, but it's grown into such a tight three piece that I prefer it more and more. I don't think it's lacking at all. We have a fantasy about doing a band record. The next one we want is true to what we've been doing. Sometimes with a couple new songs I say, 'Oh, I can really hear a violin on this.' Whatever my little whim is that day. But the next one I'm going to try and keep it close to a band record. I'm hoping when we get home we'll be more collaborative instead just my ideas or the producers ideas. I want it to be more of a band experience.

What are you listening to in the van?

AL: We've been listening to a lot of Captain Beefheart. It's funny, I have trouble reading in the van. It makes me sick. I get car sick. If I'm lying down it doesn't bother me.

What are you reading?

AL: This trip I've been reading Cormac McCarthy's *The Road*.

A girl who sings Bob Dylan and reads Cormac McCarthy—what a dream.

AL: (laughs) I read *The Road* in the first week.

Read some of the older stuff like *Outer Dark*, *Suttree*, and *Blood Meridian*.

AL: I'm almost finished with *The Crossing*. When I bought it, I didn't realize it was the second one of the trilogy.

It's all great—but *Suttree* and *Blood Meridian* rank as his best.

AL: I've heard about *Suttree*, I think I'll read that one next. It's been a Cormac McCarthy tour for me.

Well, next week, I'll try and bring you a copy of some old music or maybe a new copy of Cormac for the road.

AL: I would love that so much. Please don't forget. That would really be awesome.

I look forward to keeping you in our rotation.

AL: Thank you so much. I really appreciate you bothering to write something about me.

I'm sure it won't be the last time.

AL: I hope not.

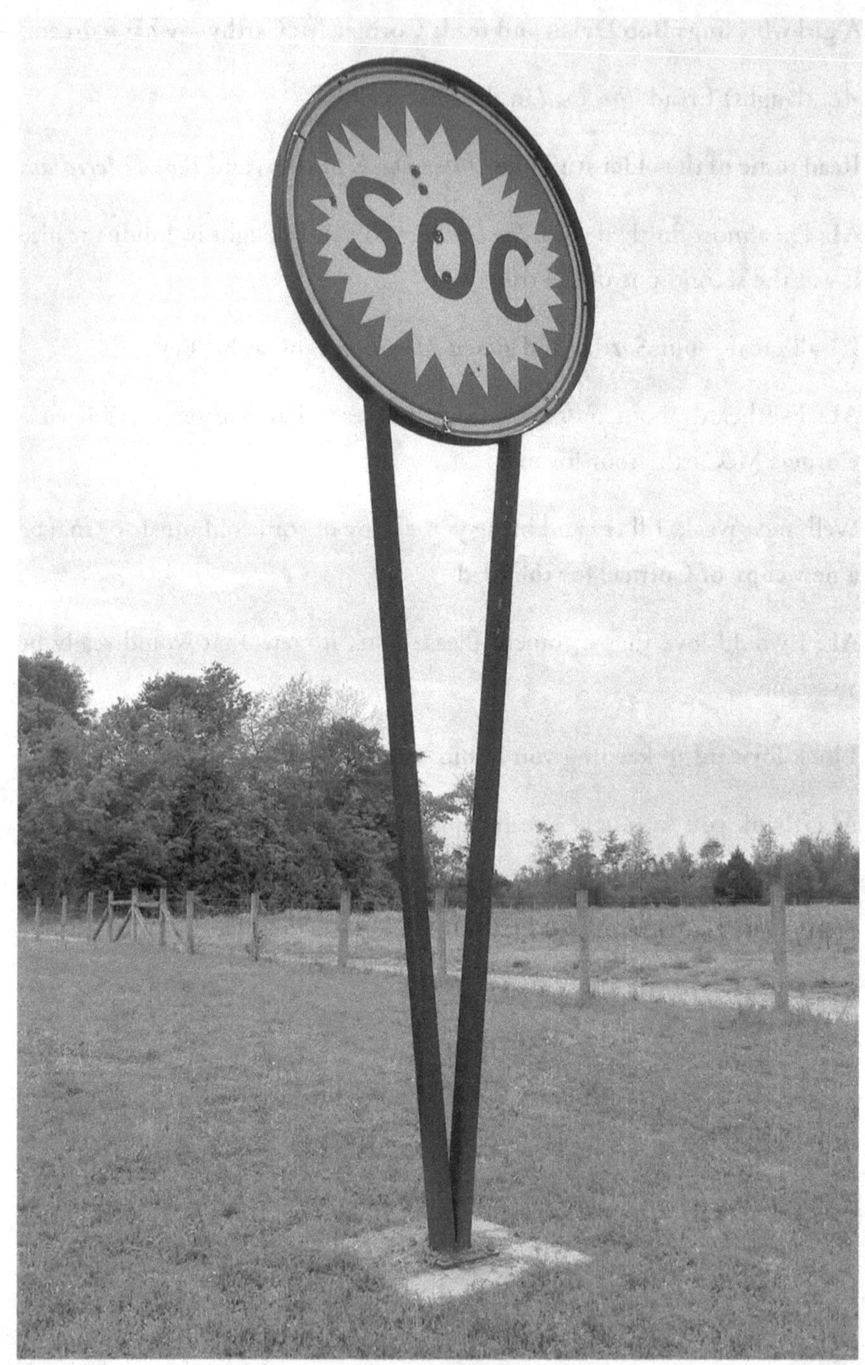

Soc Sign

John Trudell: *AKA Grafitti Man*

John Trudell died on December 8, 2015. This review of his album AKA Graffiti Man I wrote probably in 2010 for Swampland, but I heard the record long before then. Trudell played a fiction role of Leonard Peltier in the film Thunderheart. He served as an advisor on the film Incident at Oglala. His work should be explored. This album proved to be another inspiration for my own spoken word recordings.

JOHN TRUDELL, A NATIVE-AMERICAN poet, recorded this classic spoken word collection twice. Trudell formed the Graffiti Band with Oklahoma Native-American guitarist Jesse Ed Davis. Davis served as Taj Mahal's guitarist as well as playing with John Lee Hooker, Albert King, Conway Twitty, Eric Clapton, John Lennon, and Willie Nelson.

Trudell played a heavy role in Native American politics until 1979, when his wife and children were killed in a fire at their home on the reservation. Twelve hours earlier, Trudell burned an American flag on the steps of the FBI building in Washington, D.C., and he believed the fatal fire was no accident.

The music behind Trudell's words infuses blues, rock, and Native-American chants that serve as a backdrop to the social landscape of life as a Native American with a voice that resonates with every citizen. Accomplished musicians such as Mike Utley (Dixie Flyers), Kris Kristofferson, Jackson Browne, Bill Payne (Little Feat), Steven Soles (Rolling Thunder Revue), and Chad Cromwell (Neil Young) appear on these 12 songs.

In 1988, Jesse Ed Davis died before this record was complete. Mark Shark inherited guitar duties after Davis' death. Parts of this collection were re-recorded for the 1992 release that Jackson Browne produced.

Bob Dylan called *AKA Grafitti Man* the best album of the year. "Rockin' the Rez" opens the CD with an up-tempo beat threaded with cinematic reels of visual images. "Grafitti Man" hinges on a great Davis electric guitar hook. Eight of these compositions were written by Davis and Trudell.

"Restless Situation" illuminates the gravity and scope Elvis Presley's music left on America and the world, including all the "unrestrained emotion" he inspired. "Baby Boom Che"—a haunting blues riff echoed by a sad Indian mantra lingering in the background as the narrator tells the story of a man and woman going separate ways—remains unforgettable.

"Bombs Over Baghdad", written with Stark during the Gulf War, eerily resembles our country's current situation: "Bombs over Baghdad/Dancers of death/Murder in the air/With the next breath/Macho queens/Selling warmaker toys/Raining destruction/Good ol' boys."

"Rich Man's War" proves a slow spoken word blues, uttering truths for every common hardworking man and woman dealing with grave matters of the soul...from Palestine to New York...

"Never Never Blues", a gritty blues song that captures the great spirit of Jesse Ed Davis' slide guitar genius. John Trudell's storytelling ranks him as a great American and an undeniable Warrior.

Chris Robinson: *Southern Brotherhood*

This article was published in the Aug/Sept 2016 issue of South magazine based in Savannah, Georgia. I caught up with Chris that July during his Macon and Augusta shows in his home state of Georgia. Last year, 2017, we hung out in Charleston, SC., when his band–The Chris Robinson Brotherhood–played a show.

ATLANTA, GEORGIA, NATIVE CHRIS Robinson called me from his Marin County, California, home to discuss his new record, *Anyway You Love, We Know How You Feel,* released on July 29. Robinson sold thirty-five million records with The Black Crowes. He's traveled the world over since he left Georgia, and experienced all the tempting trappings of fame. These days, Robinson prefers a grassroots mode of operandi with his new group The Chris Robinson Brotherhood.

Robinson's parents Stan and Nancy were musicians. Stan Robinson earned a hit with "Boom A Dip Dip" in 1959, and even appeared on the Dick Clark show. In 1984, Chris and his younger brother Rich formed a band in Atlanta, Mr. Crowes Garden, that later transformed into the multi-platinum group. The Black Crowes. In 2015, Chris and Rich decided The Black Crowes would never play together again. The pressure, internal conflict and brutal mechanisms of the business burned Robinson out on his old band.

Since 2011, Robinson's new group, The Chris Robinson Brotherhood or The CRB—cultivated a dedicated following based on their "Farm To Table Psychedelic Rock-N-Roll" ethos. True to form, Anchor Brewing brewed 'Brotherhood Steam Beer' inspired by Robinson's group. The CRB fourth album—*Anyway You Love, We Know How You Feel*—captures the band's earthy essence. The CRB tour continues until the end of the year.

Robinson moved from Georgia to California in 1992. We discussed how his family visited St. Simons Island when he was a kid, and I asked if he missed the south.

"I miss the barbecue and some food and sensory things. I see the world through southern lenses. That's where I grew up. My interest in football is waning, but there's still something about the Red & Black—I'm still a Dawgs fan. But, I'm content with my California reality (laughs)."

The appeal of Robinson's music resides in the soulful sound he augments into his songwriting through infl uences he absorbed at an early age.

"Yeah, well I always pursued—and everyone in the CRB are inspired by roots music—whether that's folk, country, blues, jazz, R&B, soul and just plain old rock & roll. That music is a cosmic wellspring of depth. It's the kind of expression I emanate. People put on music at funerals and they play music at weddings. It's always been that way."

Robinson explained how *Anyway You Love, We Know How You Feel* sounds different than the group's previous work.

"I think the musicians and artists we aspire to be—it's been three years since the last record. That's another three years of living with good and bad stuff. As people living in a world that's teetering on chaos, anxiety, fear and suffering—that's all we see. Of course, we're going to be affected and things should be different.

"The pragmatic difference...the one thing The CRB has since we started are our hunter-gatherer skills. We use our environment for our survival. Every year The CRB does a little better. With this album we had more time in the studio. We recorded here in Marin County during a beautiful California winter with La Nina, fog, rain and landslides that kept us in our musical cocoon. It's not showbiz magic. It's magic magic."

The CRB operates beyond any parameters of atypical music-biz—not a luxury Robinson experienced in The Black Crowes.

"We have a good level of communication. Everyone is grown up. Everyone has each other's back. There's no agendas here. There's no whispering behind somebody's back to the producer to the manager to the record company telling you what to do. That's how it is in a corporate setting for bands."

Anyway You Love, We Know How You Feel does emit a funky, soulful countryish resonance in songs such as "Narcissus Soaking Wet", "California Hymn" and "Some Gardens Green". Robinson explained why they recorded in a secluded studio in northern California.

"I think it's been my favorite studio I've worked in. I've recorded in New York, London, Paris, Los Angeles, Toronto, Nashville, Atlanta—I've done a lot of recording. This place was fantastic for weirdos like us. We could set up in this big spacious room.

"To be in Los Angeles—where we made the last record—at Sunset Sound, which is a great sounding studio. Everyone from the Doors to the Rolling Stones—Prince recorded 1999 in the same room we recorded our last record. They have beautiful gear and are wonderful people. But, you're on Santa Monica Boulevard. There's no windows—you're in Hollywood, man. Now, we've expanded and we had all this other stuff available—like the weather—on the side of Mount Tamalpais, and we let it flow."

Anyway You Love took about a month to record. Robinson produced a Gary Louris & Mark Olson (The Jayhawks) album called *Ready For The Flood*. Olson said this about Robinson:

"Chris has a wide range of knowledge and the world around him. He has business smarts and he's also tough. He loves music and he's a positive force. He knows his stuff and relates to the beauty of it all. He is always leaning forward into music and life."

I asked Robinson what's the biggest difference in the record industry when he started with The Black Crowes in the late 80s, and now in 2016.

"Well, some of it's the same in a far left way when I was a kid. Now, if you're gonna be on a major label you're working for a big corporation.

And you have to make them money. I'm blessed that people like the music I make. Now is an amazing time.

"If I was a young person from Atlanta or Savannah or Chattanooga or Columbia all you need in this day and age is a few people. Play records you like. Have parties. Get a band together. If there's no scene—make one. So, for me now things are much cooler. From the beginning of The CRB we never felt anyone was trying to manipulate the scene behind our back. There's nothing to manipulate. It's just us."

Robinson takes pride in his songcraft. In the CRB, he operates as lyricist and rhythm guitarist. The lyricism on the new songs according to him "are a little more clear cut melancholy". I mentioned a few of my favorites including "Some Gardens Green" and he explained the tune's universal quality.

"The basis of that song is that nothing is what it seems. Success isn't what it seems to people. Love isn't what it seems. There's a duality. Life these days is dictated by status and people look up to sellouts. They look up to people who dumb down what they are or what they stand for because of money. In a way, it's about that not everything is for sale."

Robinson's thirty year career allows him to reveal brutal lessons. I asked him what's been the hardest thing to learn after all these years.

"That's easy. The hardest thing for me to learn was that people I'm with or closest to me don't love music like I do. Or they're not interested in artistic ideas. It doesn't stop me, but I've emancipated myself from situations I don't want to be in because joy is a much bigger commodity."

Robinson recently scored a new radio show on Sirius called "Gurus Galore". It's interesting for music aficionados and worth hearing.

"It's fun. I've always DJ'd at my friends shows or my own when the doors open. Especially in New York, San Francisco and Los Angeles. When promotional things are afoot radio stations ask me to leave them a playlist. Last winter I was at Sirius and my friend there said, 'Why don't we do a show? You can play anything you want.' I said, 'Be careful when you say anything I want.' He said, 'Anything'. So, it's great to throw vibes out there and play some esoteric or obscure music because somebody has never heard it before—who don't even know what deep—new edge music was like in the mid 70s or LSD magic music. Weird stuff. I can play anything."

Robinson's vast record collection hovers around six-thousand albums.

"The last few years, I've gotten rid of five or six thousand records. I'm moving into my 50s and I see where I want my collection to go."

Anyway You Love, We Know How You Feel contends as one of Robinson's most variegated albums, and he's happy where he's at these days.

"I didn't get into music to be told what to do. If something screws up—it's ultimately my problem, but I know how it's supposed to be. I got into this to be independent of the business. That's music. It's a deep, deep thing."

Check out The Chris Robinson Brotherhood...it's like supporting your local musical farmers.

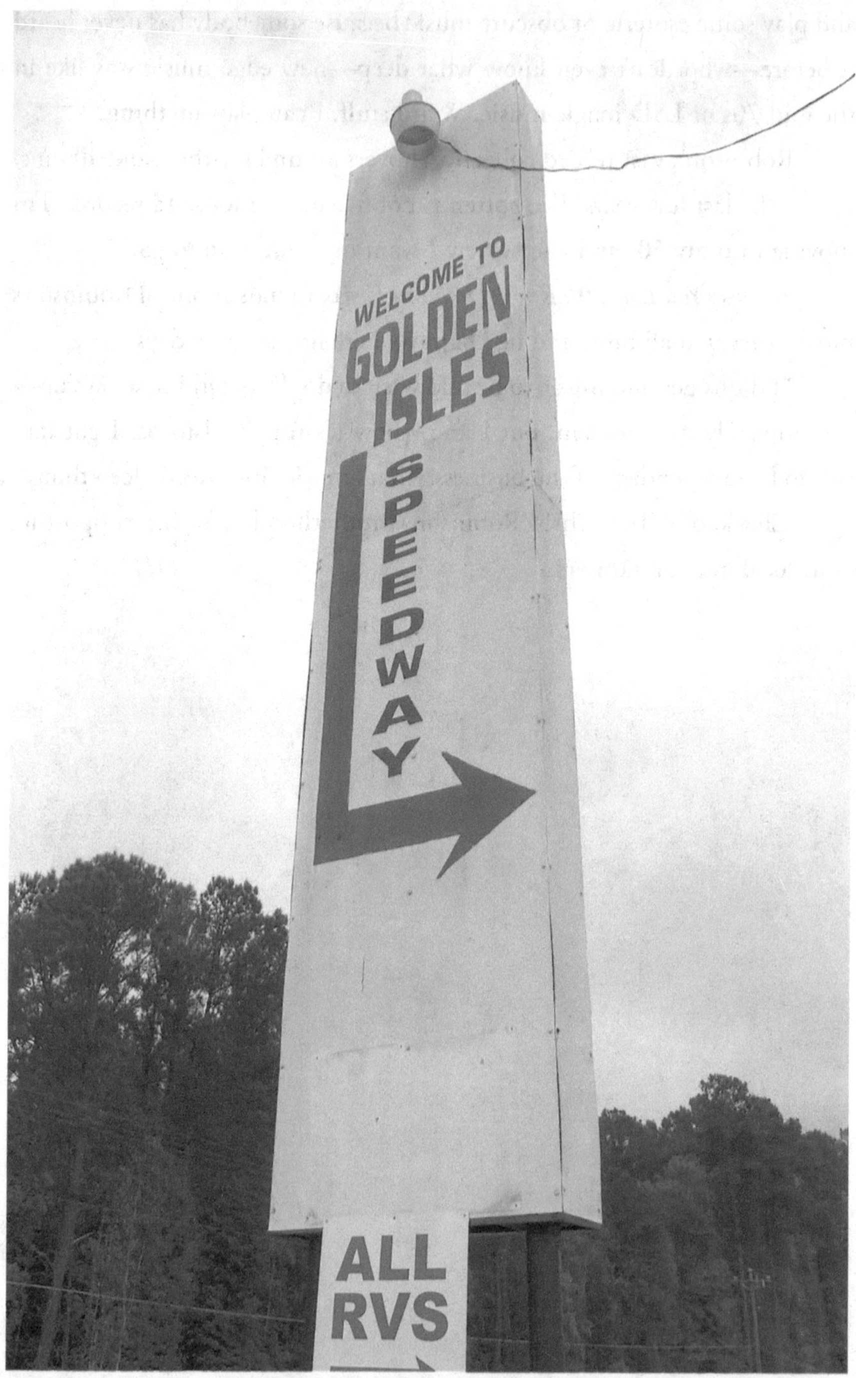

Golden Isles Speedway Sign

Sam Shepard: *Day Out of Days*

Sam Shepard died on July 27, 2017, in Midway, Kentucky.

SAM SHEPARD'S NEW BOOK *Day Out of Days* proves the award-winning playwright-actor still possesses his old literary fire. Shepard is a Pulitzer Prize-winning author of more than 45 plays. He's appeared in over 30 films, and received an Oscar as well as won 11 Obie Awards.

Some of this writer's favorite Shepard books rank as *The Rolling Thunder Logbook, Seven Plays, Motel Chronicles, Cruising Paradise, Fool For Love, Simpatico* and *Hawk Moon. Day Out of Days* contends as one of Shepard's best. These stories were written in the last several years. Composed usually in transit—from out on the road or roadside somewhere—these highway stories (over 24 specific highways are mentioned) paint vivid landscapes of contemporary American life. Shepard's stark style still cuts to the bone. It's no wonder why he's written with Bob Dylan, T-Bone Burnett and Wim Wenders.

Day Out of Days contains poems, over 100 stories and various dialogues. "Kitchen" opens as a detailed description of our narrator's pulse of the house. "Haskell, Arkansas" begins a series of stories about a severed head a man finds by the side of the road. Decapitation runs as a thread through this book. An assassin who surgically removes the faces of his dead victims appears throughout *Day Out of Days*.

Shepard maintains in his trademark style in this book. Dialogue tales—straight playwright script—like "Thor's Day", "Reason", "Livingston, Montana", "Interview in Café Pascual", "Boca Paila, Mexico", "Land of the Living" and "Black Oath" adhere to Shepard's sheer economy of words.

Throughout his books, the father/son struggle reappears, and there are a few here such as "Orange Grove In My Past", "Descendancy" and "Lost Coin". Shepard writes stories revolving around musicians such as Fats Domino, Thelonious Monk, Eric Dolphy, Hank Williams, Howlin' Wolf, Little Richard and Ralph Stanley in this book. He's always operated on the main artery of American music. He once lived with Charles Mingus' son and dated Patti Smith. He was even the drummer for the Holy Modal Rounders...

Stories and ghosts of Sitting Bull, Crazy Horse, Hurricane Katrina, The Lakota, Casey Jones, Confederate soldiers, Kit Carson, Dostoyevsky, firefighters, Richard Hugo, Marlon Brando, horses, speed freaks, Robert Blake and old friends from the past lace these pages. In many of these stories, the fine line of fact and fiction blurs the identification of the narrator, but if you know Shepard's work you know almost all of these stories are true. Even in the tales concerning wife and children, you can almost hear his wife Jessica saying, "Do you have a girlfriend?" just like the wife in one of these stories.

Shepard still retains the spirit of an old medicine man. This book counts as a timeless work from one of America's most talented artists.

Tift Merritt: *A Poetic Songbird*

Another Swampland interview…

"I can't keep quiet
Oh, I can't hide
I want to shout and sing
And shine, shine, shine…"

　　　　　"Tambourine"

—Tift Merritt

Her voice sounds flawless. She crafts her own songs, plays her own instruments and her ability to convey emotion to a crowd renders her a rare songbird in any generation. She adds soul to any song she sings. Tift Merritt, born in Texas, grew up in North Carolina—began playing music in her early teens. She spent years honing her songwriting while searching for musicians to fit into her overall sound. Her first album released in 2002, Bramble Rose, proved a reflective collection of introspective songs that marked the work of a budding musical poet. Her 2004 disc, Tambourine, found her rocking out a little more and exploring a STAX-like sound that earned her a Grammy nomination.

Tift's latest work, Another Country, finds her in a state of grace. These quiet songs, written in France, during a time she wanted to get away from anything familiar—define Tift Merritt as a serious songwriter. Her live performances, such as the one on Austin City Limits, illustrate her power as a performer.

In this interview, Tift discusses her early music influences, career moves, recording, writing, singing with Emmylou Harris, literature, photography, Another Country, future plans and a glimpse into the future. Tift Merritt emerges as one of the south's finest female artists today. She also proved an interesting conversationalist—a real southern belle.

Hello.

TM: James?

TM: I'm so sorry. I Sunday'd out…

It's okay.

TM: In fact, when the phone rang I was about to go running and I wondered who could be calling me on a Sunday night from a number I don't know. The funny thing is…I had a big sign on my desk: 'Don't forget—Interview Sunday Night!'

No problem. So, you've got a little time?

TM: Of course. How about you?

I'm just wrapping up something I wrote about seeing The Black Crowes on Friday in Chattanooga, which is relevant to our conversation because George Drakoulias produced the Crowes' first two records and he produced your last two.

TM: Wow. In fact, we just cut a track in London with Paul Stacey (Stacey played in Chris Robinson's band, *New Earth Mud*, produced *The Lost Crowes*, and served as the Crowes' lead guitarist from late 06 to mid-07 and he produced The Crowes' latest disc *Warpaint*).

Really? He's a great guitar player.

TM: He is a great guitar player.

I have to congratulate you—*Another Country* sounds mighty fine.

TM: Oh, thank you. George deserves thanks too—Dave Bianco—and all the musicians.

Let's go back all the way. You were born in Texas and you grew up in North Carolina.

TM: Oh, wow. We really are going all the way back.

We won't get lost back there, but what are your earliest musical memories?

TM: My earliest musical memories are singing with my dad or watching my dad play music and me trying to sing along. Just him teaching me cool old songs and just spending time with him…

Was his guitar always around and you'd pick it up?

TM: Well, he played piano and guitar. So I started playing piano first. Then I guess I was 13 or so when I started playing—ah that was so long ago—I should be so much better at it. At 13 or 14 I started to take an interest in his guitar. He had a beautiful old Guild. He always said he won it in a pool game, but that is so unlike my father that I just don't believe him. It's a great story but I don't think it's true. So, I eventually got a little guitar of my own by the time I was 14 or 15.

What kind of music were you buying and listening to at that time?

TM: I was always a bit out of sync. I was doing what most folk musicians do. I was fi guring out the songs that I could play. What I listened to was what I could fi gure out how to play. So, I listened to a lot of Bob Dylan, a lot of old soul and Joni Mitchell. I had *Blonde On Blonde* and this Michelle

Shocked record. Anything I could hear and latch onto and try to figure out on my own and try to sing what I was really interested in hearing.

How did you get your first band together?

TM: I played with people a little in high school, but mostly I was just by myself. I played in bars for a while when I was in my late teens. I was by myself and I couldn't drink and I didn't know how to handle drunk boys and I looked really young. So I didn't like that much. I tried playing with other people but nothing really stuck. I was pretty introverted. I eventually went to college. I just kept writing because that seemed to make the most sense to me. Then I met Zeke (Hutchins) and we put a band together and that just stuck.

Was songwriting your angle at that age?

TM: I was always a writer first. In fact, I thought that I would write stories and novels. Songwriting was really a natural part of that, but I wanted to be a writer. I didn't necessarily have to have a band.

Speaking of writers, what's the last book you've read?

TM: I'm reading a biography of Alan Waters right now.

Have you ever read any Cormac McCarthy?

TM: Oh, he's one of my favorites. In fact, I read *The Road*…it wasn't the last book of his I've read. In the past year, I've read *The Road* and that was incredible, but I love *The Border Trilogy*…

That's his sweetest stuff.

TM: I know. Some of the other stuff—like *Suttree*—that was really hard. He gets pretty dark.

His early works are not for the faint of heart.

TM: I think he writes about violence in such a beautiful way.

So, around 1999 you're playing around Chapel Hill, and that's when you and you're band crossed paths with the Two Dollar Pistols.

TM: Yeah, we had our band and we opened a lot for the Two Dollar Pistols and they would get me up on stage to sing a duet.

Around that time you met Ryan Adams, right?

TM: Yeah, it was all around the same time. Ryan wasn't living in North Carolina at the time. It was probably around 2000-2001. We were just playing clubs and doing our thing and so it was around then. Let's see, I signed to Lost Highway in 2001—yeah, it was 1999 or 2000 when I met Ryan.

***Bramble Rose* was your first real record. It's a pretty laid back affair with well-constructed compositions. You even got Tom Petty's great keyboardist Benmont Tench to play on the record.**

TM: Benmont is wonderful. We were working with Ethan Johns (Glyn Johns' son) who has a great community of musicians around him. It was all very natural. There was nothing tricky about it.

You attracted some critical acclaim over *Bramble Rose*. What was happening in between *Bramble Rose* and your next record *Tambourine*? I know you were out on the road some.

TM: I went out on the road for a while, but not long as you would have thought. We were out for about six months. Then I got the call that I needed to go home and write another record.

That's about the time you came across George Drakoulias, right?

TM: Well, while I was writing that record *(Tambourine)* I met George. George has always been a dream producer for me. I picked up the Maria McKee record when I was a teenager and just had this gut feeling that George would understand what I'm trying to do. There was a fair amount of pressure put on that record in the beginning…'we need a hit'…when that ideology is touted—I'm not saying it's anyone's fault, it's just part of the deal (laughs). That was a good time for me to say I want to work with George. Also, I felt like *Bramble Rose* is such a part of me…it's special, but I'd never been on the road before. I really found myself in a new place as a writer and as an artist after being on the road. We had this amazing capability as a rock band, and as a performer I was getting my own confidence. That record had so much tenderness on it. I really wanted to make sure that I made a record that stayed as genuine and sincere, but it didn't have so much time spent on the introverted—wanted to rock out. We played so many ballads on that tour that it was very natural that I wanted to rock. It wasn't so much that I wanted to go in the other direction as I wanted a balance of all the colors. I think George has a really amazing way of handling sincerity and energy. That was how I met George. He and I hit it off immediately.

So, since Drakoulias worked with Tom Petty in the past—he recruited Mike Campbell and Benmont Tench to play on your second album *Tambourine*.

TM: Yeah. We got lucky there. It was pretty scary because they are so good.

Emmylou Harris' band member Don Heffington also played on *Tambourine*.

TM: Yeah, he's played with everyone.

***Tambourine* is a great record too. It's got a little more rocking on there. At the end of the *Tambourine* tour was when you taped your great *Austin City Limits* session, right?**

TM: Yeah, it was late in the album cycle when we recorded that.

It was a great way to highlight the band.

TM: Absolutely, that was a great band.

So, what sort of headspace were you in that made you want to live in France? Those songs you wrote there make up your latest CD, *Another Country*.

TM: Well, I was doing a tour over in Europe and the record cycle was done, and I didn't know what was next. I just decided to stay in Paris—just to take a vacation. So I rented an apartment with a piano in it. All of a sudden I just started writing. So, I called home and said I was coming home.

How many songs did you write in France?

TM: Well, once it was all said and done—more than that, but by the time we went in to do the session it was very clear what was going on the record. I write a lot more songs that go on the record—some are finished—some aren't. Some are just pathways to other songs. It's a process for me…not really a number.

Where did you record *Another Country*?

TM: In California.

Drakoulias once again produced it. Bob Dylan's old guitar player, Charlie Sexton, plays on *Another Country*, but your band plays on all the songs. Not too many guests on this one.

TM: Yeah.

You've got a Letterman appearance coming up.

TM: Yeah, I have two. One I'm a backup singer for Emmylou Harris.

Her new record *All I Intended To Be* is great.

TM: Oh, it's beautiful.

You're in good company. Was *Another Country* your first record you really got to do what you wanted?

TM: Yeah. When I was writing this record I didn't even know that I was writing a record. I was just hanging out in France trying to give myself some time. I'd been working really hard on the road for a long time. We were nominated for a Grammy and that made everything crazy. Then everything just stopped. I didn't know what was going on (laughs). I wasn't even sure I wanted to make another record y'know? I was just totally writing for myself. I brought these songs back to the States and kept writing and kept going back to France and kept writing and then eventually this record was dropped. So by that point, I knew where to go because these songs made things self-evident for all the right reasons because that's what it is…I wrote the songs because I wrote them. I just followed the songs.

Were you feeling any pressure during that time?

TM: I think the concept of pressure is a funny one. There was pressure on this record, but a very different kind of pressure. It was a pressure of I didn't think I had anything to say. I didn't think I had it inside. I don't want to draw lines between personal and professional pressure. I do what I do because I mean it. Of course, sometimes there's pressure in the soup… somebody's calling up saying you have to do this or you should do that. I do what I do and say what I say because it's real. Whether any of those things are there are not. So, I think you're right—this record is an exceptional experience. (Pause) It wasn't the same as my other works. I think really what happened with this record is it's so apart from the music business that even talking about it in a music-business sense makes it even less special. I stepped away from my whole life and went to another country where I didn't even speak the language. It's a kind of freedom we only get a few times in our life.

Well, I must say, for someone who says they don't speak the language the last song on *Another Country*—is a beautiful song you sing in French called "Mille Tendresses".

TM: Well, I do speak the language, but I'm not fluent. I can certainly get by, but it's still an experience while just communicating with one other person is something you can't take for granted.

You've got some pretty serious tour dates coming up.

TM: Yeah, we've been out for about three months already. We did six weeks in New York and a month in Europe.

Tuesday is your next date. You're in Philadelphia Tuesday and then it's back to Europe. I'd like to try and catch your show in July at the Grand Ol' Opry.

TM: That would be great. I think they're going to televise that show.

At this point, being in the business, what's been the hardest thing for you to learn?

TM: That's a good question. The music business is not real. There are days it feels real for good or bad and you certainly have to make it work somehow. I don't know if it's been the hardest thing to learn but it's a constant reminder that I'm a working artist, and I'm glad to be working. I just want to be a good writer and a good musician. It's always been about storytelling, but somehow that doesn't seem personal enough. I think it's important to remember music is real but the business is not.

Regardless of the business, music, writing, or whatever you're just trying to move the audience—to make them laugh, cry or reflect.

TM: Ah, semantics are very important when you're talking to a writer (laughs). I would say when I'm performing, I am a storyteller because I'm not trying to illicit a reaction from the crowd—I'm trying to tell a story as true as I can. I have a radio show where I talk to artists about the kind of things you're asking a little bit. Sometimes the road is such an insular place you should be really careful that you're bringing new…uh…

…That you're not amputating yourself from real life…

TM: Absolutely! I couldn't say it better myself.

Maybe there are semantics involved (collective laughter). You're not a greenhorn anymore.

TM: We're all thankful we're not green anymore.

Obviously a Grammy nomination is up there, but what are some of your other highlights?

TM: Well, the first time I sang with Emmylou Harris in my hometown with my parents there. That was really amazing. That will always be a highlight. That was in 2002. It was a landmine benefit. I was a surprise on the bill because someone had to cancel. Emmylou introduced me in my hometown and chimed in on a song with me and I thought I died and gone to heaven. My mother told me I'd never get anything else for Christmas (laughs) since I got everything I ever wanted. There are definitely times—there are highlights of writing—highlights of performing…it's important to remember it's one of those great things about being a musician. It's not a one-sided career. You're a performer—you're a business person—mostly a writer and a musician. So, there have been moments on stage or moments in my own privacy when I was writing when they would touch that place you're trying to touch. Sometimes I get there without effort…and those are the ones you say 'I can't believe that happened'.

So, like many folks, you take photographs.

TM: Oh, I'm a hack. I started taking pictures. If I could draw or paint—I'd be a painter—but I can't. I don't have the gene where your hand expresses what you mean on canvas. Photography is really important to me for a couple of reasons—one, I think it's good to think in pictures and not think in words—as a writer it's a practice of using my eyes and challenging the words. I think it's important to look. As a performer—I really got serious about it when I was on tour because I was so desperately tired of myself and I just didn't feel interesting at all and I'd go look at other people and it was a really important part of what made me happy every day.

You can distract attention away from yourself.

TM: You get outside of yourself and that's important for all of us. Then you have this love for your step-child (laughs) and there's no pressure for you to be any good at it.

The expectation is low.

TM: Yeah, so it brings a special kind of happiness.

So, who are the guys you've got out on the road with you behind *Another Country?*

TM: Well, Zeke Hutchins—he's been my musical partner and business partner and boyfriend for a long time. Jay Brown has been with us for ten years—he's the bass player and harmony singer. Danny Eisenberg has been with us for about five years now. Scott McCall has recently started playing guitar with us—he's a North Carolina man. He's wonderful.

You're upcoming tour schedule is rigorous.

TM: You should have seen it three months ago (laughs).

Yeah, when we first set up our interview, I remember thinking that's two months from now. You're home now, right?

TM: Yeah, I'm at home in New York right now. I play Philly, New York— then I do Letterman. Then I go to Norway!

Then back to Colorado.

TM: Crazy routing, eh?

I look forward to the Letterman performance. I'll remind you in a couple months about contributing.

TM: Yeah, let me give you my email. As you know I don't have a bunch of time on my hands, but I'm always interested in writing—getting my thoughts together for something particular…

Even if you wanted to write something around some Norwegian barbecue joint you take a picture of on tour (heh heh heh).

TM: That would be a story! (laughs). That would be awesome.

No pressure. No forced march towards the deadline.

TM: Or some dreaded homework paper.

Only submit things that give you a buzz.

TM: Awesome.

Well, since you'll be singing onstage in Philadelphia less than 48 hours from now--and you're not going to have much down time this summer--I'll bid you goodnight.

TM: I enjoyed this--it was fun. It was really nice talking to you. Please forgive me for being late.

Of course, you're forgiven.

Sam Peckinpah:
Bring Me The Head of Alfredo Garcia

2004 MARKS THE THIRTIETH anniversary of Sam Peckinpah's *Bring Me the Head of Alfredo Garcia*, a film that still resonates as a disturbing volume in American cinema. Peckinpah, "Bloody Sam", contends as a pioneering filmmaker best known for his violent and nihilistic stories that reveal dark complexities relevant for every generation. Other influential Peckinpah work includes *Ride the High Country, The Wild Bunch, Straw Dogs, Pat Garrett & Billy the Kid*, and *The Killer Elite*.

Sam Peckinpah was born in Fresno, California, on February 21, 1925, into a family of lumberjacks, cattle ranchers, and frontier lawyers. Young Sam played under the rural shadow of Peckinpah Mountain named after his grandfather. After serving in the marines, Peckinpah moved to Hollywood. In 1955, he landed a job writing scripts for the famous TV show, *Gunsmoke*. Soon Peckinpah's talent led to a position as writer on legendary television shows *The Rifleman* and *The Westerner*. Peckinpah left an indelible print working as an actor, director, and writer for many movie and television projects including *Zane Grey Theater, Noon Wine, Trackdown, Broken Arrow, Have Gun Will Travel, Route 66*, and *Invasion of the Body Snatchers*, among others.

In 1961 Peckinpah directed his first full-length film titled *The Deadly Companions*. The following year he achieved a break-through with *Ride the High Country*, starring Randolph Scott. This beautiful film remains a Peckinpah gem epitomizing an undertone of "salvation and loneliness" in a story about two old lawmen.

Peckinpah fought with movie executives during filming of his next project, *Major Dundee* (1965), featuring Charlton Heston, Richard Harris, and James Coburn. The *Dundee* Civil War plot unfolds around a Confederate group of POW's led across the Mexican border to pursue renegade Apaches. Studio executives cut a great deal of the vital scenes out to make the movie shorter. Peckinpah's resistance with high-ranking production bosses led to his blackballing from Hollywood. Peckinpah later said of the film, "Dundee was one of the most painful things that ever happened in my life."

In 1969, Peckinpah's vast scope culminated in perhaps his greatest motion picture, *The Wild Bunch*. The unforgettable opening scene shows giddy children tossing wounded scorpions onto a swarming anthill as The Bunch rides up in a moment of eerie premonition that remains a classic moment on 70mm celluloid.

In *The Wild Bunch* Peckinpah's trademark shift in perspective, the same event viewed from a variety of camera angles, revealed a new cinematic technique. The ultra-violent film, starring Warren Oates, Ernest Borgnine, William Holden, and Robert Ryan, tells a grim tale of an aging gang of outlaws who become involved with Mexican revolutionaries. Upon release, the movie stirred wide praise and outrage. During the Vietnam era, *The Wild Bunch* reminded the public how violent America remained throughout history as well as current times. Peckinpah explained,

"You see, people begin to see the violence within them, the violence just below the surface. It's in all of us, as the film shows, whether we be criminals, lawmen, children (who learn from their elders), or old men. Violence usually begins with a reason, with some principle to be defended. The real motivation, however, is a primitive thirst for blood, and as the fighter continues reasons or principles are forgotten and men fight for the sake of fighting."

Peckinpah's next film, *The Ballad of Cable Hogue*, released in 1970, emerges as one of Peckinpah's most lighthearted and romantic films. Peckinpah claimed *Cable Hogue* ranked as his favorite work. *Cable Hogue*, like *Ride the High Country* and *The Wild Bunch*, continued to prove Peckinpah's genius cinematic presentation of any austere countryside.

In *Straw Dogs* (based on the Gordon Williams novel *The Siege of Trencher's Farm)*, Dustin Hoffman portrays a pacifist living in the country with his wife. Soon the couple discovers their home is invaded by a violent a gang of local thugs. A haunting rape scene lingers as one of Peckinpah's most disturbing. Peckinpah mentioned at the time, "*Straw Dogs* is about a guy who finds out a few nasty secrets about himself, about his marriage, about where he is, about the world around him…it's about the violence within all of us. The violence is reflecting on the political condition of the world today. It serves as a cathartic effect. Someone may feel a strange sick exultation at the violence, but then he should ask himself: 'What is going on in my heart?'"

Fired from *The Cincinnati Kid* in 1965 Peckinpah managed to maintain a relationship with the film's star, Steve McQueen. McQueen starred in Peckinpah's next two formidable films, *Junior Bonner* and *The Getaway.* The latter proved a major hit amplifying the off-screen chemistry between McQueen and Ali MacGraw in an adaptation of the Jim Thompson novel.

In 1973, *Pat Garrett & Billy The Kid*, including cast members James Coburn, Kris Kristofferson, Harry Dean Stanton, Slim Pickens, and Bob Dylan (who wrote the movie soundtrack) disappointed critics although the film displayed flashes of brilliance. A simple shot of a cactus against an overcast mountainous skyline arouses a mysterious melancholy in Peckinpah's trademark shots of desolate terrain. This underrated film weaves a sad theme of friendship and betrayal between two legendary old friends Pat Garrett and William Bonney. *Pat Garrett and Billy the Kid*, another film causing a war with studio executives, signified Peckinpah's last western.

Perhaps Peckinpah's most autobiographical work surfaced in *Bring Me the Head of Alfredo Garcia* (featuring Mexican sex goddess Isela Vega) where Warren Oates portrays a down and out American pianist looking for one last big paycheck. Oates' character accepts payment from a wealthy landowner that wants to find the man who impregnated his daughter. Filmed around

Mexico City and Cuernavaca, Peckinpah's mastery renders the film worth seeing just for the vivid Mexican landscape. Garcia remains a gritty tale of dangerous characters inspired by revenge, greed, and black humor—verifying, once again, Peckinpah's films do not sit well with the weak of heart.

In later years, his alcohol-cocaine fueled lifestyle affected his health, but Peckinpah managed to create *The Killer Elite* (1975), *Cross of Iron* (1977) (Orson Welles called this the best anti-war movie he'd ever seen), *Convoy* (1978), and his final film, *The Osterman Weekend* (1983).

In 1984 Peckinpah shot two music videos for Julian Lennon, "Valotte" and "Too Late For Goodbyes", that launched the young singer's career. Peckinpah began adapting several stories for the big screen months before he died of a heart attack in Inglewood, California, on December 28, 1984.

Peckinpah's hypnotic films weigh heavy in any historical context since the world continues turning on a violent axis. His work reflects savage truths the audience must face in everyday life. In the words of legendary filmmaker Martin Scorsese, "There is no doubt when seeing Peckinpah's films that you are looking at one of the great masters of American cinema."

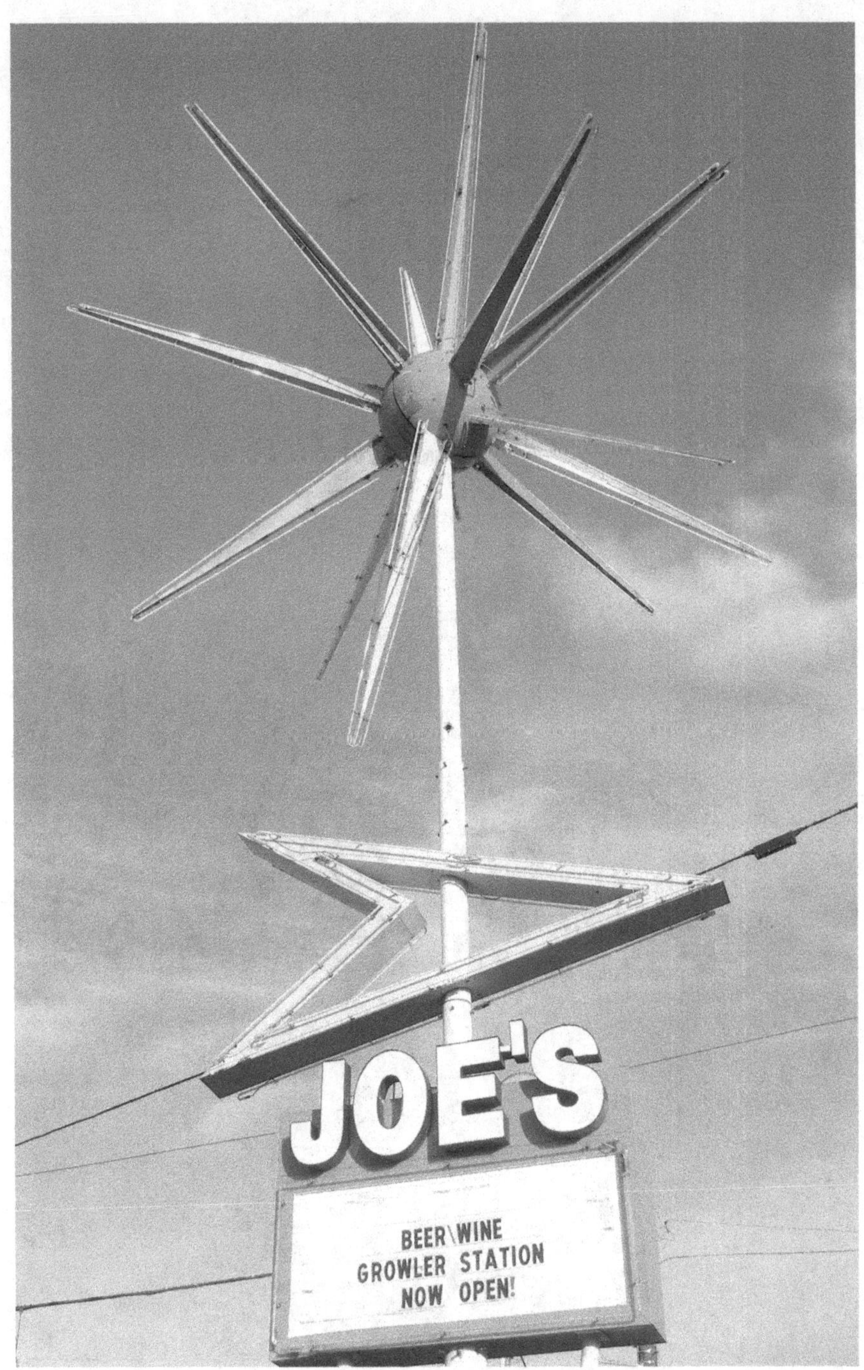

Memphis, TN

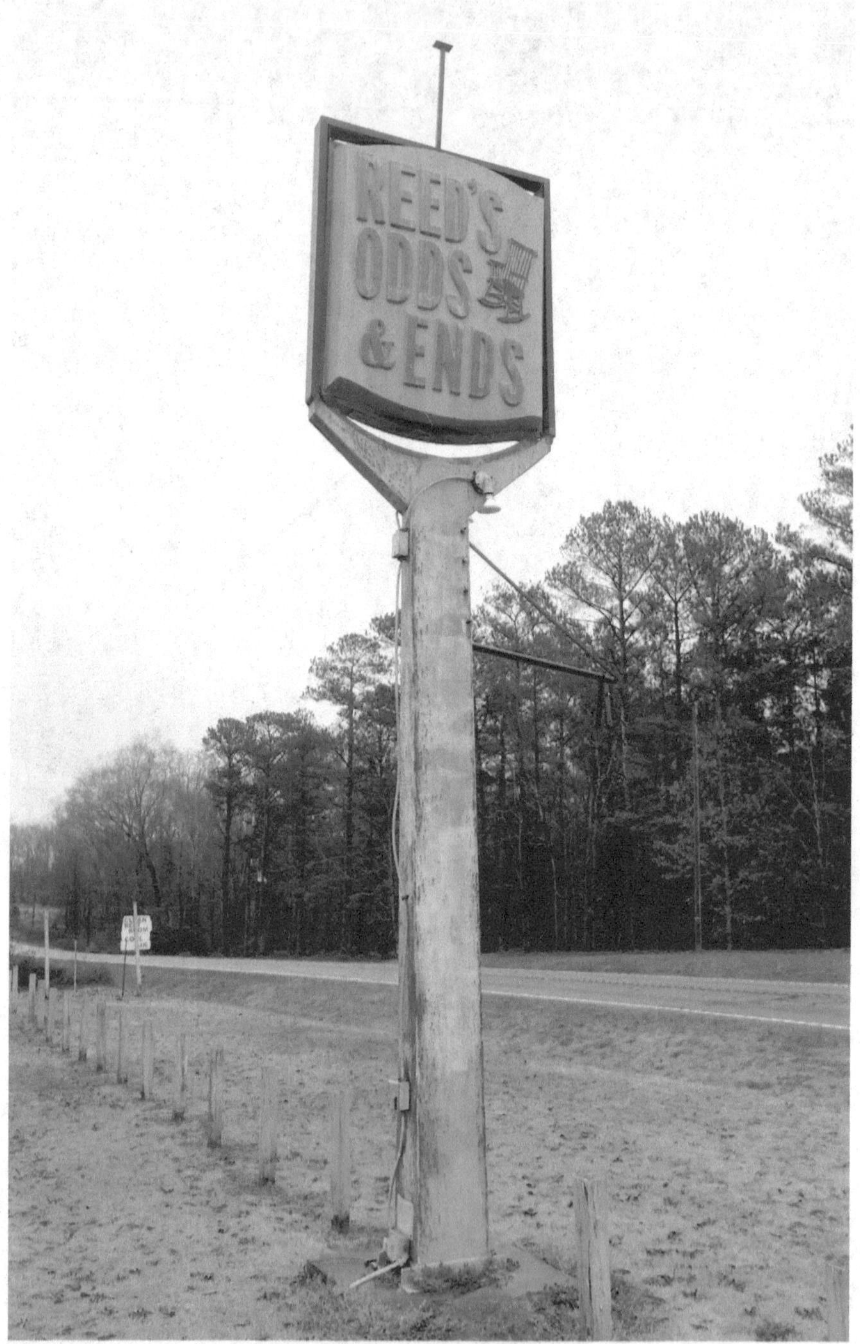

Reed's Odds & Ends

Luther Dickinson Interview:
The Secret Code of Memphis Guitars

I interviewed Luther Dickinson various times. This interview transpired in January of 2008. Luther just recorded Warpaint during his tenure in The Black Crowes.

"I'm gonna leave Memphis and spread the news/ Memphis women don't wear no shoes."

—Furry Lewis

Luther and Cody Dickinson grew up in the Mississippi hill country, where country blues music remains fertile. Their father, Jim Dickinson, played an instrumental role in the North Mississippi Allstars latest record, Hernando. The Allstars recorded this hard-rocking, blues-filtered collection at Jim Dickinson's Zebra Ranch. Jim Dickinson played with many great artists such as Aretha Franklin, Ry Cooder, Duane Allman, The Dixie Flyers, The Rolling Stones and Bob Dylan to name a few, but his musical roots and instincts allowed him to produce other artists such as The Replacements, Screamin Jay Hawkins and Big Star. Dickinson and Sons serve as a beacon of light in the environs of Coldwater, Mississippi. Luther and Cody fell into their father's footsteps while they continually advance towards preserving and continuing some of America's oldest musical idioms.

Hernando, the name of their hometown, wastes no notes. These songs will transfer well to a live audience. The hard-rocking album also cements the Allstars as a great American trio. In this interview, Luther discusses Hernando, the origins of the Allstars, growing up in hill country, musical influences, his father, his brother Cody, Stanley Booth, his local community, the old days, recording with John Hiatt last fall, upcoming super groups as well as recording with and joining The Black Crowes.

This interview took place the night before Luther was set to go out on the road for about a month and a half to promote Hernando, The Allstars fifth studio release. I've invited Luther to contribute periodically, and he's up for it. So, this interview preserves a clear insight into Luther's (and Family) accomplishments, intentions and in between some very landmark sessions as well as a peek into the future.

Our paths first crossed in Memphis in 1990. You and Cody were playing with your Dad at the Memphis Blues Festival as Jim Dickinson and the Hardlycan Playboys.

LD: I remember that.

Stanley Booth and I made the trip. Stanley and your dad are luminaries on the Memphis music scene, and they go way back.

LD: Yeah, man they're old friends.

So, tomorrow is the first show of the tour, right?

LD: Yeah, it's a six week tour. I'm excited.

You're one of the few guys who grew up in a perfect environment for a serious music education.

LD: Yeah, we were lucky.

The band has evolved since 1996 and three GRAMMY nominations later—would you say times have changed?

LD: We have gone through a lot of changes just growing up. We started touring in 1998—with 10 years on the road we've gone through different musical influences of being on the road. Sometimes you tour with bands and you're exposed to different scenes but we've always drawn on strength and power from the home-front. The biggest evolution in the home scene has been—since that period of time—the elders of the hills have all passed away. That was really hard to deal with…especially more so for the family members more than us—we were just friends. The cool thing is down here—I'm not really talking about my band—but the community that we come from and represent it's so cool because Gary and Dwayne Burnside— David Kimbrough—The Turner Family—everybody is keeping their thing going. What really flips me out is that there's a whole new batch of young dudes. Just teenagers and cats in their early twenties from our hometown of Hernando who are playing great and hanging out with the families and grew up doing what I grew up doing. Not only that these cats Dwayne and Gary, they're the new elders and that makes me feel so cool. It's such a cool thing to see.

How does *Hernando* fit into the Allstars history or approach?

LD: Well, I'm real proud of it…there's a couple of things. In the past, the songs you write you try to write them to fit the band—even if it isn't your forte. On this record we had the time and took my Dad's advice and demoed up like 22 songs. Then he picked which ones he wanted us to do. He picked all the rockers which is really great because the original plan was to make a classic, straight-up blues rocker. Then I started writing and all these different kinds of tunes cropped up and then they kind of seduce you. It's funny how songs do that—a song will come and you'll have to give it respect and you gotta follow it through, but it may not be the right song for the time or for your band, you know what I'm saying? This is the first time that we had enough material in the demo process…we put the record together before we recorded it. Usually it's in the studio. It's a real concise record and I really thank dad for keeping me true to my original vision of just doing a straight ahead blues rocker.

So, once again, father Jim played an instrumental role.

LD: Oh yeah. He was keeping me on task. We did it at home which to me—we've done our last two records in Memphis and I love Ardent and I love Memphis, but I think in this day and age with the record industry the way it is and the technology—I think it's important to capture the atmosphere, and some character. In our home studio we've been nurturing the scene and the vibe and the sonics for years. I think it's more important to have some character on your record instead of some cold studio. Listening to the Black Keys kinda turned me onto that because they got some real charmingly lo-fi sounding records. And I thought that was really cool—here's some cats making their own records and they don't sound great, but they sound cool. Lots of fans would rather listen to a bootleg tape of a concert. So I think the more character you can put into your records in this day and age, the better. That's part of why I wanted to record at home. I do other things other places, but for us I think our home studio is part of what people like about our early records. What's also cool is that we've focused so much that we have our home studio at our parents place, and I can come home and be in the studio at our parents place and I can come home and be in the studio working but it feels like I'm just hanging out with my family and friends. To have that is great because a studio can be a really stuffy, intimidating place, but to be in a studio with family and friends—you can't beat that with a stick.

I suppose it was the same old Jim Dickinson strategy of, 'What take do you like boys? First one or second?'

LD: That's exactly right. (laughs) Exactly. The way it works is the first complete take…y'know, no false starts.

Any guests on *Hernando*?

LD: It was just us. Dad played a little piano. I had a couple buddies sing some background vocals.

It would be nice to have your dad hit the road because he would be a dynamic addition to the band.

LD: He doesn't travel too much because of his health and all. Plus he's got his studio. He's got his whole career invested in that place. It's too bad though.

How long did it take to record *Hernando*?

LD: We did it pretty quick—about three weeks I guess. We cut the basic tracks in five or six days. This was in September and we cut the basic tracks and spent time doing the vocals and tightening up the lyrics, and overdubs here and there. Then we mixed it. So we cut it—did some vocals and overdubs and then we mixed it in three weeks. It went pretty quick.

You knew going it this record would be a flat out rocker?

LD: Oh yeah. I was definitely listening to a lot of early ZZ Top, Black Sabbath, Zeppelin, AC/DC, but there's so much blues in that stuff and we never claimed to be a blues band…we just rock and roll.

I think you're exposure at an early age to your father's music, Furry Lewis, the Dixie Flyers, Fred McDowell and those old blues men, leaks into your interpretation of rock and roll.

LD: Yeah, you're right man. It was cool for me because I always knew I wanted to be a guitar player. I was never rebellious against my father. I always looked up to him and his friends because they were so fucking cool.

And you could always coax them to give you a little music lesson.

LD: Oh hell yeah. Just Dad's record collection was a wealth of knowledge—it was my responsibility being in the position I was in—to learn as much of that traditional roots music as I could. It really paid off. Man, it's funny you mention Stanley Booth because there's this one—I can't remember the name of the story in *Rythm Oil*, but he's talking about the band being on-stage and they're playing the guitars and speaking in the secret language of Memphis guitars, or something like that. I talked to my dad about that and I said 'What is that? I want to sound like that…what is the secret code of Memphis guitars? He was like, 'Well, you know it's a bunch of songs you gotta learn. It's the language of what we all do.' So, that's what I went after.

Just the geographical influence of where you grew up proves a fascinating ghost map of old blues legends. You're even a real close ride to Memphis.

LD: Yeah, 45 minutes to Memphis on some back roads. I grew up hanging out in Memphis a lot—especially as a teenager. In the 90s when I realized there was modern day country blues right down the road it just changed my life. That was when we started going to Junior's (Kimbrough) and hanging out with R.L. (Burnside), and hanging out with Otha's (Turner).

What was your first guitar?

LD: I was five when I got my first electric. I had a plastic acoustic. But Cody, he was a natural. He learned "Casey Jones" right off the bat. I was not a natural. I had the desire and the drive to do it, but I learned a lot from Cody because he was so damn talented. I always knew what I wanted to do and I worked my ass off. Cody was just a little bitty kid playing some guitar.

Stanley and I spent the evening at Jimmy Crosthwait house, and he was the guy who taught Cody how to play the washboard.

LD: That's awesome man. Yeah, I guess we're products of the underground Memphis counter-culture.

You were talking about recording at home—once you get to the point of becoming a touring band did you begin to see the evil underbelly of corporate record companies?

LD: Man, as far as creative control we were always rebellious, but we found our own way. It's funny we signed our record deal in 1999—and our first record came out right at the end of the old school record industry, because by the time our second record was finished people started talking about ripping and downloading CDs and I didn't know what they were talking about. I said, 'You burned it because it was so bad?' (laughs). That was when everything started changing—the technology. It was pretty cool because our first record sold a lot and it opened up the whole world for us. We did a world tour. I think our best advantage at that point was the fact that we waited so long to put out a real release. We had a fan base in the southeast because we'd been touring but then with that record deal we got bought and sold like a piece of property three or four times and we just got out of it last year. That's when we started our own record company—Songs of the South. *Hernando* is our third release and we have a fourth release on the way. I think our rebelliousness is coming out now. We've got our fan base, we're not going after some fantasy to get on MTV or sell a million records. We're gonna do what we do and we're going to do it on our own and control it. I think it's the way of the future. All my friends are doing it. Robert Randolph is the only cat I know that has a record deal.

The Songs of the South label presents some wonderful opportunities to expose some real artists.

LD: As of now, we're releasing our own product. My brother has his own record label, Diamond D, and he's got like 30 some artists…it's download only—no physical CDs. It's doing really well, so he's got that covered. I would, in the future, be interested in doing some of my friends' records, but I really don't want to get into that right now. We're really just getting it off the ground.

You should check out a label here in Atlanta called Dust To Digital. They put out these amazing box sets like *Goodbye Babylon, The Fonotone Records* collection and old sacred harp recordings. One of the Goodbye Babylon CDs is just sermons.

LD: Wow. I will have to check that out.

So, you hit the road tomorrow.

LD: Yeah, it's a rocking record to take out. There's no acoustic instruments on it. We did an acoustic record right before *Hernando* that was all traditionals so we got that out of our system. This one is nasty rock and roll. I'm real proud of "Keep the Devil Down", "Soldier", "Eaglebird", "Shake What Your Mama Gave You"…

You wrote all the lyrics?

LD: I did some collaborating with Jimbo Mathus, but yeah I pretty much wrote all the lyrics. Most of the time it works best when I have some lyrics I'm working on and some music and then all of a sudden it comes together into one thing. Luckily, for whatever reason I never had to sit down with some music and say, 'Man, I gotta come up with something.' Sometimes songs fester and I take my time. There's one old song on *Hernando* that Mudboy & The Neutrons used to do "I'd Love To Be A Hippy"—that's a Champion Jack Dupree song. There's another cover, "Long Way From Home" that my old jazz guitar teacher wrote, it's a real cool tune. The crazy thing is—he's kind of a world traveler—a psychedelic warrior—Stanley probably knows him, but since he taught me the song he disappeared and I can't find him. So that's why there's a special thanks to him in the liner notes.

You'll go out on the road behind *Hernando*, and then you join The Black Crowes for the *Warpaint* tour. You recorded their new album with them. You're now officially a Crowe—congratulations.

LD: Yeah, I'll jump right into their tour. I'm really excited about it man. What a band.

One of the greatest rock and roll bands in the last 20 years.

LD: Absolutely. I grew up listening to those guys, but over the years I became friends with them. I can't think of another band that would put such a jolt into my life, and it really feels like the right thing to do for rock and roll. I think there's a lot of potential in the chemistry.

What was it like recording with The Crowes?

LD: Oh man, it was cool. Once again, it's really live—they were fresh songs we worked up. It was very organic, just a bunch of dudes in a room looking for the one take. When it came together, it was magic…it was a story like the Rolling Stones recording in Muscle Shoals that my dad would talk about.

I've got a 400 page draft of a Crowes book I've been writing, and you joining the band proves a very interesting twist.

LD: It will be very interesting.

Before I forget, talk about getting back with Robert Randolph in December for those *Word* shows.

LD: It was really cool to watch Robert because by the third and fourth night he really came back to this place that musically was where he was when we first met him. That was really cool. He said it was good for him to do something different again. It was fun because it was really improvisational.

Do you think being a full-time member in the Black Crowes will affect other musical commitments?

LD: Well, you know, I just made a record with John Hiatt as well. He's touring in April and I wish I could join him. We made a record and toured two summers together. He just made a largely acoustic record that I'm real proud of and I haven't heard it since we did it. He's got a home studio now. He engineered it, produced it, wrote it, performed it—he didn't want anybody extra in the process. He really did a fine job.

Do you know what the Hiatt record will be called?

LD: I don't know, the working title was *He's with the Band*, or something like that. But James, we cut this thing last week that was a motherfucker! I wanted to do a blues supergroup thing, and I always say we're not a blues band, we play rock and roll—blah, blah, blah—but I wanted to do a record where we just say fuck it—we're doing a hard ass blues album. So, it was Charlie Musselwhite, Alvin Youngblood Hart, Jimbo Mathus, my dad and us. We cut like 22 songs in three days and I'm telling you that shit is badass. The basic tracks are done. Dad's gonna finish it. My thing was I didn't want to sing. I instigated the whole thing, but I just wanted to play guitar and do blues. We all sat in one big circle in the studio and played quiet with a bunch of microphones—we kinda shot for a Chess Records or Sun Records feel…no headphones—just singing out in the room and playing it right there…it was fucking bad.

22 songs in three days—I'm anxious to hear that stuff.

LD: It was tight. You want to know the name of the band?

…Of course…

LD: …The New Moon Jellyroll Freedom Rockers…

Charlie Musselwhite is the real deal.

LD: The real deal for sure.

Alvin Youngblood Hart is going out on the road opening up for y'all, right?

LD: Yeah, exactly. He's great.

I interviewed David Barbe last week. He records all the Drive By Truckers' albums—even Bettye Lavette's in Muscle Shoals with them. Have you heard *Brighter Than Creation's Dark*?

LD: Oh man, I love it. I'm so proud of those guys.

The Allstars will do a few shows with the Truckers towards the end of your tour.

LD: Yeah, we'll join and play with them out in California. *Hernando* is a real simple album we're touring on. We didn't want a lot of guests—so it will be great live. It will be great to cross paths with the Truckers.

What will Cody have going on when you're with the Crowes?

LD: He's got a bunch of stuff going on. He, Chris, and the Burnsides are gonna be a Hill Country band, which I think is really cool. He just produced a bad as record on Dwayne—that we all played on and helped out. He's got one in the can that's a motherfucker. Cody did a great job. And Cody just produced the two records on the Burnside Exploration, which is Gary's band, so Cody's got a lot going on back home. Then also, Chris Chew has come to the forefront as a singer doing soul music—so we're working on doing Chris' solo record. He's stepping out because he's got a really good soul voice.

The Allstars aren't coming through Atlanta on this run. I guess I'll see you in March when the Crowes play the Tabernacle.

LD: Yeah, I don't think the Allstars hit Atlanta. When I get a break from the Crowes we'll go down south. This time around we'll (The Allstars) start in the south and end in the south but we don't hit it all. That's our home base. The SEC is it. Yeah, the Crowes hometown show in Atlanta will be a fest. The new Crowes record is so cool. Like I said, it's so honest and raw—it's a bunch of guys making some real rock and roll on the spot. So, I did our acoustic record, then I went to New York with the Crowes for that record, then we recorded *Hernando* right after that. So, late last year I was on a roll.

The Crowes will play *Warpaint* in its entire sequence. I don't think they've ever done that before.

LD: You're right. On this promotional tour of clubs—like the Tabernacle—they've never done that before. I remember Chris (Robinson) talking about it. He was like, 'Man, I'm so proud of this we're going out and playing the fucker in its entirety.' Those guys are really inspired as far as I can tell.Chris was writing and singing his ass off. And Rich, I mean, he's a great, great guitar player and we really see eye to eye and that's partly what's so appeal-ing…we have potential to be a classic, all-time, dual guitar team. Nobody is trying to outshine the other. We just try to make each other sound better. We became friends before we played together.

Yeah, Chris sang on the *Hill Country Revue* record.

LD: We met them years ago. Then Chris started sitting in with us, and that was great shit. Then we opened for the Crowes at Madison Square Garden. That's when I got Rich's number. We started chatting, became friends and then we did our side project, *Circle Sound*, which was fun and we have a really good chemistry. Then later Rich called me up and said 'Hey man, you want to record?' I was like, 'With the Crowes? Hell yeah…'(laughs). I love our power trio—I love what we do, it's special. But the Black Crowes got a big band—keyboards, guitars, backup singers, bass and drums.

Now you've got a guitar player to play with and someone to cover the singing.

LD: Yeah, man. I can't wait. I don't want to do any singing in the Crowes. Hell, I've got over a hundred songs I'm learning to play. I've got a lot of work to do before I bring anything to the table. Chris and Rich are family and they are a great collaborative team.

How long did it take to record *Warpaint*?

LD: That took three weeks also. The Hiatt record went really fast too—we did that in something like a week—nine days. That was all just building my confidence—it made me feel like I was really on the right path. Then when we went in to do *Hernando* we just let it hang out.

Well, I'll let you have your last evening at home for awhile to you and the wife. I'll catch up with you in a few weeks.

LD: Okay man. Thanks. Just give me a holler.

Thanks for talking Luther. Godspeed out there…

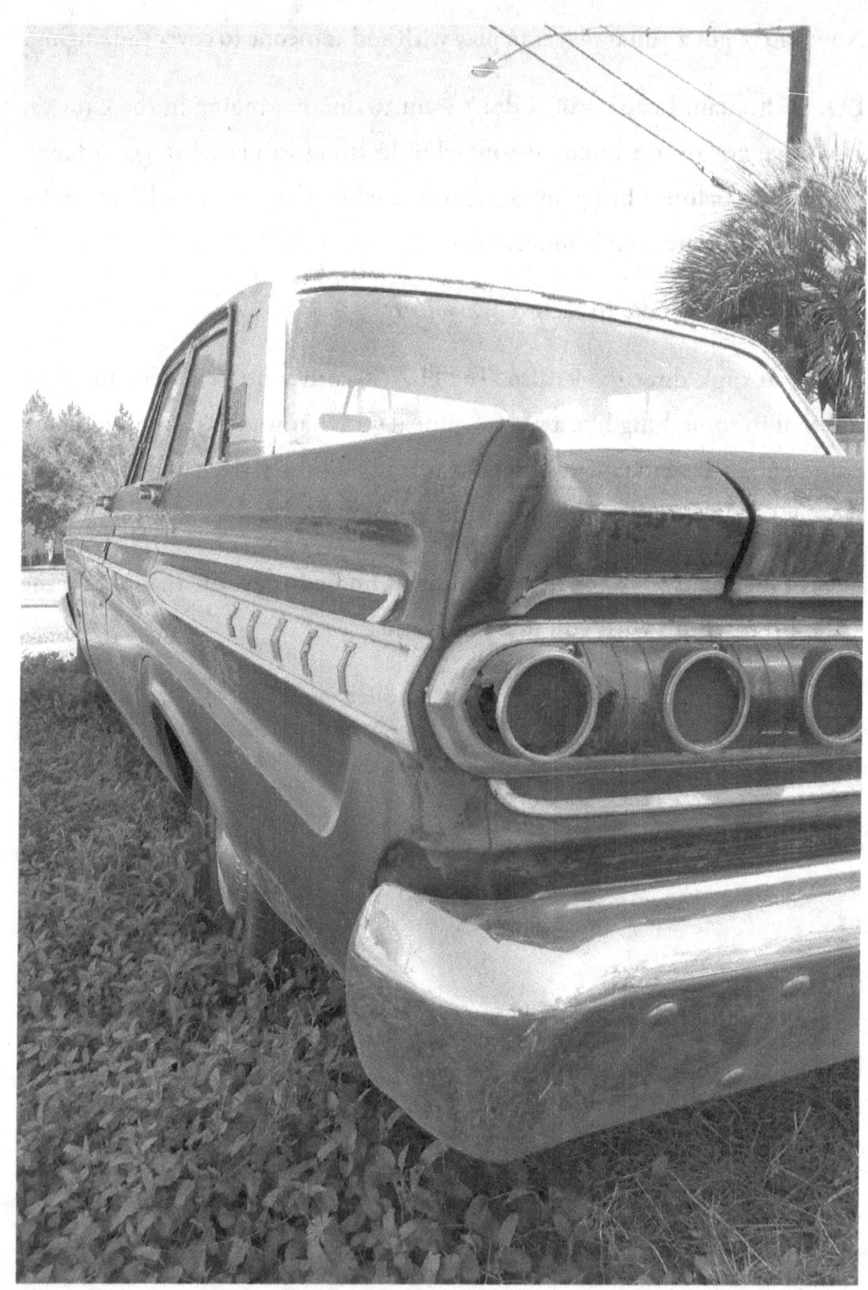

Ford Comet

Drive-By Truckers *Southern (Dis) Comfort: It's Only Rock and Roll*

> *"People need trouble——a little frustration to sharpen the spirit on, toughen it. Artists do; I don't mean you need to live in a rat holeor gutter, but you have to learn fortitude, endurance. Only vegetables are happy.*
>
> —"William Faulkner

> *"…stories of corruption, crime, and killing yes it's true, greed, fixed elections, guns, drugs, whores and booze…"*
>
> —Mike Cooley

ON A WARM MAY evening, The Drive-By Truckers stormed the stage at the Atlanta Music Midtown Festival. Some of the largest acts in the business perform at this annual music gathering. The Truckers' main man, Patterson Hood, grins at the festive crowd wearing mirrored sunglasses, a grizzled beard, a light short-sleeve shirt, blue jeans, smoking a cigarette, and glances over at his longtime musical sidekick, Mike Cooley, who prepares to sing the opening song, called "Where the Devil Don't Stay", from the Truckers new CD, *The Dirty South*.

In the past several years, The Drive-By Truckers managed to carve a niche in the industry by presenting unrepentant southern-style music to a cold and schizophrenic music business. *The Dirty South* propels the Truckers closer into the company of classic southern groups and songwriters like

Eddie Hinton, Otis Redding, Steve Cropper, the Allman Brothers, Lynyrd Skynyrd, Tony Joe White, Spooner Oldham, Donnie Fritts, and Dan Penn.

Onstage, the triple threat of the Truckers appears evident with three talented songwriters and guitarists in Patterson Hood, Mike Cooley, and Jason Isbell sharing duties which never allows a dull musical moment. It's been many years since anyone has seen a band like the Truckers. The grim narrative on the Trucker's new venomous CD, *The Dirty South*, told in a merciless and unforgiving tone, reveals tales of natural disasters, cancer, unemployment, corruption, war, and weak economy with a brutal truth that leaves no room for soft hearted nonsense. Rock and roll with a vengeance…

Recently, the Truckers' musicianship carried them to television—in mid-May, they covered Tom Petty's "Rebels" which appeared on Fox's show "King of the Hill." These same songwriters once wrote, "to the fucking rich man all poor people look the same")…

The Truckers performed a great set at the Music Midtown for an enthusiastic Atlanta crowd. The band appeared relaxed. They played with a trademark jackhammer intensity including new songs in the setlist such as "Where the Devil Don't Stay", "Carl Perkins' Cadillac" and "Daddy's Cup".

As Cooley sang the lowdown lyrics ("deal from the bottom/one ace in the hole/one hand on the jug/but you never do know") from a new tune about bootleggers and poison whiskey, the jubilant Atlanta crowd seemed to celebrate a homecoming with open arms for the next great southern band.

II

"The artist penetrates the concrete world in order to find at its depths the image of its source the image of ultimate reality."
—Flannery O'Connor

"George A. was at the movies in December 41
They announced it in the lobby what had just gone on
He drove up from Birmingham back to the family's farm
Thought he'd get him a deferment there was much work to be done

> *He was a family man, even in those days*
> *But Uncle Sam decided he was needed anyway*
> *In the South Pacific over a half a world away*
> *He believed in God and Country, things was just that way."*
>
> —Patterson Hood

Patterson Hood grew up in Florence, Alabama, near the Tennessee River. Patterson's father, David Hood, played bass in the legendary Muscle Shoals Rhythm section called the Swampers (recently inducted into the Alabama Music Hall of Fame). This talented group played on recordings made by the Staple Singers, Aretha Franklin, Wilson Pickett, Jimmy Buffett, Willie Nelson, Jimmy Cliff, Traffic, Solomon Burke, Clarence Carter, Arthur Conley, Etta James, Percy Sledge, James Carr, The Rolling Stones, Duane Allman, Bob Seger, Bobby Womack, Paul Simon, and many more.

Muscle Shoals is one of the (Quad) four small towns including, Florence, Sheffield, and Tuscumbia. Twenty-two miles from Mississippi, and eleven miles from Tennessee, Muscle Shoals is known as the hit recording capital of the world, an unlikely place for a hotbed of popular music. A place where white and black musicians ignored the racism and prejudice from locals in the 60's and 70's to produce more than a few hits that helped change the sound of modern music. The beautiful area also remains the site of the Wilson Dam. Browns Ferry, a local Nuclear Power Plant, holds the distinction of the world's third worst nuclear power plant accident, which caused grave pollution to the people and waterways of the area.

Since his father owned a great collection, Patterson Hood was exposed to a wide variety of timeless music. He recently told me, "Soon as I was old enough to sneak those records back underneath the covers I did because he was very picky about his records just like I am. So I started raiding his collection pretty regularly around eight years old. Any allowance I could get, I'd buy records. My first job when I was 16 was at a record store. I worked there five years so I blew pretty much every penny I could come up with on records and keeping my old car running."

Hood began writing songs in the third grade and picked up a guitar when he was 14. He graduated from high school in 1982. In 1985, he began playing in a band with Mike Cooley. Cooley "The Stroker Ace" grew up in Tuscumbia, Alabama, the same town as Helen Keller. As a boy he took guitar lessons from blue-grass legend Al Lester and watched saw Carl Perkins play at the Hayloft Opry. Cooley told me of his early exposures to music: "I took lessons from Al Lester for a couple of years. I can't remember exactly. I was around 8 or 9 years old. I kinda picked guitar up on my own. My parents are somewhat musical; neither one of them learned to play any instruments, but they could both sing, they had really good feel for pitch, rhythm, melody, and those kinds of things.

"My Dad always loved music. He would have probably played something if he could've started playing when he was young. There was an old movie theater in downtown Tuscumbia—they stopped showing movies there long, long ago, but for a short time a group of people went in together and bought the place. They were all local musicians that had this country band. Every Saturday night they did this Hayloft Opry thing. They'd have some of the same people rotating every week, they did it very much like a Grand Old Opry performance, but that's where I saw Carl Perkins and Red Sovine…"

Hood and Cooley played in a band called Adam's House Cat for six years. Cooley revealed the provenance of his musical relationship with Hood: "I was 19. We didn't know each other, but we ended up being roommates. I was rooming with a guy that Patterson knew, and we had an extra room, and he was looking for a place to live and he moved in. He saw I had a couple of guitars laying around, and we got to talking and the next thing you know we were dropping out of college." Adam's House Cat eventually broke up. Then Cooley and Hood moved to Memphis, Tennessee. Later, they moved to Auburn, Alabama, where they played shows as an acoustic duo (Virgil Kane) and another band (Horse Pussy) before going separate ways.

In 1994, Hood moved to Athens, Georgia where he started playing solo shows anywhere he could book a gig. In 1996, Cooley and Hood reunited to originate the Drive-By Truckers. Cooley explained their regrouping. "We started getting back together some and just fooling around with four track demos. After Patterson lived in Athens long enough to get to know quite a few people, he just kind of assembled a group and got some studio time to go in and cut some songs. So he gave me a call and asked me to come over and play on it. He didn't know these guys that well. I'd never met them before in my life.

"We got together the night before, and kinda rehearsed for a little while and went in the next day and cut five songs. Two of em' ended up on our first release. We called the band the Drive-By Truckers to give the release a name. Patterson just started booking gigs as the Drive-By Truckers. Everybody in the band had other commitments—there was six of us, and it was like whoever showed up, that was the band. It was the drummer from the Possibilities, Matt Lange, a guy named Adam Howell who we knew from Auburn—the Horse Pussy bassist, Barry Sell, and John Neff."

In 1998, the Truckers released their full-length debut album, *Gangstabilly*, a punk, country, and rockabilly collection. Cooley explained the line-up changes the band began experiencing, "Shortly after we released *Gangstabilly* we started hitting on the road. Barry Sell left the band right after we cut the album—actually he'd already left the band but he went on and played on *Gangstabilly*. We started getting on the road and then Rob (Malone) came in just before we started to cut *Pizza Deliverance*."

The band released *Pizza Deliverance*, a humorous title that shed light on the band's philosophy and mode of operandi. Hood explained to me the dichotomy between the Truckers humorous and dark songwriting. "I've always been drawn to dark subject matter—dark stories. I started writing young and I wrote for years and years and everyone always said, 'you're songs are so goddamned dark.' I've been doing this shit for years, so out of frustration, I started letting humor ease into the songs. If I could tell this story in a way that made it more entertaining then I would. Then I'd hear, 'all your songs are joke songs.' You can't win.

"I like the ones that insert a little humor cause I don't really think of it as being a bad thing. Our later records don't have as much humor as some of the earlier ones when we were playing small clubs, competing with loud crowds and kinda had it a little more tuned up, in your face, just to get some attention."

Alabama Ass Whoopin' was recorded live in Athens, Georgia, during the fall and summer of 1999 at various clubs. This record, released in 2000, displays the band's feverish live dynamic. During this time the band already seemed to capture it's own style. However, they found difficulty in cementing a line-up. Cooley explained the band's intention, "We got together and started looking for a bass player cause the plan was to move Rob to guitar and have three guitar players to bring in a full time bass player, and we went through a few different people and Earl "Bird Dog" Hicks was working with the band and played some bass before and finally he just got disgusted watching us try and try and try to keep cutting and recutting the album and not being able to get anyone to commit to the bass. So Earl decided, 'screw it, I'll do it myself.' He became the full-time bass player for a long time."

The band went through an arduous process in 2000 of recording *Southern Rock Opera*, a release that captured the "rock critics" interest. A concept album released by the band, *Southern Rock Opera*, tells the story of a fictional band, Betamax Guillotine, based roughly on growing up in Alabama and the tragic fate of the great southern band, Lynyrd Skynyrd. Songs like "Ronnie and Neil", "72 (this highway's mean)", "The Southern Thing", "Road Cases", "Shut Up and Get On the Plane", "Greenville to Baton Rouge", and "Angels and Fuselage" mark the *Southern Rock Opera*, a formidable release.

In the liner notes, Hood explains the album's intention: "In the six years that we've been brainstorming, writing, learning, playing, and recording this album, we have given a lot of thought to how this record would be received by the fans, friends, families, and surviving members of Lynyrd Skynyrd. This work is delivered with the utmost respect for them and the legacy that they left behind. Even the seemingly irreverent title is in keeping with the spirit of the band that performed "That Smell" and the man who wrote the line "oak tree you're in my way" to tell of his band mate's near-fatal collision. We hope that it is taken as the absolute highest possible form of flattery and honor."

This double CD collection solidified the Trucker's authenticity while furthering the southern music movement in a modern day tradition. Around this time, Patterson Hood recorded a solo album he never intended for release, later titled, *Killers and Stars*. Hood explained the current psychic weather of the time in the liner notes of his solo debut: "I recorded *Killers and Stars*, by myself in the dining room of the house where I was living, in early March 2001. I had just gotten divorced, was fighting with the band (DBT) and a good number of my friends. I recorded the album in two consecutive nights, then ran down some rough mixes about a week later. The band (DBT) was taking some time off the road to finish mixing our new album (*Southern Rock Opera*) and generally cool off from a really intense time of touring and recording. It was also a time to deal with some personal demons that were ravaging our personal lives and were beginning to spill over into our relationships with one another." *Killers and Stars* would not be released for another three years.

In 2001, when the Truckers released the *Southern Rock Opera*, they hit the road hard, and in the fall of 2001 Lost Highway picked up the album and re-released it the next summer. Jason Isbell joined the band midway through the SRO tour. On a half-day's notice, Isbell learned the songs on-stage in Norman, Oklahoma. Two days later, he wrote the title track for the upcoming record, *Decoration Day*.

Most of the songs written during this period surfaced on a record The Truckers recorded at David Barbe's studio in Athens, Georgia. Isbell earned a publishing deal with FAME before he joined the band while working as a session guitarist at the Muscle Shoals studio. He told me during a phone conversation while driving with his wife Shonna (Trucker's new bassist) from Nashville to Columbia, South Carolina for a solo gig, of his musical origins: "Well, with me it was a family thing. My parents don't play, but they were about the only two people from either family that didn't play any-thing. Everybody else around me when I was a kid played…my Granddad played, my uncles played, my cousins played, so it started out as a family thing since everybody would get together as early as I can remember. I pretty much picked it up from there. My Dad's brother gave me a guitar when I was 7 or 8 years old and I was playing mandolin before that because my hands weren't big enough to play guitar. My family was my first big influence. My Dad was real big into the rock and roll records of the 70s like Queen, Free, Skynyrd of course, and the Allman Brothers records. Dad listened to that stuff all the time—so I inherited his record collection."

Once Lynyrd Skynyrd heard *Southern Rock Opera* they offered the Truckers the opening slot on their tour. The Truckers were also selected by Farm Aid in 2002 to perform alongside legendary acts such as Neil Young and Willie Nelson.

Isbell augmented the threat of two guitar playing songwriters in the band. Cooley and Hood finally found what they'd been looking for in a third guitar player (much like Skynyrd discovering Stevie Gaines).

Decoration Day, recorded at David Barbe's Chase Park Transduction Studio in Athens, Georgia, was released on New West Records in June of 2003. This collection of 15 songs emerged as the group's greatest accom-plishment to date. It's more mature, personal, and controlled than any of the previous recordings. With three songwriters-guitarists, the group trans-formed into a leaner, even meaner rock and roll locomotive. David Barbe played guitar, keyboard, and wurlitzer piano as well as produced the re-cord. However, the unsung hero on the *Decoration Day* remains the killer pedal steel guitar player John Neff. Neff, an original Trucker, has played with other Athens bands like the Star Room Boys, Japancakes, Bloodkin, Barbara Cue, as well as composing movie soundtracks with David Lynch such as *Blue Bob*, and *Mulholland Drive*.

The short film, *The Accountant*, by Ray McKinnon won the Academy Award for Best Live Action Short Film in 2001, inspired Hood to write

"Sink Hole" a memorable song that tells the story of a family losing their farm in a sad plight of the American farmer.

Other *Decoration Day* gems stand as "Marry Me", "Heathens", "When the Pin Hits the Shell", "Loaded Gun In the Closet" (special appearance on Wurlitzer from legendary Spooner Oldham), and the title track proving the Truckers were a fierce musical force. The importance of family remains a theme in many of these songs dealing with death, incest, poverty, suicide, love sickness, and addiction with sad twangs of country music. *Decoration Day* achieved #27 on the Top Independent chart as well as wide critical acclaim.

Once again, the band endured changes with the departure of long-time bassist Earl ("Bird Dog")Hicks. Hicks' replacement, another Muscle Shoals player, Shonna Tucker, who later married Isbell (on Hood's birthday) made her first appearance playing stand up bass on the *Decoration Day* tune, "Sounds Better In the Song." Isbell explained the new dynamic of having his spouse in the band: "On a professional level we all communicate with each other real well so it's pretty easy to keep everything going like it's going right now. With Shonna and me it makes it a whole lot better—we get to spend more time together and for travel arrangements and stuff like that it works real well. I don't have to share a hotel room with a bunch of smelly bastards (laughs). We can go over stuff with each other, and she's a great player, which is the bottom line.

"That really makes more difference than anything else especially when you're considering hiring someone to play. She fits in really well with the band and we all have a good time I think. She was also a Muscle Shoals studio musician back home. Before I was in the band we used to do some local and regional touring—like we're doing now (Isbell solo gigs) as a two-piece while the bands off the road for a few days. We used to do that a lot. We met that way—she was a musician before I knew her. We met at a songwriter's night when we were both teenagers. It's something she's been doing long as the rest of us. It changes the atmosphere a little bit, but I think in the right way. Plus, you don't really want to fuck up onstage with a pretty girl watching you. She keeps us on our toes with her playing."

The Truckers solidified their song craft while touring across the States, and Europe, behind *Decoration Day*. After running the industry gauntlet, the band decided on returning to sweet home Alabama and record their meanest record yet.

III

> *"The man who believes that the secrets of the world are forever hidden lives in mystery and fear. Superstition will drag him down. The rain will erode the deeds of his life. But that man who sets himself the task of singling out the thread of order from the tapestry will by the decision alone have taken charge of the world and it is only by such taking charge that he will effect a way to dictate the terms of his own fate."*

—Cormac McCarthy

> *"You can throw me in the Colbert County jailhouse,*
> *You can throw me off the Wilson Dam*
> *But there ain't much difference in the man I wanna be*
> *And the man I really am."*

—Jason Isbell

On August 24, 2004, New West Records released the Trucker's sixth record, *The Dirty South*. Once again, Athens musical sorcerer, David Barbe produced the album. This time, the band returned home to Muscle Shoals and recorded at the famous FAME studios.

A few days after the Music Midtown Festival, New West Records released Patterson Hood's new solo record, *Killers and Stars*. Hood played various solo gigs in June and July, fresh from a honeymoon trip to Amsterdam and Paris. Hood and I sat backstage at Smith's Olde Bar in Atlanta, Georgia, over tall cans of PBR, before his solo show with his band, the Necessary

Evils. A southern gentleman, Hood talked about growing up in rural Alabama, "There's really nothing there—it's beautiful because of the rivers and the dams, but all the buildings are ugly. We were a dry county so you have to drive to the Tennessee State line to get any beer—it's not dry anymore, but it was until I was an adult. Which was good as a teenager because it was a lot easier to buy beer illegally when it's illegal anyway. When I was sixteen I knew everybody on the state line on a first name basis."

When asked about returning to his hometown to record, Isbell remarked, "It's great, I love it down there. Not to mention the history of the place which is obviously overwhelming. It's a really good room, and it's easy to get a good sound down there. A lot of people don't realize that studio is still up and running still making really, really good records on a regular basis. The room still sounds like a million bucks and they still got all the old instruments—organs, pianos, and stuff they recorded all those hits back in the 70's with. It's a great place to make a record, and it's real close to the house."

Hood agreed that recording *The Dirty South* in Muscle Shoals ranked as inspirational. "It was incredible. It was a thrill for me because I'd never really been there until the year before. We did Jason's solo record there. We finished his solo stuff right around the time we started making this new one. We cut nine songs in four days. We mixed it in Athens, but that's all. Then there was a half an album of songs that didn't make the cut because we had all the new songs and we wanted to put the newest songs out. I don't second-guess any of the songs that made it onto the record. They were the 14 songs that needed to be together, but I really like the songs we left off.

"There was a song we left off called "Good Field's Road" that was still in the running until the last minute—it was a tough decision because that was probably my favorite piece of writing. I always liked that song, but I don't think we had the quintessential take. "Lookout Mountain" was one take. "Where the Devil Don't Stay" was the first take, so was "Tornadoes". "Buford Stick" was maybe a second take. There was at least a couple more first takes. Then several first takes we left off."

Cooley commented on recording in Muscle Shoals where the 'Swampers' thrived, "Well, we'd talked about it for awhile. We just thought it would be cool to go and record there. David (Barbe) was excited about producing and engineering in such a legendary place. It was like, why not? Those songs took shape in that studio."

The Dirty South sounds much darker and grittier than any of the group's previous work, containing even sharper, more concise songwriting. Williams Burroughs once wrote that a writer can only write about what's in front of him, and this 70-minute CD revolves mostly around the band's home state of Alabama. Unlike *Decoration Day*, a collection of songs about relationships, *The Dirty South* reveals desperate people with no choice sometimes but to turn to a life of crime. Once again the "duality of the southern thing" manifests itself through pride and regret. "Lyrically, it's darker than *Decoration Day*, but I think it might rock harder which might save it from being too awfully depressing, but it deals with some very serious situations," Isbell told me.

In the liner notes, Hood explains the album's mission: "Welcome to the Dirty South. It's a tough place to make a living, but we ain't complainin'. Just doing what we got to do. Trying to raise our kids and love our women. Do right by the ones we love. But don't fuck with us or we'll cut off your head and throw your body over a spillway at the Wilson Dam. We'll burn your house down. We mean business and it ain't personal. Hell, I always liked ya. I might not want to get my hands dirty, but I got this buddy…In the end, I'll continue loving my family. I'll try not to fuck up too bad. Maybe I'll live to tell the tale."

When this writer asked Hood the meaning of the title of the new CD, he explained: "One of the only things we all agree on music wise to listen to in the van is Hip-Hop. We all love Hip-Hop. So it was kinda a nod to Atlanta's hip hop scene and it fit. It was a nod, a tribute, a salute, but it was also tongue and cheek because what we do is the dirty south too—in a lot of ways our subject matter is not real different. Like on the new record, a lot of the songs are about people who, out of desperation, turn to a life of crime.

They end up doing things they never thought they would do, but they were forced to, and all that somehow tied in. I think it's a perfect name for the record. It was the working title for a long time. We kept thinking another title would come along that would be the real title, but in the end that was the only thing to call it."

From the opening song, "Where the Devil Don't Stay" to the fading notes on "Goddamn Lonely Love", *The Dirty South* stands as a classic rock and roll record. Of course there are always critics who'll claim the record is not up to par. This happened to the Rolling Stones (who recorded three songs in Muscle Shoals for their *Sticky Fingers* album) with records such as *Exile On Main Street* that received lukewarm reviews when released, but years later emerged as a classic. It may take folks a few years to catch up, but *The Dirty South* stands as timeless electric countrified-blues.

Each indelible member of the songwriting team contributes strong compositions to this disturbing collection. Mike Cooley's tunes, "Where the Devil Don't Stay", "Carl Perkins Cadillac", "Cottonseed", and "Daddy's Cup" vie as the album's strongest compositions. The glorious opening tune, "Where The Devil Don't Stay" tells the tale of bootleggers and prohibition behind one of the fi nest triple guitar attacks ever. "Carl Perkins Cadillac" contends as a hit single ("I tend to have the five-minute plus curse that keeps me off the radio" said Cooley) which brings back great memories of Sam Phillips, Elvis, Jerry Lee Lewis, Carl Perkins, and Johnny Cash.

"Cottonseed" stands as one of the album's darkest tales, and the only song that contains one man playing an instrument by himself in lone troubadour fashion. Cooley told me about the tune, "Yeah, it's based on a real person. I tried to make sure I didn't connect anything to him because he might kill me. He was a bad, bad boy. Definitely a southern Tony Soprano." "Daddy's Cup", one of the positive songs, tells a fine tale of a father passing on his knowledge to his son that most racing fans will love. This song would make for a great NASCAR theme song

Isbell's songs "The Day John Henry Died", "Danko/Manuel", "Never Gonna Change", and "Goddamn Lonely Love" indicate why he was asked to join this band, and scored a publishing deal with FAME studios. "The Day John Henry Died" reveals a tale of industrialization coming of age in a time where machines began replacing flesh and blood at the workplace. "Danko/Manuel" is based on the story of the Band. Isbell revealed, "I know a lot of people who learned how to sing by listening to them. They wrote great songs. I love the Band—it just turned out to be kind of a sad story about being on the road for too long, and not getting out of it what you deserve."

"Never Gonna Change" stands out as the most polished song on the album. "A tale of a North Alabama man who refuses to live in fear," explained Isbell. The final song on the album, his "Goddamn Lonely Love" a sad ballad ("I ain't falling asleep/I'm fading to black") serves as the slowest, and prettiest tune on the collection. Isbell, only 24 years old, shows all the signs of being as a technical songwriting master.

The Trucker's fearless leader, Patterson Hood's songs cast the most ruthless tone and messages. "Tornadoes" was written in 1988 after a tornado ripped through Hood's hometown during a local performance, as he explained "the day God decided she didn't want me to be a rock star." This serves as a fine song dealing with the savage facts of life—natural catastrophes, and how people's lives are wrecked by something which they have no control. Anyone who's experienced trouble can relate to this album, or this band. "The world is like that and at the same time I hope it's fun and at times maybe a little beautiful—the world is like that too. The older I get, and the more different places we go the more the reality is to me is that duality of the world…life sucks, but I want to keep living it," said Hood.

"Puttin' People On the Moon" conveys a sharp political insight. Yankee musicians will step aside, scratching their heads in wonder at these mean ass country boys revealing such cut-throat political insight. Hood wrote in album notes about this song: "I wrote this one in the van, shortly before we completed the album. Sort of my latest and best attempt at a song that I've written and rewritten at least a dozen times since the mid-80's. This song deals with 'rocket-envy', a non-diagnosable psychosis affecting people in an economically depressed community, located just 60 or so miles from the

NASA Space and Rocket Center. To make matters worse, our community is downstream from industry, contributing (surely) to our massive cancer rate." A sample verse:

> *"Mary Alice got cancer just like everybody here*
> *Seems everyone I know is getting cancer every year*
> *And we can't afford no insurance, I been ten years unemployed*
> *So she didn't get no chemo so our lives it was destroyed*
> *And nothin' ever changes, the cemetery gets more full*
> *And over there in Huntsville, even NASA's shut down too."*

Like Skynyrd, or Hank Williams Sr. this ain't no act. They're not pretending to be country boys with no other choice in their lives but to play music. The next Hood song, "The Sands of Iwo Jima", constructed with subtle banjos, harmonica, Rhodes organ, and guitar parts, he revealed to me as probably his favorite: "I feel pretty strongly about this bunch of songs. "Sands of Iwo Jima" is a real personal thing for me cause it's about a good guy that doesn't do anything bad or wrong. That made it a harder song to write as opposed writing a song about a guy who killed someone. It's easier to write about the darker characters. The song's about my great Uncle, George A, and capturing that in a song and do it justice that was the hardest thing I've ever done as a writer. I feel real happy about that song. It's probably the best piece of writing I've ever done. I guess that's my favorite, but at the same time, I don't play it live very much because it's so hard. It's not a song that lends itself to a really loud rock show. I'm really proud it made the record. In some ways it doesn't fit the record, but to me it kinda did because the recurring theme on this record is people not having as choice. In most cases, people not having a choice meant them doing very bad things—really terrible things in a sense of desperation. In the case of my great uncle, it made for a counterpart to that because he was forced to go and be part of this horrible day in history, and by surviving it, he came home a greater man. He truly did. It was something that shaped a big part of his personality. The more I've traveled the more I realize what a unique man he was. One night while watching the old John Wayne movie (*The Sands of Iwo Jima*) on TV, he simply said that 'he never saw John Wayne over there'." Great songwriters immortalize the common man…

"The Boys From Alabama" tells the story of Buford T. Pusser (remember the original movie, *Walking Tall*?). During the beginning of the song, Hood's monologue explains "this is the other side of that story…"

The song is based loosely on folklore surrounding the "red-neck mafia" which inspired countless books and movies through the years. Although three guitars propel the band's dynamic, there are no indulgent solos on *The Dirty South*. Lyrics reveal the Truckers hard boiled tendency to lean towards dark truths:

> *"Friends on the inside*
> *Friends on the outside*
> *Sneak up beside you*
> *So keep on the good side*
> *Don't piss off the boys from Alabama*
> *Better take it like a man*
> *Ain't nobody gonna stick anything up your ass*
> *If you remember who your friends are"*

Dark stuff.

"The Buford Stick" is another tune based on the Pusser tale from his enemy's point of view. A faint musical reminder of Crazy Horse comes to mind on this one. Hood noted, "I wrote this one night in the studio at FAME right before we wrapped the album. It was originally set to be a country type song, but (producer) David Barbe suggested we put the pedal to the floor on it. We love David Barbe."

The old Cooley/Hood song "Lookout Mountain" was written years earlier, and first appeared on *Alabama Ass Whoopin'*. Hood claimed, "Cooley and I have been playing various versions of this song since about 1990

(*Adam's House Cat*). It has always been one of our favorites to play, but was a last minute addition to this album. In the mixing stage, we swapped a song called "Goode's Field Road" for it because we wanted a harder rocker for this spot on the album. "GFR" was one of my favorites on the album but I stand by this as the better call."

The Dirty South tells a ruthless tale with vengeful moxie serving as a paragon for any underdog, drug store truck-driving man, sick hearted soul, hardworking folk, or good ol' boy or gal down in the world with hard luck. This is why *The Dirty South* will transcend the last two decades of music, and rank as an all-time great record—above or below the Mason-Dixon Line. For those who seek music to rise above depression, loss of loved ones, and savage fate, then this album will serve as a great musical companion. In fact, it will give you faith, but if your life is easy and painless, you might be scared away. If you're not into the Truckers, as Bob Dylan once wrote, "next time you see me comin', you better run…"

Hood looks down at his beer, minutes before stepping onstage with all sorts of distractions surrounding him, as if he knows the hellhounds sniffing on his trail never lurk far behind says, "Most of the people I meet are pretty nice across the world. There's no shortage of things to really get mad about, upset about, cry about, but in the end you do what you can to fix what you can and find a way to do whatever you can to make a little piece of it better, and you revel in that. To me that's kinda what it's all about. That's definitely where our heads are at with this new record without sounding lofty about it. At the same time, it's a fucking rock record—I don't want to get too cerebral about it. That's why I love having three guitars to go along with all those dark messages…"

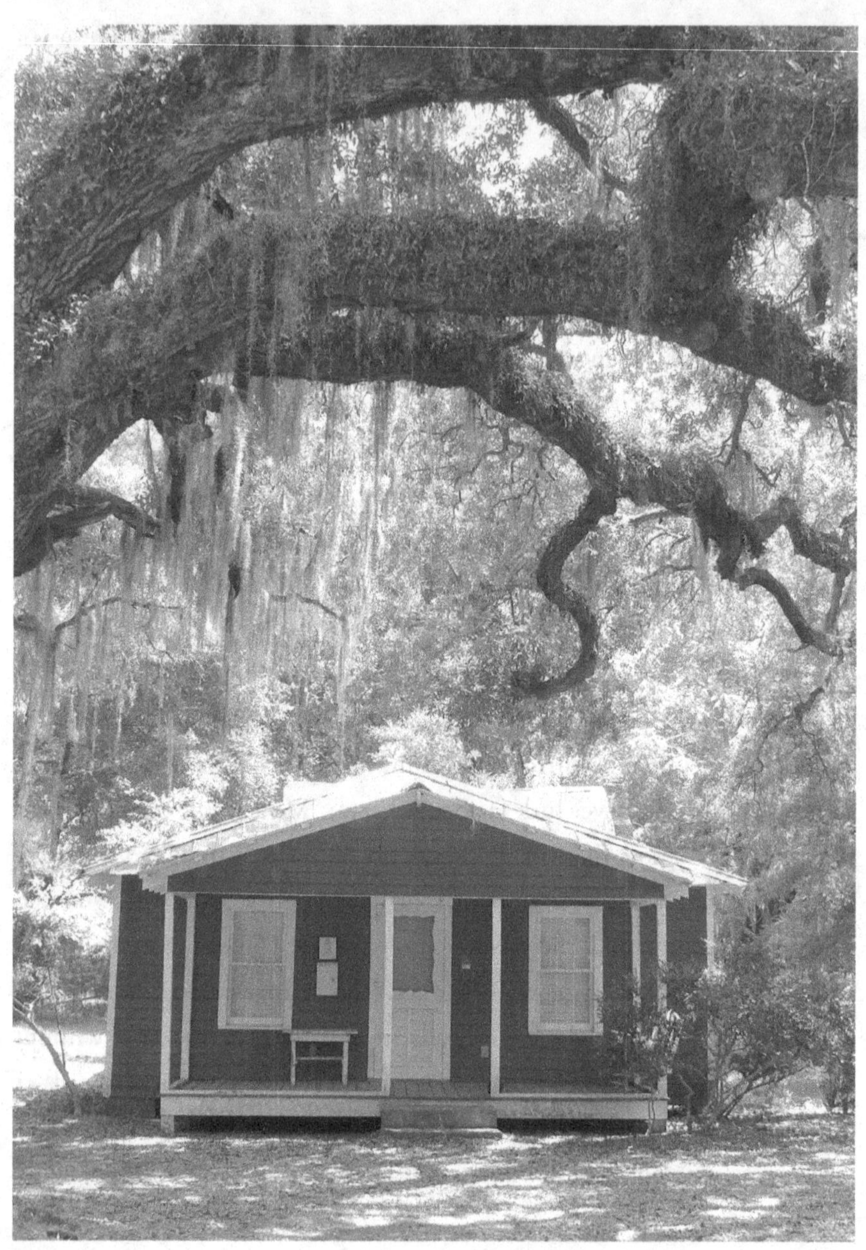

Gullah Cabin

Cheyenne Mize:
Shades of Blue & Grey

Cheyenne Mize operates as a key player in the Louisville, Kentucky, music community.

"If I could think of a way to do it right now, I'd head back to Louisville, sit on the porch drinking beer, drive around Cherokee Park for a few nights, and try to sink back far as I could into the world that did its best to make me. It's not hard to get tired of the interminable palms and Poinciana, and I could do it at the moment with a single elm tree on a midnight street in the Highlands."
—Hunter S. Thompson

HER VOICE UNLOCKS SOMETHING in the soul. Singer/songwriter/in-strumentalist Cheyenne Marie Mize hails from Louisville, Kentucky, along with Muhammad Ali, Hunter S. Thompson, Johnny Depp, Will Oldham, Joan Osborne and My Morning Jacket to name a few. The daughter of radio DJs, Mize caught the music bug early in life. Not many musicians can play seven or eight dif-ferent instruments—or play all the instruments on their albums.

The Louisville music community proves a fertile one, and Mize plays an instrumental role in that scene. She's a relatively new artist. At 30, she begins her musical ascent. Her moody songs, versatility and resonating soulful voice indicate she retains a staying power. Her latest release, *Among The Grey*, culminates all of her musical magic.

Mize's previous groups include Arnett Hollow and Maiden Radio. In 2009, she recorded an album of parlor songs (from 1860-1915) with songwriter, actor and photographer Will Oldham (aka Billy 'Prince' Bonnie) titled *Among The Gold*. She's also collaborated with Ben Sollee and Daniel Martin Moore. Her voice evokes the ability to fuse the past, present and future into one streamline of the moment. She takes the listener on their own personal journey through her music. That's art.

Her previous solo releases include *Whereas Before Lately* (2010), an EP *We Don't Need* (2012) and her latest collection *Among The Grey*, which was recorded in a Louisville Church. Mize is quite pretty, but even if that was not the case the listener would still be mesmerized by her hypnotic voice. I looked forward to interviewing her because I knew she possessed cognizance. She stands as an artist steeped in earthy American folk music, but her latest release finds her exploring more progressive sounds...from the soil to the stratosphere...

She's an accomplished instrumentalist. During our Q & A, I asked her about when she obtained her first instrument. "I started taking piano lessons when I was eight years old. My aunt played piano. So, I really wanted to play piano. My uncle and grandma played guitar, so around ten or eleven I started learning guitar. For my twelfth birthday I got a Martin guitar. I started violin in the fifth grade. From there, I played anything with strings I could get my hands on.

"I can play dulcimer and autoharp, but those things don't take a lot of skill—once you can play the violin all the other string instruments are pretty easy. I play cello on one of my records, and I've played upright bass, but I'm not great at those things. I play banjo quite a bit. On my song "Wishing Well" I played drums and all the percussion. I play electric bass sometimes."

I wanted Mize to take me back to her rural childhood days, so I asked her to discuss early musical influences: "Where I lived in southern Kentucky until I was 10, there was nothing but country music, so I definitely grew up on 80s and 90s country mixed in with old country music. My grandma used to listen to The Carter Family a lot.

"Then my parents were also radio DJs back in the 70s so they were huge into 60s and 70s album rock so it was a kind of mix of Jimi Hendrix, Pink Floyd, Led Zeppelin and Bob Marley. I still turn on classic radio stations and know most of the words to all of the songs. Then in middle school and high school I got more into modern music like Radiohead. I have some of my Dad's record collection, but he hasn't given it all up yet."

Perhaps her close-to-the-soil musical diet led her to more experimental genres. When I requested Mize to nail down her seminal influences, she responded, "Definitely Radiohead as far as immersion of my musical mind. I've spent more hours of my musical life listening to Radiohead more than any other band. That was my high school soundtrack. I think Pink Floyd is a big one too. To me on a lot of that stuff there were sounds that were never made. I try to take on that spirit of creating new sounds.

"I've had a heavy dose of Fiona Apple, Tori Amos and Tracy Bonham as a teenager. Recently, I've gotten into a woman named Shannon Wright out of Chicago whose got an incredible mouth and voice."

I asked Mize to elucidate on the Louisville music scene, which she plays integral role. "There are so many different kinds of music here in Louisville. I went to college for music therapy. I went to the University of Louisville, and in college I played with several local bands including Arnett Hollow, but some rock bands and super heavy—almost heavy metal bands. I was playing violin and singing every chance I could get. Then I started playing with Arnett Hollow regularly.

"But the Louisville music community...one person might play in three different instruments in three totally different bands and genres. Everybody kind of helps everyone else out. It's not a competitive environment around here. It's really nice. It pushed me in the direction of performing more because there were so many friends and bands I loved—and the more I got to play with them, the more I was playing with other people."

Mize's participation with the group Arnett Hollow opened up a new avenue for her own music and she provided insight on what that group did for her own music: "Arnett Hollow was the first time I realized the thing

I get out of music is playing with other people, not for people. It's always been that way—that's why I went to school for music therapy.

"So, playing with Arnett Hollow was the first time that I realized I could get that much enjoyment playing with people while playing for people and playing on a higher level than I ever expected to. The Louisville music scene has a lot to do with that and I still play with a lot of people randomly with whatever they need. There were two Arnett Hollow records. The fi rst one I really wasn't part of the band—I just played some violin stuff and that worked really well. Then I started kind of playing with the band. This is around 2006-2007. Then we recorded another record in 2009, and that one was more of a band effort. I played fiddle and sang. It was more of an Americana-rootsy band. We pulled from a lot of things.

Being interested in the work of Will Oldham, I urged Mize to elaborate on her musical relationship with prodigious actor/songwriter (aka Billy Prince Bonnie), which led to an EP they recorded together titled *Among the Gold*. "Well, I was playing a lot with Arnett Hollow, and then in 2008 I was acquainted with Oscar Parsons who was putting together a show to back Will up. He was going to be doing all of Will's songs in a hillbilly vein and that was when *Lie Down in the Light* was coming out. Since that had so much fiddle and female vocals they didn't have a female or fiddler in the band so Will basically told Oscar to find a woman who could sing and play fiddle and then everything was set.

"The first couple of months I was not even sure it was going to happen because Will was on tour overseas and we practiced without him for the first couple of months, and I was like 'I wonder if Oscar even knows this guy' (laughs). It was hard to tell. But then we had our first couple of rehearsals with Will and it all went really well. We had just one full rehearsal and we clicked. Then Will asked me to think about the idea of touring with him starting in 2009, which was 7 months away at that point, but that got the gears turning."

Mize kept busy until it was time for her record the amazing record, *Among The Gold*, with Oldham. "So, yeah that winter I was playing with

Picket Line. We did one show in the summer then we played a winter show. And in the middle of that I talked to Will about some old songs I came across in my music studies from older generations. And you don't hear older songs like that anymore with these complex chord progressions and super sweet songs.

"We basically needed a room and a microphone and someone to help me record it and Will happened to have a room and a mic and he helped me out with those songs and he helped me pick a couple out. We recorded one of them as a duet, and it worked so well and sounded so good we decided they all needed to be duets so then it became a duet record. Most of the songs were from around the turn of the century—from the 1860s to the 1920s." Oldham's musical influence on Mize emerged in subtle ways.

I inquired about her collaboration with Ben Sollee and Daniel Martin Moore, and she explained the seeds of that project. "Ben and I went to college together and I knew him for a long time. I played a little bit with him here and there, but it wasn't until 2010 in February-March that I went on tour with his band.

Mize's next musical step was her involvement with a group called Maiden Radio. Maiden Radio comprised Mize, Julia Purcell and Joan Shelley. It was recorded at the Funeral Home in Louisville. All the songs had unknown authors except "Dear Someone" (David Rawlings & Gillian Welch) and "Go To Sleep Little Baby" that was composed by T-Bone Burnett, Alan Lomax and Gillian Welch.

She revealed how that group operated. "Maiden Radio kind of started in 2009 and I had known Julia for a few years because she moved to Louisville for a music therapy job. We bonded over traditional music that we loved to sing. In the summer of 2009, I met Joan through some other friends and we shared that same connection of singing old traditional tunes. We decided it would be amazing if we could get all three of us in a room together. It was an immediate connection. We weren't trying to make a band, we just wanted to play. Then we put some songs together, did some shows and we decided to make a record.

"We recorded a short self-titled record first. It was 6 songs. It was traditional. One was a Carter Family song, and we also did "Weary Blues" by Hank Williams Sr. Then two years ago we did the *Lullabies* album. We're slowly but surely working on another batch of songs. Hopefully, we'll get it out by next spring.

"The lullabies were all traditional, but nobody knows who wrote "Bye Bye Lulu". Julia was pregnant during that time and we recorded it as a gift to her and her baby. We wanted it to be used particularly as lullabies for babies. They were super sparse arrangements—really quiet dynamics. Once we recorded that we had friends who really wanted us to put that out so we did on Daniel Martin Morris's label.

Up until this point, Mize focused on traditional music. Knowing songwriting is the fulcrum for any musician, Mize elucidated on the impetus for writing her own music. "Historically, I've not really been a songwriter. I'm sure I wrote a few when I was a teenager, but I didn't really write a lot. I would just put on an album and play along to it to figure out a song. I was more interested in that than the songwriting aspect—if I did write I was just a teenager, and don't have any record of them.

"I guess in 2007 slowly I'd write a song every four to six months. I'd do some demo stuff on 'garageband'. Then the touring I did with Will in 2009—that was a huge tour—we did 75 shows in 90 days...it was crazy. When I came off that tour it allowed me a little time to concentrate on my songs and make sure they sounded well. Those songs are what became Before Lately."

Whereas *Before Lately* was also recorded in Louisville with musical cohorts Ben Sollee, Duane Lundy, John King and Kevin Rotterman lending musical contributions. *Before Lately* stands as a sparse testament to Mize's ability to craft songs, and also where her true soul began to shine through. It retains a subterranean, quiet quality with sparse instrumentation. "On that record I played all the instruments." The only cover song was a version of a Stephen Stills tune called "The Doctor Will See You Now". Mize told me about that one cover tune:

"Crosby, Stills, Nash and Young were always in heavy rotation for me. I got my hands on a demo album called *Just Roll Tape* with only Stephen Stills laying down songs at the end of someone else's session, and he asked if he could just throw the songs on tape. It had "Wooden Ships" and "Judy Blue Eyes" as well as "The Doctor Will See You Now". I'd never heard that one before and I don't think it's recorded anywhere else so it made sense to make an arrangement of it it that spoke to me."

The music business—what's left of it—is ugly. Money is tight—non existent, even. I was curious how Mize fused the phase between *Before Lately* and the variegated EP she released titled We Don't Need. "*Before Lately*, I decided I wanted to pursue something in the solo realm and play some shows. I had a theme. I had been working with Sonablast out of Louisville, but we kind of started to pursue things with other labels and I knew a full album wasn't going to happen for a while, and I had a group of songs I didn't think would go on my next full length record so I just wanted to get them out there. There is a lot of variation within those six songs on *We Don't Need*. It's meant to be a collection of six singles instead of one whole album.

"There is more instrumentation on it. My co-producer helped with the soundscape. He played drums. My current drummer played drums on "It Lingers". Part of it was a natural progression and getting more comfortable with writing. I started pulling on more modern influences than I had in the past. Around Halloween of 2010 I played in a trio where we played all of PJ Harvey's *Rid of Me* so that started to influence my musical thinking in the way I approached singing and guitar. I haven't listened to too many of her albums because I thought it might be too much of an influence. So, I'm really only familiar with three of her records."

Mize records all of her music in Louisville and I asked if *We Don't Need* was recorded in the same studio as the rest of her recordings. "*We Don't Need* was recorded in Kevin Ratterman's Funeral Home Studio. At that time his studio was located on the second floor of a studio home. There is a chain of funeral homes here in the area. His studio was located on the second floor of one of those. It's a totally beautiful home that had been converted—so most of that EP was recorded there. He's since moved to a studio where he's building his brand new studio and in the meantime he was at The Church, which is where I recorded *Among The Grey* and also where My Morning Jacket recorded *Circuitual*."

We Don't Need stands as a brilliant EP. The Stax-sounding "Going Under" and the gritty "It Lingers" stand out as the true gems on the collection, and testimony to Mize's musical vision. I wore the disc out. Then I asked Mize, "By the time you released We Don't Need did you have the songs together for *Among The Grey?*"

"Some of the songs on *We Don't Need* were written after the songs on *Among The Grey*. I was hoping to release *We Don't Need* early in the year of 2011 and *Among The Grey* would come out right after that, but Yep Roc decided when they came on board to help and we pushed *We Don't Need* to January of 2012 and at that time I already recorded the bulk of *Among The Grey*. In the following months we finished the overdubs and the mixing.

"So we pushed *Among The Grey* to 2013. We added a new song—the title track. We used the extra studio time to wrap the whole record up. For several reasons we kept pushing it back and it came out in June of 2013. The wait was worth it. It was a huge undertaking as far as the time put into the record—especially the emotional energy. I wanted to be able to get it right and get it out to as many people as possible. So, it was worth the wait."

Among The Grey contains more instrumentation, a murkier vibe with more musicians involved. Mize agreed. "Yeah, that was a conscious decision because before then I mainly had the experience of playing most of the instruments myself. On this record I had in mind what I wanted. I started playing with this woman Emily Hagihara who is just one of the most incredible musicians I've ever met. She can play everything. She's a percussionist by trade, but she's a killer bass player, singer and she can play everything else as well."

I mentioned two of my favorite tracks from *Among the Grey* were "Through The Window Pane" and "Raymaker", and Mize responded,

"Well, those are the two in major keys of the whole record. I think all of the other songs are in minor keys." The lyrics "Through The Window Pane" retain a universal quality: "As the light shines through the window pane/I can see it in your eyes/It's been building for sometime now/It should be no big surprise."

Recently, Mize toured the midwest. I asked her if she has a new batch of songs ready to record. "Some, but you know, I'm not a super prolific writer. I'm not the kind of person that writes songs all the time. Usually when I get in that mode, I write a lot in a short period of time.

Among The Grey was such a big undertaking and took up so much of my brain space that honestly I've had a hard time moving forward as a writer until the record came out. Also, we've been playing some of those songs live for three years so we're starting to have new material. This past week I wrote a couple of new songs that we can play on this new tour.

"It's funny because I haven't felt the need to write new songs, yet since performing those because so many people are coming to my music for the first time so when I play a live show it's probably a good portion of those people have never heard my music. So, it doesn't matter if it's new or old music to them. I hope to record some new stuff this winter. I have a couple of other projects going on as well. "I hope to make it down south by early spring."

Rest assured, Cheyenne Mize will be welcomed with open arms in the wild blue yonder...

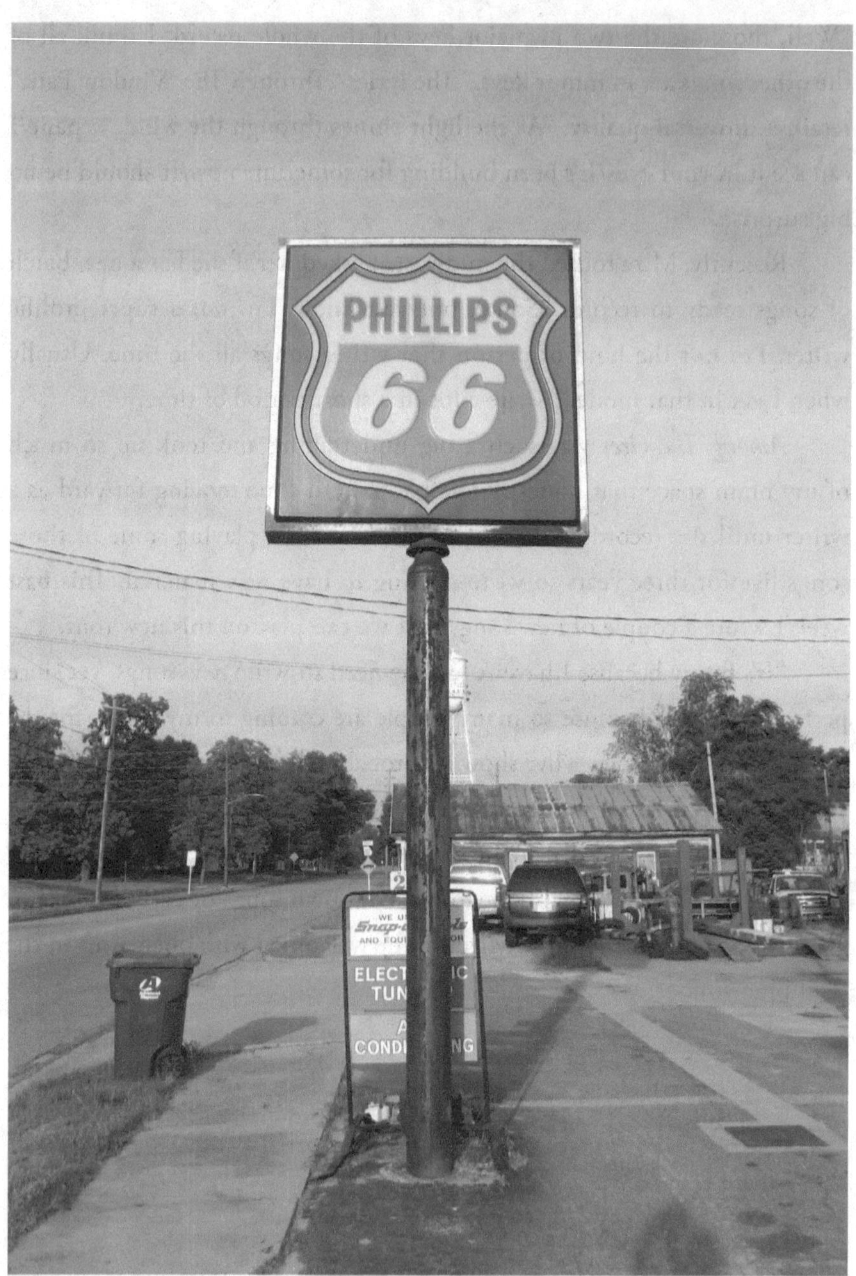

Phillips 66 Sign

Farther Down The Road with Taj Mahal

This article first appeared in Hittin' The Note magazine during the 1990s. Mahal always interested me because he once played with Ry Cooder, Jesse Ed Davis, Music Maker Relief Foundation, Keb Mo, Ali Farka Toure, Wynton Marsalis as well as continuing his own variegated music styles. Mahal exists as a modern day musician steeped in old American music traditions. He's still out there playing his special blend of blues...

TAJ MAHAL REMAINS A craftsman of many musical styles. His career reveals a vast scope submerged within traditions of roots music. This year Columbia released four Taj Mahal classics: *Taj Mahal, The Nach'l Blues, The Real Thing*, and *The Best of Taj Mahal.*

These reissues focus on the early years of Taj Mahal's thirty-five year career in music. Each new CD edition contains original packaging, liner notes, and newly commissioned essays by Keb Mo and Stanley Crouch.

Born in New York in 1942 to musical parents, Mahal also developed an ear for music at an early age. After graduating from the University of Massachusetts, he moved to Los Angeles in 1964. In L.A. Mahal met the great guitarist Ry Cooder where they started a band called the Rising Sons who opened up for acts such as Otis Redding, Sam the Sham, The Temptations, and Martha and the Vandellas.

Mahal incorporates various styles of music into one stream-lined sound. He's a GRAMMY award winning artist and has played with great musicians such as Etta Baker, Rory Block, Mike Bloomfield, Alvin Youngblood Hart, Algia Mae Hinton, John Dee Holeman, B.B. King,

"

Ziggy Marley, Big Bill Morgan, Nitty Gritty Dirt Band, Neal Pattman, the Rolling Stones, Carly Simon, Ali Farka Toure, Joe Louis Walker, and many others. Mahal also composed numerous soundtracks for fi lms.

In a recent interview, Mahal spoke about the origins of his versatile musical career: "All the folks I learned my guitar music from were in Louisburg, North Carolina. The other side of it is, the kids who played music up the street were from Stovall, Mississippi, and that was another infl uence for a fifteen year old kid with a guitar he got from his stepfather who came from Jamaica.

So, I'd heard a lot of music, played a lot of piano and messed with trombone and clarinet, but the sound of the harmonica grabbed my soul.

"At school I studied agriculture—I figured you couldn't go wrong with music or agriculture. From about 1965, when I first came to the West Coast and the music scene, I'd been playing all kinds of different music over the years, and I found that there was an open format for folk blues. The people I heard about I could finally go and see. Eventually I got to the point where I could play those kinds of clubs, but then I realized it was too much of an ingrown thing. This was because I was in Boston with a bunch of people just talking about the blues, and I knew I could take this thing to another generation of youngsters. So I left the east coast for the west coast because I heard there was a lot of action going on there. Then I got hooked up with Ry Cooder and by September of 1966, we were signed to Columbia. Then I met Gary Gilmore and Jesse Edwin Davis. There's so many levels that music can come off at, and I just wanted to play music. If you're there playing with a big band or just up there with a guitar or banjo, harmonica, or piano—by yourself—you can turn it into a show.

"I've played all kinds of music—country, calypso, R&B, blues, jazz, reggae, Latin music—but it always ended up on the margin. So I thought, why not just play the kind of music you want. This was American music too, whether people wanted to recognize that or not…which makes those English groups—like the Rolling Stones—important because they went directly to the source. I've done about fifty projects, and there are thirty-seven or thirty-eight of them that are directly under my name, and then there are things I've contributed to."

Taj Mahal was originally released in 1967. This record introduced the world to not only Taj Mahal, but guitarists Ry Cooder and the late Jesse Edwin Davis. Davis, the inimitable Oklahoma guitarist and pianist toured with Conway Twitty before he moved to California and met Mahal. Other Oklahoma natives Chuck Blackwell (drums) and Gary Gilmore (guitar) played on Mahal's fi rst two albums. Davis, Blackwell, and Gilmore comprised a vital part of the "Tulsa Sound".

This is an album of straight-ahead electric blues covers. The most notable songs are Sleepy John Estes' "Leaving Trunk", Robert Johnson's "Walkin' Blues", Sonny Boy Williamson's "Checkin' up on My Baby", and Blind Willie McTell's "Statesboro Blues". It's been documented Duane Allman spent hours learning the Jesse Ed Davis bottleneck solo to "Statesboro Blues' from Taj Mahal.

The *Natch'l Blues* was no sophomore slump when released in 1968. The album is more reflective—and of a country-acoustic nature—as opposed to the debut album. The *Natch'l Blues* consists mostly of Taj Mahal compositions, aside from William Bell's "You Don't Miss Your Water" and the Banks/Parker tune, "Ain't That a Lot of Love". Mahal classics such as "Done Changed My Way of Living", "She Caught the Katy", and "Going up to the Country" reveal just how mean and diverse his music had become.

Taj explained to me his approach to the material before he recorded for those albums: "Most of the stuff—maybe only one or two times did I have lyrics in the studio—all that was head stuff we played. That's why it sounded like it did. After three takes, we'd all say, 'It's number one or number two'—we didn't leave stuff lying around the studio like a lot of bands. We always destroyed all the takes except what we used. So, on the new version of *Natch'l Blues* that's out, there's three extra tunes; one's an alternate take of "The Cuckoo" one is "I Think It's Gonna Work Out Fine" we did as an instrumental, and the other one is called "New Stranger Blues".

The Real Thing was recorded live in 1971 at Bill Graham's Fillmore East in New York. This was the first Taj Mahal album to follow *Giant Step/ De Ole Folks at Home*. This variegated collection of eleven songs is testimony to how well Taj Mahal's music transfers in a live atmosphere. The band on *The Real Thing* includes a brass section that emits a lush, free flowing, jazz mood—even when Taj plays along on the banjo.

The Best of Taj Mahal is essential to one's music collection. The CD not only highlights his blended styles with classics such as "Leaving Trunk", "Corrina", "Take A Giant Step", and the killer reggae song "Johnny Too Bad", and several live songs, but also obscure gems like "Chevrolet" and a previously unissued studio recording "Sweet Mama Janisse".

For an unknown passenger, just one of these classic Taj Mahal albums is a musical vehicle rolling through deep country, blues, folk, R&B, and gospel destinations en route to his later albums and musical abodes of African, Caribbean, Hawaiian, jazz, and Zydeco descent. There are valleys of discovery in every album, and as for Taj Mahal's musical journey, he reveals: "For me, music has always been a learning thing—to hear something I've never heard."

John Coltrane: *Stellar Regions*

THE COMPOSITIONS ON *Stellar Regions* were recorded five months before John Coltrane's death in 1967 at the age of 40. However, *Stellar Regions* was not released until 1995. Coltrane's wife, Alice, discovered this lost session in 1994. Only one song from these original compositions ("Offering") were ever heard before this album was released.

Alice Coltrane was responsible for the song titles on *Stellar Regions*. The band on this session included Coltrane (tenor & alto saxophone), Alice Coltrane (piano), Jimmy Garrison (bass) and Rashied Ali (drums). Coltrane's health was failing during the time of these sessions, but it's hard to tell from how exuberant he sounds. His avant-garde explorations are captured on these 8 tracks. Three alternate takes are also included on this disc.

"Seraphic Light" opens the album with a calm that evokes a rising sun. "Sun Star" traverses a galaxy of sound where only Coltrane's inimitable tone overtakes the soul. "Iris" emits a golden loom that only Coltrane could create. "Offering" epitomizes Coltrane's command over his instrument.

The band explores uncharted musical territories in a frenetic fever of "Configuration". "Jimmy's Mode" offers a laid back musical landscape best heard when the sun begins to set. "Tranesonic" counts as the final track on *Stellar Regions*, and finds Coltrane traveling on trails of cosmic dust. *Stellar Regions* ranks as a vital recording in Coltrane's prestigious discography.

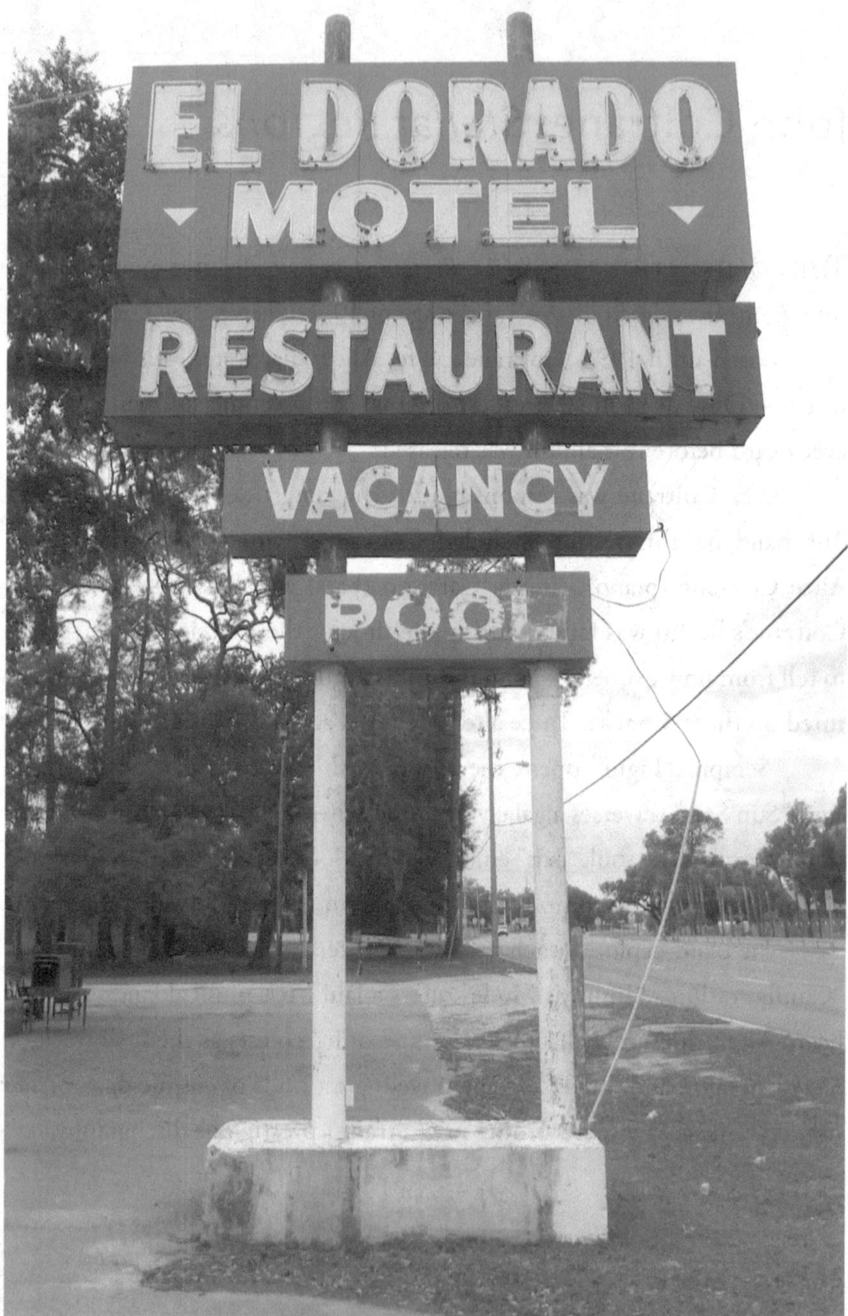

El Dorado Motel

Willie Nelson:
The Complete Atlantic Sessions

Jerry Wexler produced the two albums—Shotgun Willie and Phases and Stages—back in the 70s. The re-released Atlantic Sessions rejuvenated my interests in Willie during 2006. Willie's contribution to American music remains undeniable.

"If America had one voice, it would be Willie's…"

—Emmylou Harris

WILLIE NELSON'S MUSIC CROSSES many generations. His life's work includes 50 years of songwriting, 50 million records sold, over 100 albums released, thousands of shows, countless collaborations, three books, and 2500 penned songs. Nelson spear-headed organizations such as BioWillie, Farm Aid, and many non-profit gigs providing donations to earthquake, tsunami, and flood victims. Many of Nelson's fans are not old enough to remember him as the rough and rowdy songwriter struggling to make a living. These days, Nelson's seminal image personifies a wise, pony tailed, grey-haired sage, dope smoking golf freak that represents peace, love, and earth awareness. Regardless of his image, not many artists can say Miles Davis named a song after them. These *Complete Atlantic Sessions* prove Nelson served as a purveyor of blending rock and roll and country cultures into one unmistakable sound.

Growing up in Abbott, Texas, Nelson began writing songs at age 7. He worked various jobs (even joined the Air Force) as a disc jockey, tree trimmer, and salesman. He soon began playing nightclubs , trying to get his music heard. In 1960 he moved to Nashville. Country great Hank Cochran scored Nelson a publishing deal. Soon, Nelson's songs "Night Life", "Crazy", "Hello Walls", and "Funny How Time Slips Away" were recorded by Ray Price, Patsy Cline, Faron Young, and Billy Walker, which all brought early success. In the early 60's Nelson experienced a string of hits.

In 1965, he became a member of the Grand Ole Opry and recorded a few more semi-hits. By 1970 Nelson became frustrated by the narrow Nashville musical confines while the Rolling Stones, the Grateful Dead, the Band, the Flying Burrito Brothers, and Bob Dylan all augmented country influence in their music. These groups helped expose longhairs to the purity and essential grains of country music in American culture.

The 2006 release of Willie Nelson: *The Complete Atlantic Sessions* mark the second ascent in Nelson's career. The handsome case contains a booklet where Atlantic mogul Jerry Wexler writes about how he signed Nelson and recorded *Shotgun Willie* and *Phases & Stages*: "I think it was 1972 or 1973 that I fi rst encountered Willie in the flesh. I was in Nashville checking the C & W scene for Atlantic; somehow I was invited to Harlan Howard's house for his annual pickers' party. Who all was there…I think I remember Ray Price, Conway Twitty, among others, and Willie Nelson minus a record contract! How could this be? Maybe because Willie was in bad odor with the Nashville establishment; he was a "rebel" (whatever the hell that was intended to imply), he sported an earring and a pigtail halfway down to his butt, and scandal of scandals, he was rumored to partake of the yerba buena. Somebody introduced us, and it was instant karma. I signed him up, and the first thing we did (mostly in our New York studios) was *Shotgun Willie*…"

Wexler, a New York City native, attended Kansas State University where he spent most of his time in dank clubs discovering Joe Turner, Andy Kirk, and Western Swing. In the late 40s Wexler wrote for *Billboard* magazine where he invented the term "rhythm & blues". Wexler kept heavy company. He stands as, arguably, America's greatest jazz, blues, and country music connoisseur. His instinct and ear remain unparalleled.

In 1953, Ahmet Ertegun made Wexler a partner at Atlantic Records. Ertegun seemed interested in music with a pop sensibility while Wexler sought out black artists in the mean streets and swamplands of the south during a time in American history when interracial relationships and friendships proved unacceptable. Wexler paved a progressive road, a link to all the sources of America's most prized source, music.

Wexler's cultivated musical amalgamations changed the music culture forever by cross-pollinating artists with different musical backgrounds to record together on specific projects. The list is too long to name every artist Wexler produced or co-produced, but to name a few: Ray Charles, Bob Dylan, The Staple Singers, Dr. John, Delaney & Bonnie Bramlett, Champion Jack Dupree, King Curtis, Duane Allman, Guitar Slim, Doug Sahm, Dusty Springfield, Aretha Franklin, Professor Longhair, Allen Toussaint, The Dixie Flyers, Donnie Fritts, Tony Joe White, Ronee Blakley, Etta James, The Drifters, Wilson Pickett, Donny Hathaway, Dire Straits, Cher, Patti LaBelle, Carlos Santana, and Willie Nelson.

Wexler signed Nelson onto the label, and they soon set to work. *The Complete Atlantic Sessions* encloses three CDs: *Shotgun Willie, Phases & Stages*, and *Live At the Texas Opry House*. Each CD contains unheard bonus tracks, outtakes, and alternate versions to the official releases.

The importance of these two albums in Nelson's career should not be taken lightly; they set the stage for the flowering of the Austin music scene. Like any great musician, Nelson suffered from a severe aversion to musical stereotypes. He wanted to reach people who didn't necessarily listen to country music. His first Atlantic studio album, *Shotgun Willie*, released in 1973 proved his ability to reach Texas shitkickers, hippies in California, jazz freaks in New Orleans, sons & daughters of the South, and cynical urbanites in New York City.

Nelson stated the album's title track was "the only song I ever wrote in New York City." In his book *The Facts of Life and Other Dirty Jokes* Willie wrote: "I did an album in New York City one time. It turned out to be called *Shotgun Willie*. I wrote the title song while I was making the album.

Jerry Wexler was the producer—one of the best producers of all time. I was looking for a record deal and he really liked my work. So there we were in New York City, doing an album. I was thrilled. At the same time though I was a little pissed because I wanted to come up with a really good new song for the album."

The booklet for these landmark *Atlantic Sessions* contains Nelson's explanation for the title track's origin. "I walked out of the studio and back to my hotel. In my room I paced from corner to corner, listening to radio waves, the old sensation surging through me. Then I went to the bathroom and sat down. I saw a sanitary napkin envelope in the sink. I picked it up and started writing: "Shotgun Willie sits around in his underwear…"

On this opening track Nelson establishes immediately that he's incorporated Atlantic's blend of R&B into his music with a brass backdrop provided by the Memphis Horns. *Shotgun Willie* was recorded in five days. Wexler allowed Nelson to choose his own band. He recruited talented musicians such as Leon Russell, Doug Sahm, and Jimmy Day to contribute to these sessions. Nelson renders Johnny Bush's "Whiskey River" so well many thought Nelson wrote the song himself, and continues to perform the tune in his live repertory.

Longtime musical sidekicks such as Bee Spears (bass guitar), Sister Bobbie Nelson (piano), and Paul English (drums) comprised the core of Nelson's band on *Shotgun Willie* and they remain in his band until this day. "Sad Songs And Waltzes" sounds quite autobiographical considering that era was a tumultuous time in Nelson's life and he sang about his daily pain and tribulations in a straightforward and honest manner that connected with the common man. Nelson tips his hat twice to fellow-Texan Bob Wills by covering "Stay All night" and "Bubbles in My Beer". Also, Nelson covers two of Leon Russell's songs—"You Look Like the Devil" and "A Song For You". The elusive Russell operated at the peak of his career during this time, having already collaborated with rockers The Rolling Stones, Eric Clapton, Joe Cocker's Mad Dogs & Englishmen, Bob Dylan, and George Harrison. Nelson mentioned his bond with the Oklahoma native: "My daughter told me I had to listen to (Joe Cocker's) *Mad Dogs & Englishmen* album. I was amazed by the arrangements. I made a point of checking him (Russell) out. I thought it was the most incredible show I'd ever seen. Not just the visual impact, but the music." Russell and Nelson later cut a record together titled, *One For the Road*. Russell recently appeared (as he has almost every year) at Nelson's 2006 Fourth of July Picnic in Texas.

"Slow Down Old World" finds the songwriter at a crossroads at 40. "She's Not For You" proves as a universal soundtrack for any man who's lost a woman he's loved. "So Much To Do" (with strings arranged by the late Donny Hathaway), tells a tale of a man forced to pick up pieces of a shattered love: "There's too much to do now that you're gone/too much to do all alone/time rolls on like a river/there's so much to do/I just can't do without you."

These songs serve as therapy for any man facing the world alone with only a bottle as solace.

These *Atlantic Sessions* contain 12 bonus tracks unearthed from the *Shotgun Willie* sessions. Two outtakes included Floyd Tillman's rocking "I Gotta Have Something I Ain't Got" and Leon Russell's "My Cricket And Me (also covered by Glen Campbell). Nelson songs that didn't make the cut for the album were "I'm So Ashamed", "Both Ends of the Candle", a heart-rending version of "Save Your Tears", and instrumental "Under The Double Eagle". These songs would prove as hits for any other artist, but Nelson decided to leave them off the album.

Phases & Stages, a concept album, was recorded in October 1973 and released in March of 1974. The first five songs are told from a woman's perspective in a disintegrating marriage; the songs reveal her unhappiness and plans to leave. The last five songs are told from a man's point of view in the same relationship when he wakes up to realize his woman is gone. These songs were written by a man in an emotional and domestic up-heaval. All the compositions on *Phases & Stages* were composed by Nelson.

The sessions occurred in Muscle Shoals, Alabama, with the Muscle Shoals Rhythm Section ("The Swampers"): David Hood, Barry Beckett,

Roger Hawkins, Jimmy Johnson, Pete Carr, accompanied by John Hughey playing pedal steel and Johnny Gimble handling mandolin and fiddle, serving as the band. Muscle Shoals became an oasis for artists because anything that contained "The Swampers" more or less appeared high in the charts. Countless great albums were cut in Muscle Shoals. Percy Sledge, The Rolling Stones, Bobby Womack, Jimmy Cliff, Aretha Franklin, Joe Cocker, Bob Seger, Leon Russell, and Lynyrd Skynyrd all recorded hits there. Not to mention great obscure recordings by Duane Allman, Little Richard, Eddie Hinton, and Bob Dylan.

Jerry Wexler spoke about industry doubts concerning Willie Nelson recording in Muscle Shoals, "Everyone in Nashville thought I was out of my mind. They said Muscle Shoals was too R&B for Willie. I said Willie was too R&B for Nashville…"

The Muscle Shoals Rhythm Section's, low-bottom, sparse, warm sound on *Phases & Stages* permeates each of Nelson's songs, which proves more subdued than *Shotgun Willie*. These tunes allowed Nelson to continue reaching a wider audience and solidifying his position as a timeless troubadour of country music.

The first three songs—"Washing the Dishes", "Walkin'", and "Pretend I Never Happened"—conjure folk, rhythm & blues, flamenco, and country ingredients in each song creating a melting pot of sonic alchemy that transcended musical boundaries.

Emmylou Harris enjoyed Nelson's "Sister's Coming Home" so much she covered the song on her *Blue Kentucky Girl* album several years later. "(How Will I Know) If I'm Falling In Love Again" sounds as if it could succeed in any musical form—country, blues, rock, soul, or even reggae due to Nelson's strength of song construction.

"Bloody Mary Morning" stands out as the *Phases & Stages* centerpiece song which Nelson continues to play almost every gig. Often Nelson's guitar prowess is overlooked, but subtle licks on this tune verify Nelson's six-string aptitude. In his latest book, *The Tao of Willie*, Nelson wrote about his early musical influence which he incorporated for these releases, "Back in

Texas, it was easier to remember all that great Mexican and Spanish guitar pickin' I'd heard as a boy, and those sounds helped fi ll out two albums I made for Atlantic. *Shotgun Willie* and *Phases & Stages* were both hits…"

"No Love Around" tells the story of a man "coming home on Saturday morning" to find a note from his wife that she no longer loves him and she's gone. "I Still Can't Believe You're Gone" ranks as a gem ("It's the very first day/since you left me/But I've tried to put my thoughts in a song/All I can hear myself singing/Is I still can't believe you're gone"). Nelson's mode of operandi always revolves around his strength in simplicity although lush string arrangements sweeten these sad songs of love and loss.

"Heaven And Hell" reminds the listener Nelson never strays far from his country roots with a weeping pedal steel and toe-tapping solid drum beat. *Phases & Stages* closes with the recurring acoustic theme just before "Pick Up the Tempo" where Nelson sings like a desperate man resigned to a hard-luck hand he's been dealt: "I'm wild and mean/I'm creating scene/I'm goin' crazy/Well I'm good and bad/I'm happy and sad/And I'm lazy/I'm quiet and I'm loud/I'm gathering a crowd/And I like gravy/I'm about half off the wall/But I learned it all in the Navy."

Ten bonus tracks from *Phases & Stages* include alternate versions of original songs on the album, essential for any real Nelson fan who played the album over and over. With each listen one hears another layer of Nelson's musical genius. *Phases & Stages* ended a golden era at Atlantic.

The final CD of this *Atlantic Collection* comprises 16 live tracks performed on June 29 and 30, 1974, at the Texas Opry House in Austin, preserving the dynamic power of Nelson's live performances. The staple songs include "Whiskey River", "Me & Paul", "Funny How Time Slips Away", "Crazy", Night Life", "Bloody Mary Morning", "The Party's Over", "Truck Drivin' Man", "She Thinks I Still Care", the Waylon Jennings/Nelson classic "Good Hearted Woman" (which set the stage for the timeless Outlaws album released a year later), and "Sister's Comin' Home." This collection magnifies Nelson's ability to assemble a band for incandescent live performances. Five previously unreleased bonus tracks close this live CD.

After *Shotgun Willie* and *Phases & Stages*, Nelson's career improved dramatically. He became an icon. These days, there's a plethora of great Nelson CDs to explore, but the *Atlantic Sessions* verify Nelson's position as an essential American songwriter.

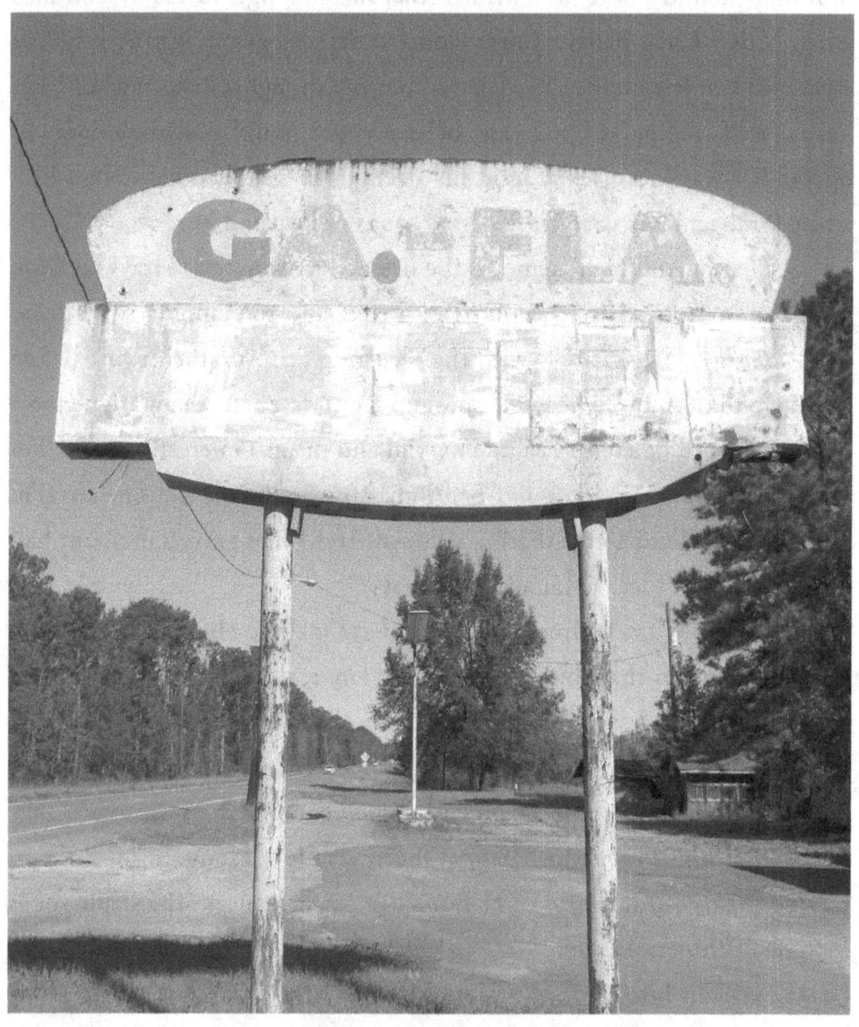

Georgia-Florida Motel

Reverend Johnny L. Jones:
The Hurricane That Hit Atlanta

Rev. Johnny Jones died in 2015.

THIS 2 CD DUST-TO-DIGITAL compilation of archival recordings from Rev. Johnny L. "Hurricane" Jones, culled from more than 1,000 tapes of live congregational recordings, can now be heard for the first time. The earliest recordings on this set began in 1957. Jones still records every Sunday service at his Second Mount Olive Church in Atlanta, Georgia.

The recordings sound raw and distorted during certain sermons, but the spirit proves unforgettable. Born on June 25, 1936 in Marion, Alabama, Jones began singing in church at an early age. Eventually he started preaching. Jones organized gospel groups, traveled and played piano in church choirs.

Over 50 years ago Jones moved to Atlanta. This compilation documents some of the most soulful and spiritual recordings ever committed to tape. Disc One begins with Rev. Wright from Durham, North Carolina, introducing the fireball preacher "Hurricane" Jones. A rumbling bass follows the introduction and suddenly drums, guitar, bass and organ all converge on Jones' "Sit At The Welcome Table" message to the congregation.

These discs contain two-dozen soul-stirring songs, sermonettes, guest soloists and priceless radio clips. Rev. Jones' ensemble ranks as one of the most powerful bands you'll ever hear. Highlights on Disc One include "I Got Drunk For The Lord/Train Is Moving", "I'm Going Through", "God Specializes" and "Sometimes I Feel Like I'm Almost Gone".

Disc Two brings Jones' Sunday services up to the latest Second Mount Olive Church era. Memorable tracks on this sequence count as "Glad About

It", "It's That Way Sometimes", "Walk with Me", "Female Choir Medley", "Don't Move My Mountains (sung by Valerie Mathis), "Tell It (sung by Sonya Dorsey) and "Psalm 23/Lord Help Me To Hold Out". Rev. Johnny L. Jones brings church to the airwaves the first and third Saturday of each month on WYZE in Atlanta.

Recently, Rev. Jones spoke about his musical mission: "We sing a lot of songs, and I guess my personal reason would be that they interest the older people and still move a lot of the younger people. I think you're going to come out better though when you learn how to mix styles. As for this new experience with Dust To Digital, I'm proud, and I just pray and trust that this will be a help to everybody who listens to it."

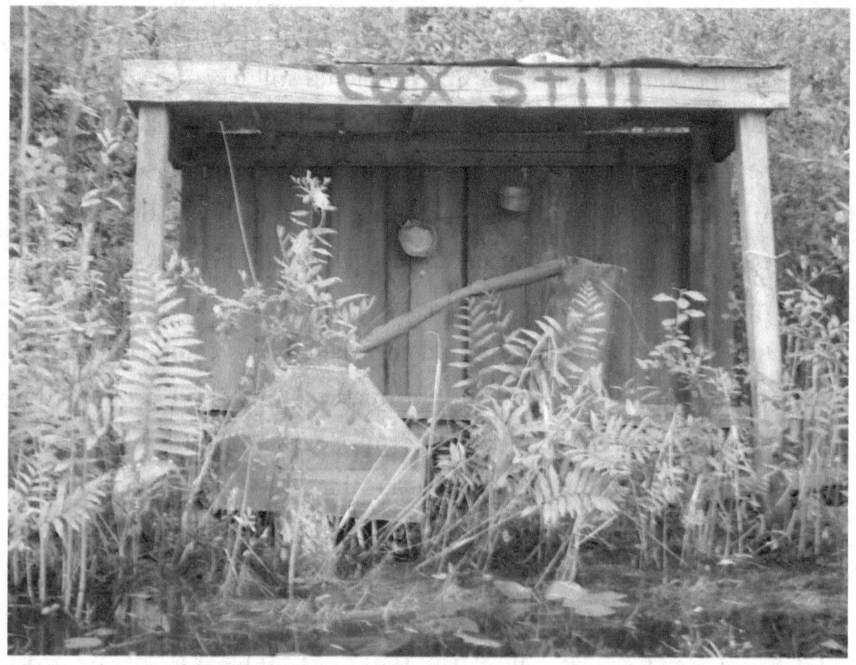

Cox Still

Don Nix: *Road Stories and Recipes*

DON NIX'S *ROAD STORIES AND RECIPES* contains personal music stories of Memphis, Muscle Shoals, dangerous juke joints, traveling tales in the 50s, 60s and 70s as well as over 60 recipes from some of the world's most talented musicians. Don Nix, musician/songwriter/producer, recounts his singular memories and experiences through the years in *Road Stories and Recipes*.

Nix tells firsthand stories about crossing paths with luminaries such as Freddie King, Albert King, Dewey Phillips, Steve Cropper, Duck Dunn, Charlie Freeman, Terry Johnson, "Packy" Axton, The MarKeys, Jim Stewart, Estelle Axton, Wayne Jackson, Stax Records, Chips Moman, Rufus & Carla Thomas, Elvis, Carl Radle, J. J. Cale, Chuck Blackwell, Leon Russell, Booker T. Jones, Isaac Hayes, Al Jackson, Furry Lewis, Gus Cannon, Charles Elmo (aka Charlie Brown), Gram Parsons, Delaney Bramlett, Jim Dickinson, John Fry, Sam The Sham, Eddie Floyd, Wilson Pickett, Sam & Dave, Taj Mahal, Jesse Ed Davis, Dale Hawkins, Otis Redding, Dan Penn, Spooner Oldham, Donnie Fritts, Eddie Hinton, Charlie Musselwhite, Jim Keltner, Jim Gordon, Sid Selvidge, Rita Coolidge, Jimmy Johnson, Roger Hawkins, David Hood, Wayne Perkins, Joe Cocker, Karl Himmel, Denny Cordell, Elton John, Robbie Robertson, Levon Helm, Bob Dylan, Paul Simon, Bobby Keys, Lonnie Mack, George Harrison, Steve Winwood, Eric Clapton, Jeff Beck, and John Mayall.

John Mayall wrote the Foreword to *Road Stories and Recipes*. Mayall revealed: "What you are about to get stuck into is the reminiscences of a truly humorous raconteur and participant in an exciting period of rock-n-roll that might have slipped your attention. Here you will find stories of the road that tell of an era of our musical history that will hopefully give you something to remember and have you on the phone urging your friends to go out and buy it. As if this memoir isn't enough, you are also getting a cookbook full of recipes from a whole slew of musicians who often "don't get to eat as handsomely on the road as they do in their own kitchens..."

Many of the 45 photographs in this book originate from Nix's personal archive. Don Nix played an integral role in American music, and these pages verify his talent and influence in the community of first-class musicians. In the Prelude, Nix wrote: "The Memphis music scene has become a phenomenon with literary midgets as well as giants doing interviews, taking notes, and writing books. The trouble with this is, of course, if you ask twenty people the same question, you get twenty different answers, twenty points of view, twenty different memories, and, in some cases, people who were on the fringe or who were not there at all, giving their opinions about what happened.

"I have read books and heard people interviewed about Stax and its glory days when I know damn well they never set foot in the place. I get angry sometimes when people look at it from an analytical point of view. They put it under a microscope, dissect it, examine it, and reexamine it. They try to make it something it ain't, cause when you get past all the books and labels, it was just people trying to make a living the best they could. creating something that had never been before without even knowing it. People who got paid very little for what they contributed but would have done it for free because they loved it. Making music meant freedom as well as a sense of belonging, but most of all it was fun."

Some of the musicians that contributed amazing recipes in this book include Tim Drummond (Green Chili Pork Stew), Butch Trucks (Sauteed Chicken & Kielbasa), David Hood (Louise's Lemon Dessert), Lonnie Mack (Mexican Delight), Don Henley (Texas Chili), J.J. Cale (Quick Dinner), Bobby Bare (Biscuits & Gravy), Tom Dowd (Fettuccine), Delaney Bramlett (Delaney's Stew), Dan Penn (San Francisco BBQ Chicken), Wayne Jackson (Lowfat Chicken Dish), Steve Cropper (Linguine with Cream Sauce), Little Milton (Catfish Head Stew), Sam The Sham (Chili Pie), Dickey Betts

(Smoked Venison), Eddie Hinton (Tuna Helper Skillet Style), Donnie Fritts (Cornbread Dressing), Jim Dickinson (Boiled Salad Dressing), Jim Stewart (Vegetable Casserole), Sid Selvidge (Jalapeno Cheese Grits), Jerry Wexler (No-Cholesterol Corn Pudding), Spooner Oldham (Salmon Gravy) and Nix's own Chicken Pot Pie recipe.

Road Stories and Recipes celebrates southern music and cooking like no other book. I keep this one in the kitchen.

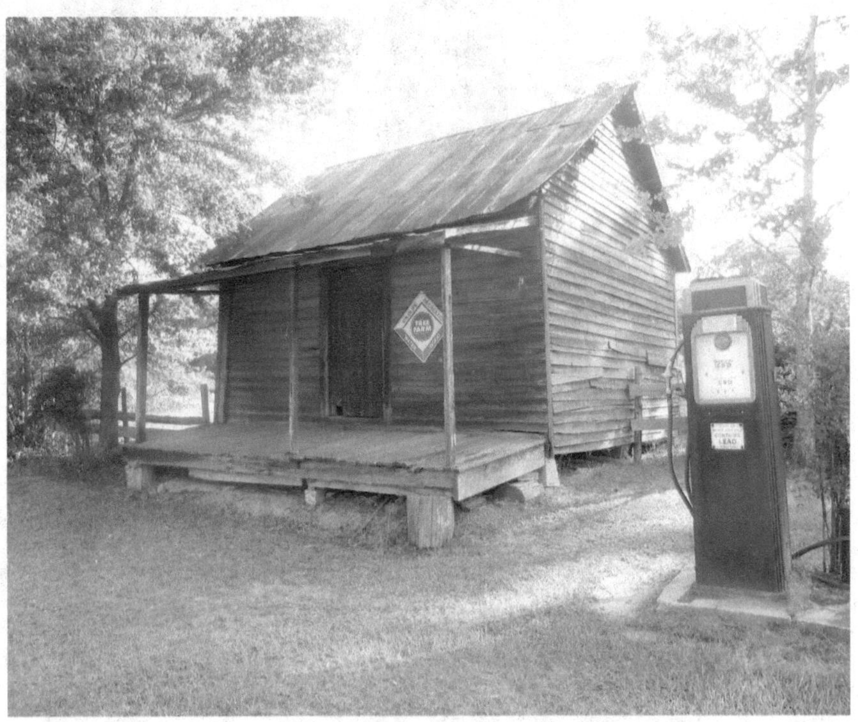

Georgia Tree Farm

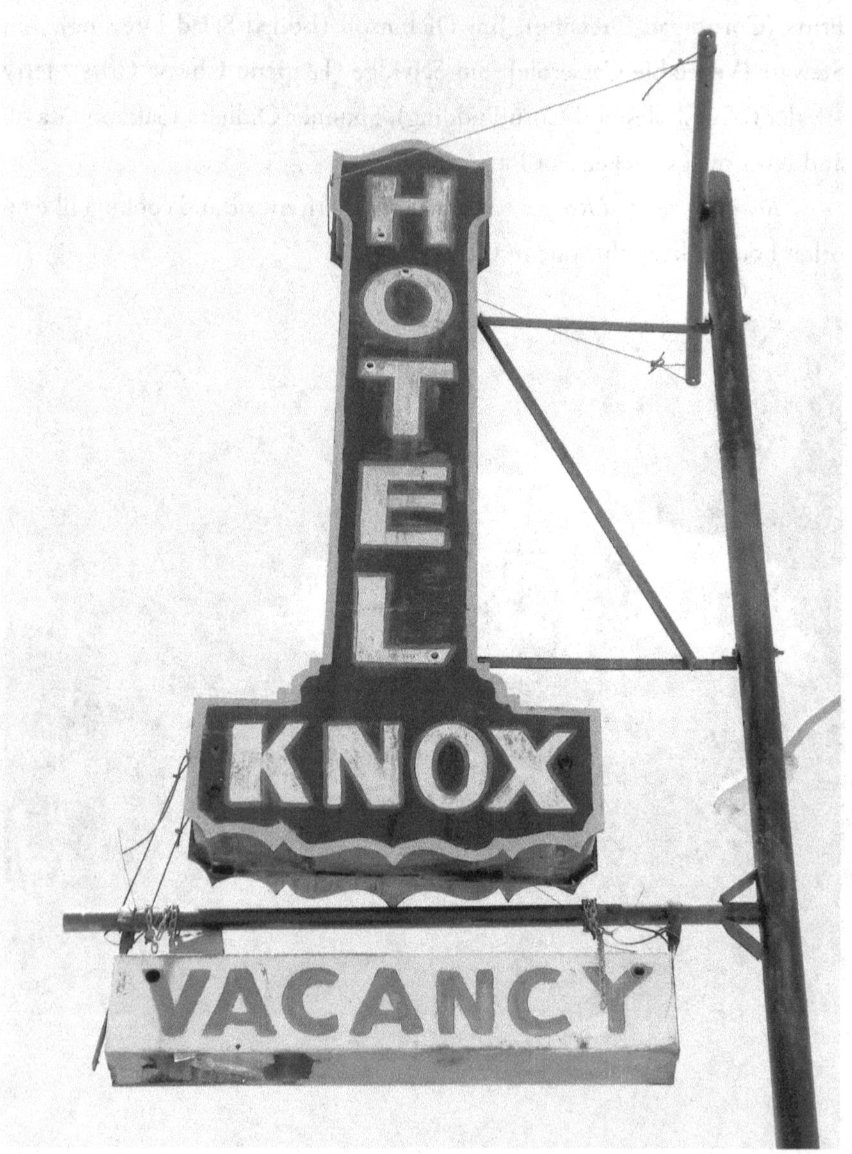

Hotel Knox

The Feelings of
Beverly "Guitar" Watkins

RECORDED AT CLEAN TRACKS Studio in Vinemont, Alabama, these ten songs illustrate the true guitar mastery of Beverly Watkins. Born in Atlanta, Georgia, on April 6, 1939, Watkins played guitar for the legendary Piano Red when she was a teenager.

This new release showcases Watkins' songwriting talent. In the album liner notes Music Maker president Tim Duffy wrote, "I met Beverly when she was playing on the streets of the Underground Atlanta. She put on a tremendous show and she was obviously a star. Music Maker started booking package shows throughout the country and Beverly was a showstopper. She tore down the house at halls such as Irving Plaza, Great American Music Hall, House of Blues, Tipitina's, and European festivals. She came up under Piano Red and cut records with him back in the 50's and 60's. She plays low down, hard stompin', railroad-smokin' blues. She'll tell you, 'People are impressed to see a black woman play like a man.'"

The first song, "As I Was Walking (Down That Lonesome Highway)", opens with a great R & B horn-laced energy. "Baghdad Blues", a political tune sheds light on our country's current situation emerges as the centerpiece of this CD.

"Sugar Baby Swing" carries heavy jazz inflections. Watkins molds her sound to any style with a slow musical precision. The evidence of her talent verifies there's no substitute for experience. "Just Make Believe", a quiet piano waltz, is sure to attract lovers towards one another. The next song, "Get Out On the Floor" invites all good timers to shake their moneymaker while Watkins plays fiery licks on the guitar.

The jubilant "Jesus Walked on the Water" features an upbeat barbershop quartet vibe you only hear on Sunday mornings that ends The Feelings of Beverly "Guitar" Watkins.

Watkins continues to play with other blues greats and Music Maker musicians such as original Ink Spot Eddie Tigner, Cootie Stark, Jerry "Boogie" McCain, and Sammy Blue. Catch Ms. Watkins live for the full effect of her guitar mastery. Until then, this batch of songs should keep you busy. Her gritty style will keep any man honest.

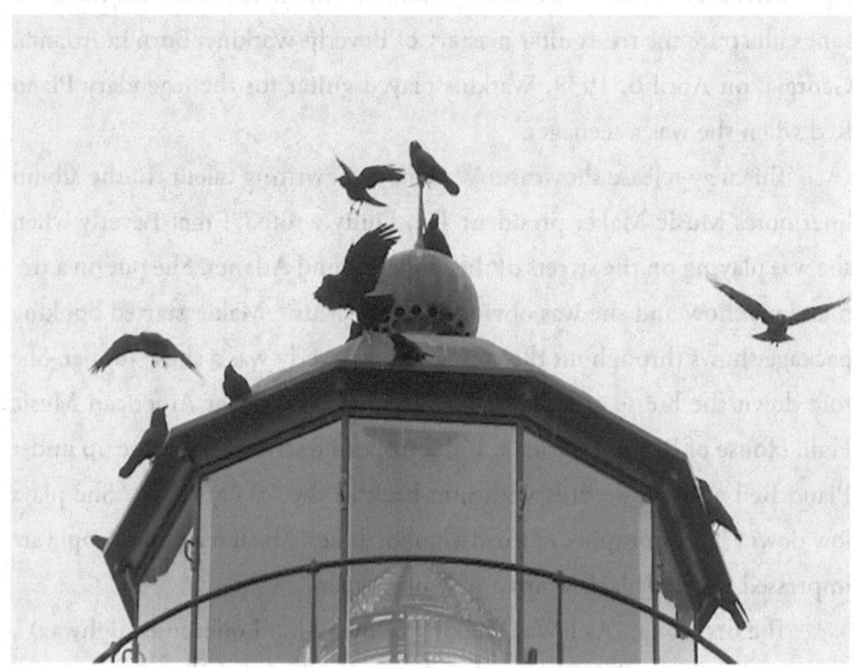

Crows On a Lighthouse

The Divine Spark of
Sly & The Family Stone

In 2016, Sly Stone (Sylvester Stewart) was awarded five million dollars in back royalties. For years, Sly lived in an RV, and before that he was homeless. The story of Sly & The Family Stone cuts to the bone. It documents the price talent and fame brings with talent. This theme seems to appear through these pages—the price one must pay for the sake of their art. Sly Stone is a survivor. This article coincided with the 2007 release of The Collection, which comprised the group's first six albums.

"Time needs another minute, at least."

—Sly Stone

FEW GROUPS EVER ATTAIN the musical power and wide commercial appeal of Sly & The Family Stone. From 1967-1974, the group proved a formidable band whose music crossed all social and musical barriers.

Sly Stone, a purveyor of funk music who influenced artists like George Clinton & P Funk, Prince, Rick James, Marvin Gaye, Stevie Wonder, Curtis Mayfield, Outkast, Weather Report, Arrested Development, Earth, Wind & Fire along with countless others, still lurks in the reclusive distance somewhere for the past two decades. Whispers of Sly's comeback have circulated for years.

Perhaps the Epic/Legacy release of the 7-CD *Sly & The Family Stone Collection* might inspire Stone to release new music and return to performing. His story is one of sheer talent, fame, fortune, and an eerie darkness that still lingers like smoke.

If they never make music together again, this handsome box set proves the undeniable greatness of Sly & the Family Stone's first 7 albums that include bonus tracks, photographs, along with original and new liner notes. The *Sly & The Family Stone Collection* highlights what this multi-racial, multi-sex group accomplished during the apex of their illustrious career.

Born Sylvester Stewart on March 15, 1944, in Dallas, Texas, Stewart participated in a family gospel group at the age of 4. Stewart's brother, Freddie (born June 6, 1946, in Dallas) and Rose (born March 21, 1945 in Vallejo, California) always played music together.

An early recording of the Stewart Four's "On the Battlefield of My Lord" never surfaced, but gave a glimpse of the family ambition and aptitude for musical pursuits. Early on, the Stewart family moved to Vallejo, California, a suburb of San Francisco.

Stewart played piano and guitar early on. He soon learned to play drums, bass and horns. He began making records at 16. Sylvester and his brother Freddie recorded doo-wop singles in 1959 and 1960. Then Sly took songwriting control when he cut "A Long Time Alone", "I'm Just A Fool" and "Help Me with My Broken Heart".

Soon Stewart met Jerry Martini, a white, horn player from Colorado, and they played gigs at North Beach bars. When Stewart was still in high school they played in a group called the Viscaynes.

A huge Bob Dylan fan, Stewart landed a DJ job on an R & B station in San Francisco where he learned to network his skills. A respected young DJ, Stewart already had a wife and three kids to support. He served as staff producer for Autumn Records where he worked with Billy Preston, The Mojo Men, Bobby Freeman, The Beau Brummels and Grace Slick who later sang in the Jefferson Airplane.

Around this era, Stewart changed his name to Sly Stone. Then he met trumpet player Cynthia Robinson who joined on with the siblings. Martini's cousin, drummer Greg Errico, also began playing with The Family

Stone. Texas bassist—Sly's cousin—Larry Graham soon joined the band, completing the lineup of the original group. A family affair, indeed.

They gigged around playing songs by James Brown, Wilson Pickett and Otis Redding among others. In 1967, the group recorded their first album, *A Whole New Thing*, in Los Angeles. The Family fused hybrids of soul, Motown, Stax, jazz, psychedelia (they were after all in the middle of San Fran's hippie Mecca) and pop into one streamlined sound.

The opening track for *A Whole New Thing* was "Underdog" which set the tone for the group's gradual ascent. "I know how it feels to expect to get a fair shake/But they won't let you forget you're the underdog/And you got to be twice as cool."

This record, like the first few, contained an unrestrained exuberance. "If This Room Could Talk" stands as a mercurial song displaying the band's capability for instantaneous virtuosity. "I Cannot Make It" provided dramatic musical changes that inspired movement…color…speed…action…sound.

Sly wrote all of the songs. Freddie Stone's guitar playing always served as a quicksilver thread through these recordings. The band congealed quickly. Bonus tracks on *A Whole New Thing* include "Underdog", "Let Me Hear It From You", "Only One Way Out of This Mess", "What Would I Do" and "You Better Help Yourself". The latter song proves a frenetic track which finds The Family channeling southern groups like Booker T & the MGs, the JBs and the Memphis Horns into one soul stew. These songs were recorded on a four track tape. Larry Graham, Freddie, Rose and Sly all provided backing vocals. *A Whole New Thing* held a big promise for the future.

Sly & the Family Stone's second record, *Dance To the Music*, came out in 1968. The title track hit #8 in April of that year. The band's unrestrained joyous tunes continued on this album. "Color Me True" represented an authentic picture of a band still connected to common folk in Sly's lyric: "Do you laugh at the boss's jokes when they're not funny?/Color me true/ You might think you talk just like a player/Would you know how to talk to your city mayor?"

"I Ain't Got Nobody" remains the dark horse song of this batch. *Dance To the Music* outsold the first record and the group's momentum continued to expand. Six bonus tracks appear on this CD, including Otis Redding's "I Can't Turn You Loose"—the only song Sly didn't write in this 7 CD box set. The single version of "Dance To the Music" is included on the bonus list as well as an R&B fueled instrumental titled "Never Do Your Woman Wrong".

By May 1968, Sly & the Family Stone played New York's Fillmore East with Jimi Hendrix. In July, the group released a single, "Life", and a b-side "M'Lady"—two positive, upbeat popular tunes that epitomized the band's vibe. That fall, at London's Heathrow airport, the band was kicked out of England for a small amount of marijuana. The group would not return across the pond until 1969.

The third album, *Life*, hit the streets in fall of 68. Freddie Stone's screaming guitar riff opens the album with "Dynamite". "Into My Own Thing"—a heady number that highlights Sly's lyrical ability and the group's musical power amazes. On "Dynamite" Cynthia Robinson fuses a horn medley from "Dance To the Music" into the song, a periodic re-occurrence on Sly's records. "Plastic Jim", "I'm An Animal" and "Jane Is A Groupie" shows outside infl uences creeping into Sly's psyche.

The bonus track "Pressure" would've fit nicely on the original LP, but at least it can now be heard. "Sorrow", another bonus instrumental, exhibits Larry Graham's thumping bass on Errico's solid beat, Freddie's quick hooks, Rose, Cynthia, Jerry providing musical Technicolor—and of course—Sly in a loose, creative space where some of their best tracks like this one never made the cut. Life didn't produce huge hits like the previous two albums, which put the group at a crossroads in their career.

"Stand, they will try and make you crawl."

—"Stand"

The breakthrough came with the fourth album, *Stand!* The title track opens the CD and upholds the group's positive sentiment, but "Don't Call Me Nigger Whitey" introduced a darker edge into the music. Serious racial and political unrest divided the country in 1969, and the masses looked to Sly—who seemed to appeal to blacks and whites—for a mystical solution for peace. "Sing A Simple Song" emerged as the band's overall simplistic overall vision.

"Everyday People" hit #1 on the charts and remains the band's signature song. Sly still preached amid chaos that trying to stay humble never hurt anyone:

> *"I am no better and neither are you*
> *We are the same whatever we do*
> *You love me you hate me you know me and then*
> *You can't figure out the bag I'm in*
> *I'm everyday people."*

The song propelled the group into instant stardom. "You Can Make It If You Try" promised hard work paid off. Paranoia leaked in on "Somebody's Watching You". "Sex Machine", a 13-minute funk template displayed The Family Stone's instrumental dynamic led by Brother Freddie. This album influenced even the most seasoned and successful musicians and led many upstarts to Sly's door.

Sly, one of the few black acts dominating the charts, became a cultural magnet during turbulent times in America as well as his personal life. On July 4, 1969, The Family shared a bill on the Newport Jazz Festival with Led Zeppelin and James Brown. In August of 1969, Sly & The Family Stone played at Woodstock (a highlight of the movie) with Jimi Hendrix, The Band, Joan Baez, Creedence Clearwater Revival, The Grateful Dead and Santana.

Soon the single "Hot Fun In The Summertime" hit #2 on the charts with a melodic hook and a friendly message that anyone could enjoy. This album would serve as the last straightforward approach or message Sly would promote. He developed a taste for luxury and drugs that began to obscure storm clouds gathering in the distance.

On a personal level the group began attracting parasites, groupies and vampires that all successful bands experience, which surely contributed to Sly's upcoming creative delay. In December, "Everybody Is A Star" and the decadent funk anthem "Thank You (Falettinme Be Mice Elf Again)" sold many copies, and shed some cognizance of the impending darkness with the lyrics: "Dyin' young is hard to take/Sellin' out is harder."

In 1970, Sly missed 26 of 80 gigs. In 1971, he missed 12 of 41. The group began to stagnate due to Sly's nefarious distractions. In November 1970 a Greatest Hits album was released that shot to #2, selling one million copies in two months.

In the fall of 1970, Sly rented a Spanish mission-style home at 738 Bel Air Drive in Beverly Hills owned by John Phillips of the Mamas and Papas. Sly spent most of his time in the spacious recording studio located in the attic. The house was used in the opening credits of the TV show The Beverly Hillbillies. At this point, Sly sat in the driver's seat. Musicians like Joe Hicks, Bobby Womack, Jim Ford, Ike Turner, Herbie Hancock, Miles Davis and Billy Preston stopped by the mansion to jam.

There's a Riot Goin On, released in 1971, marked Sly & The Family Stone's fifth studio album. These songs sounded much different than the previous four albums. Songs from *Riot* sound murkier, darker, mellower, less-danceable, and funkier than any of their previous work. *Riot* is a late night record. Sly began employing a drum machine on these sessions, and Larry Graham suspected Sly of erasing his bass parts and re-recording them. Soon band members felt alienated. Chaos descended on 738 Bel Air Drive.

Riot's opening track, "Luv N Haight" contains a disturbing yin and yang narrative within a deep rhythmic groove. "Just Like A Baby' sounds like a zombie-powdered love song. On "Poet", Sly looks into the magic mirror: "My only weapon is my pen/I'm a songwriter."

The centerpiece song, "Family Affair" rose to #1. "Brave And Strong" showcased Sly's new sparse, tight-bass approach including fewer horns. "Time" finds Sly at his blissed-out, Zen master best when he mumbles the line: "Time, they say is the answer…"

"Spaced Cowboy", another laid-back hedonistic ditty reveals: "Everything I like is nice/That's why I try it twice." It began to sound like the band was descending, and the critics issued their doubts on the band's creative spark. Riot's bonus tracks "My Gorilla Is My Butler", "Do You Know What?" and "That's Pretty Clean" are all groove-oriented instrumentals founded on thick bass, organ and a steady beat. One can only imagine the rarefied air surrounding this recording session.

Later, Larry Graham and Greg Errico quit the band. Rusty Allen replaced Graham on bass and Andy Newark fi lled the drum position. When original members of a successful band quit the community musical dynamics change on various levels. Yet, Sly Stone still had a few tricks up his sleeve.

In 1972 Sly began recording *Fresh*. Existing in the storm for so many years, Sly began showing signs of understandable weariness. Longtime members leaving the band, record company pressure, drugs, women and money can destroy even the most seasoned creative souls.

On *Fresh's* opener, "In Time" (later rendered by Miles Davis), Sly sings "There's a mickie in the tastin' of disaster/In time, in time you get faster." Sly's fascination with time continued. *Fresh* contains some of Sly's most cryptic and clever insights. Gone was the pop element to the music. Now, it was funk-plain and simple. Ingredients of soul and R&B never disappeared, but Sly seemed disinterested with radio-friendly rehash.

"Let Me Have It All" mirrors the professional pressure Sly felt for a while: "You have turned into a prayer/I can feel I'm almost there/Closer closer to the top/Lookin' down is quite a drop." "Frisky" conjures a dense beat, but Larry Graham's bass licks are missed. However, without question, Fresh contends with Sly's first three albums.

The classic "Thankful N Thoughtful" ranks as one of his finest augmentations of gospel-tinged lyrics into his own funk: "Sunday morning, I forgot my prayer/I should be happy I still be there/Something could come and taken me away/But the mainman felt 'Syl' should be here another day."

"Que Sera, sera" was a song made popular in Alfred Hitchcock's *The Man Who Knew Too Much*. Sly's version was a sardonic, soulful resignation to ruthless change washing over passing time. "Babies Makin' Babies" reflects a stark realism an epidemic of young people raising children: "From the womb/To the tomb." Fresh bonus tracks include alternate versions of five of the album's songs; amid distractions, disintegration and flux, *Fresh* remains a classic.

A year later, in 1974, *Small Talk* was released. The record was a moderate hit. Around this time, Sly got married onstage in front of 20,000 paying fans before his Madison Square Garden show.

Small Talk completed the trilogy of mellow, low-bottom, laid back funk records in the vein of *Riot* and *Fresh*. *Small Talk* sounds cleaner, but spontaneous like *Riot*. Violinist Sid Page plays with a prominence on these compositions. The title track opens *Small Talk* with Sly trying to console his fussing infant son. Sly tries to remain positive on this record, but it's a struggle—his weariness prevails.

"Mother Beautiful", an ode to all mothers, isn't danceable but emits an organic mood best heard with the shades drawn, relaxing on the couch. Sly's honesty overflows in "Time For Livin'": "Time for livin'/No time for making up a monster to sell/Time for livin, time for givin'/No time for breakin' out a lie to tell."

In "Can't Strain My Brain" Sly sings "I know how it feels to worry all the time." Mysteriously, Brother Freddie sounds low in the mix on *Small Talk*. With "Loose Booty"—the album's gem—Sly once again pulls a rabbit out of the hat with a sheer joyous 3-minute song harkening back to the old days.

"Holdin' On" spells out Sly's mentality at this point in his career and life. "Better Thee Than Me" employs complex horn progressions few jazz ensembles ever master. "Livin' While I'm Livin" and "This Is Love" (a full-circle return to Sly and Freddie's doo-wop days) end the album with not a bang but a whimper. A bonus track, another instrumental, "Positive" proves Sly's throwaways might result in a hit for a band with lesser talent.

Small Talk marked the end of Sly & the Family Stone's musical endeavors. Sly made various solo albums and other collaborations with various musicians such as George Clinton on P Funk's *Spanking of Electric War Babies*, but then Sly disappeared. Various stories and reports resulted through the years, whispers of demise and comebacks. Inducted into the Rock and Roll Hall of Fame in 1993, rumors persisted Sly & the Family Stone might return, but the events never materialized. A 2006 live Sly—blonde Mohawk and all—performance at the GRAMMYs teased fans concerning his recent activities, but Sylvester Stewart remains elusive as ever.

Even if we never hear from Sly & The Family Stone again, this latest 7-CD Collection embodies the divine spark of a musical genius.

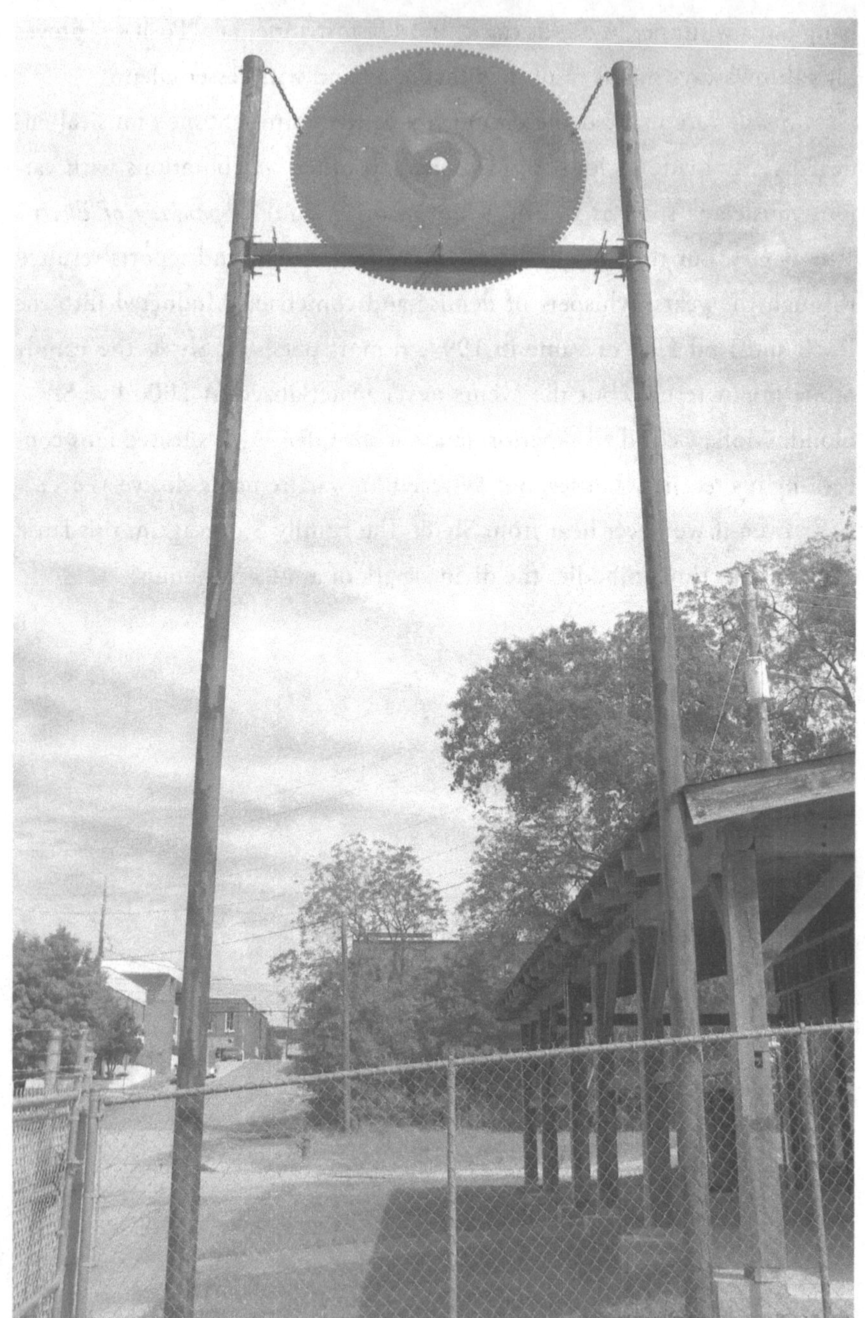

Saw Sign

Through A Crooked Sun:
The Rich Robinson Interview

This counted as my second interview with co-founder of The Black Crowes, Rich Robinson. This conversation took place almost two years before The Crowes regrouped for the last time in 2013. What follows is a documentation of Robinson's on goings at the time. He just released Through A Crooked Sun, which retained some of the Woodstock mojo The Crowes achieved on their last album Before The Frost...Until The Freeze. By the time Robinson recorded his next solo album, The Ceaseless Sight, he knew The Black Crowes were finished. He's now making music with his group The Magpie Salute.

"The prodigy of my youth is now broken Leaving what's left beneath the stars..."

"Bye Bye Baby"

BORN IN 1969, THE same day as Bob Dylan—May 24, Rich Robinson formed The Black Crowes with his older brother Chris in Atlanta, Georgia, during the 1980s. At 17, Robinson wrote songs for The Black Crowes album, *Shake Your Money Maker*, which eventually sold 7 million copies. Following Black Crowes albums such as *The Southern Harmony & Musical Companion, Amorica, Three Snakes & One Charm, By Your Side, Lions, Warpaint* and *Before The Frost* compile a formidable rock & roll songbook.

Robinson retains a rare degree of insight concerning success, the music industry and musicianship. The Crowes dealt with the sudden curse of

"

fame with talent and perseverance few bands possess. On the craft of writing, Ernest Hemingway once wrote: "...real seriousness in regard to writing being one of the two absolute necessities. The other, unfortunately, is talent." If you've ever heard it, Rich Robinson's undeniable music speaks for itself in terms of talent.

Over the years, Robinson and The Crowes performed with Bob Dylan, Neil Young, The Grateful Dead, The Rolling Stones, Jimmy Page and many others. Looking back, it seemed the better The Crowes became as musicians the fewer records they sold. The early 90s MTV boom earned The Crowes global exposure, but they soon became jaded once they discovered the echo in the hollow shell of the record industry. Regardless, The Black Crowes have sold over 35 million albums, but as Rich Robinson will tell you there is a price for such success. Like them or not, The Black Crowes gave no quarter when it came to songwriting and keeping the show on the road. The band's turbulent story is well-known in music circles. There's a dark side to anything that deals with money...

Rich seemed to always stand in the shadow of his older brother. Yet, Rich operated as the musical engine of The Black Crowes. Rich released his first solo album—*Paper* in 2004, which showcased his stellar, but underrated guitar playing, as well as his lyrical capabilities. In all these years, Rich learned a few lessons about creativity, commerce, family values and funneled his vision into a new timeless, salt-of-the-earth album that transcends soul and money titled, *Through A Crooked Sun*. Recorded in Woodstock, New York, in April 2011, Robinson's 12 new songs feature Larry Campbell (Bob Dylan, Levon Helm & Phil Lesh), Warren Haynes (Gov't Mule, Allman Brothers Band & The Dead), John Medeski (Medeski Martin & Wood, The Word), Karl Berger, Joe Magistro and Adam Widoff.

Through A Crooked Sun revolves around material change, everlasting spirit and strong songcraft. Exposure to illusions and excesses of the 'rock star' lifestyle forces the most enlightened artist to keep an ear open to the common man and what's going on in the street. Today's economy affects everyone from the factory worker to hard working musicians. However, Rich always maintains an everyday manner of expressing himself. He's quiet, thoughtful and chooses his words carefully. *Through a Crooked Sun* was released on October 11. When I interviewed Rich three days later he was in Burlington, Vermont, and already touring to promote his latest release. In this interview, we discuss *Through A Crooked Sun*, songwriting, painting, historian Howard Zinn, the economy, Woodstock musicians, art & life in the 21st Century, deals with The Devil and more.

James Calemine: It's been almost seven years to the day since we conducted an offi cial interview. *Paper* was just released in 2004. In the last seven years there have been changes afoot. *Through A Crooked Sun* is a great salt of the earth record.

Rich Robinson: Well, yeah. I think it's about the human experience. People who do what I do or people who write articles like you, working in the world or whatever, we all have similar experiences. At least in the sense of what we all deal with—our feelings, family, jobs, fear, raising kids and the shit we have to deal with just to exist in the world. It's like that age old thing—when you have kids and they go to school and they feel alienated and all of these common or universal things emerge—and everyone feels that sooner or later in their lives. Everyone feels these universal experiences. If you can tap into it, and kind of write about it, you can listen and hopefully heal the connection to what's going on in your life.

You produced and recorded *Through A Crooked Sun* in Woodstock, New York, at Applehead Studios in April. How long did it take to record?

RR: It took about three weeks to record.

Larry Campbell, and Warren Haynes make amazing contributions to this record. Talk about the rest of the players.

RR: Well, Joe Magistro is on it, and he was on my last record. Steve Molitz played on the record and he's in a group called Particle—he played keyboards. Then Larry Campbell came out and played on a couple of songs.

Warren came out to play on a song. We had a guy named Adam Widoff who played with Lenny Kravitz for years. He played some guitar, harmonica and keyboards. John Medeski came and played on some stuff, which was good to have him. Then this guy named Karl Berger who is in his 70s and he was famous for playing with Ornette Coleman. I was very fortunate. In Woodstock it's really cool that way because it has so many great musicians right there. It's such a small little hamlet. I'd say to my engineer, 'I need some vibes on this.' And he'd say, 'We'll call Karl Berger. He lives right up the street.' There's sitar players up there. Anything you want. It's pretty amazing.

They're all hard-boiled experts up there in some weird Appalachian-wooden instrument sort of way. They're not about fl ash, that's for sure.

RR: Yeah, these guys just play man. They wanted to move out of the city and live up in the mountains and do their thing. Joe lives up there and he knows a lot of people there. It was a great thing to be part of. Just to have all these great musicians come and play on my album was just great. Any time you have great musicians come and play on your stuff is always a good feeling.

Are most of the songs *Through A Crooked Sun* pretty new?

RR: Yeah. Most of the songs were no more than six months old. Some of them I'd just written right before I went into the studio. When I went in to record some of them were about six months old.

It's an acoustic-based album. These songs like "Bye Bye Baby", "Falling Again", "All Along The Way" are strong tunes. It seems your song "What Is Home" from *Before The Frost* indicated some stepping stone or new direction that perhaps foreshadowed this latest batch of songs.

RR: I just write music. So, I do feel kind of like "What Is Home" was a song I had, and I guess you could sort of say it was a stepping stone for this record. It was something I felt really good about when I wrote it. It didn't take long to write the song. I actually wrote it for Chris to sing on, but he was like, 'Nah, you go ahead and do it.' So, I wrote lyrics for it. I was up in

Woodstock and I just wrote this song. I literally felt the connection, and I wrote the lyrics. I obviously wrote the music, but I had to write the lyrics which is something I've always been very reticent about. The whole lyric thing kind of freaks me out sometimes, but either way I wrote it and I felt like I really captured something. In Woodstock, for some reason I really like it up there. It's beautiful. There's mountains and there's a vibe. And like you said, they are very serious musicians—there is no flash. Larry Campbell would pull up in his pickup truck, brought out his lap steel or pedal steel and just set it up. There's no techs or 20 people running around. This is what I do and it's incredibly fulfilling. It's such a cool thing to see because it should be that easy. You don't need all that bullshit. You should just be able to pull up with your guitar. And Larry does it, man. John Medeski—same thing. That guy came in so unassuming and he was phenomenal...a people player. We were all just watching and lis-tening to him going, 'Holy shit. He's great.' He's very unique, but he understands styles.

"All Along The Way" contains some amazing instrumentation.

RR: "All Along The Way" is me playing the B-bender. You know what a B-bender is?

Yeah, Clarence White invented it. It's that guitar-type instrument that Jimmy Page can make twang so beautifully, right?

RR: That's right. I was going to get Larry to do it, but he had a Midnight Ramble that night so I just did it. I did my best Jimmy Page "Tangerine" intro best I could (laughs).

"Follow You Forever" was written for your father, right?

RR: Well, yeah. He wasn't doing so well. So, I moved down to Atlanta to be with him. Right now he's doing okay and things have taken a turn for the better. He had lung cancer. It's good. I'm just staying kind of near him now.

Explain the cover art for *Through A Crooked Sun*.

RR: Actually a friend of mine did it. He's a director from Paris. He put an image to the emotive feeling of the record and the music. He was around while we were recording and visually he made the vibe of the record come to fruition. He was around to see the setting of where the studio was, which is on this beautiful piece of property in Woodstock on 12 acres with llamas and horses around. I took some pictures and also sent them to him. He loves music and he really loves to do that stuff. He laid everything out. The pictures were like a collage and touched visually all the aspects of the recording process and what the whole record is kind of about.

Are you still painting? I know you painted the cover art for *Paper*.

RR: Yeah, I haven't been painting much in the last year because I've been moving and working. But when I get home and have time to find the space I can get in there and get it going. I work in bursts. I'll go for a year without painting and then I'll go in and on the last round I did about 30 paintings. Then I'm done with it for a while.

Hey, before I forget...Scott Kinnebrew from the Truth & Salvage Company told me you gave him a favorite book of mine, *Don Nix's Road Stories and Recipes*. To me, just Eddie Hinton's skillet fried tuna fish recipe is worth the price of the book.

RR: (Laughs) Absolutely. Those guys were out on the road with The Crowes for a while. They were cool guys and I thought they might enjoy it. He seemed to really like it.

I want you to talk about working on Howard Zinn's project *The People Speak*. I forgot he lived in Atlanta for years.

RR: Howard Zinn was a historian. He actually fought in WWII. He was a patriot of our country. He went to war and saw things that made him uneasy. He felt Hitler was obviously a bad guy and he wanted to fight for his country so he went there. He saw disturbing things like when he came back to America after the war. By the way, Howard lived an incredible life. He was an incredible human being. It was a true gift for me for me to be able to meet him just before he passed away. He was just one of those guys. He was an integral figure in the Civil Rights movement. He was at the center of it. He held hands with the students and encouraged them, and in my opinion he was a true American.

The government really fucked with him, and called him a communist.

RR: Totally. That's what happens in America if you don't agree with these jerkoffs. If they're afraid of you they call you a socialist-communist-fascist even when they don't understand what those terms mean. Back then they were trashing this gentle, caring, intelligent human being in a way that anyone could understand was wrong. He gave his life for America and humanity. He saw what he thought was injustice and in a non-violent way fought it. I have nothing but the utmost respect for him. I did a play, that was the format at first. They were doing it around New York, and Steve Earle was doing it. And I did a couple of those—I was nervous as hell, but I did it. So, when they decided to turn it into a movie they brought it all these artists that were involved and it was about finding these protest songs on the music side of things. Protest songs that really convey a message. The whole point of the movie was to show that every day common people can make a huge difference just like the people on Wall Street right now. They've had enough of what's going on and I commend them. I'm all for them. Good for them man. These people in charge are fucking everything up. They're just putting money in their pockets. The movie is a great testament to the American spirit. So, Chris and I played (Neil Young's) "Ohio". It's a song that really captured a moment when Vietnam protesters, college kids in Ohio, are shot and killed by their own American National Guard because they were doing what the first amendment of the U.S. Constitution protects. They killed college students, and so for us to be able to do that song and put it in perspective. I just felt incredibly honored to be part of the whole thing. Bob Dylan did a song. Bruce Springsteen did a song. Eddie Vedder did a song. When we went to L.A. they had a lot of other bands out there like X. Chris and I got to play with X. Jackson Browne, John Legend and all these people, so it was an amazing thing to do. I felt honored to be part of it.

You may have insight or an opinion on this, but it seems art and our culture is drifting a little...perhaps creeping back to the dust bowl blues of the 20s, 30s and 40s kind of vibe. It's hard. There is an eerie feeling of fear in the air. There's no time for excesses of the 60s, 70s, 80s or 90s—across the board.

RR: Well, it's definitely heading there. Right now we're just teetering. A lot of it I feel is just perception. With all the media-owned multinational companies with an agenda, and they own media outlets and push their agenda to people. Anytime the truth comes out, people throw a lot of money and untruths at it so that no one knows what the hell is going on. I think a lot of times, we're on the tip of something if things don't change soon of really falling into a deep financial problem. This is stuff, regardless of people's politics, we all know something has to be done because you have these other people that steer. It's all a distraction.

When one percent of the country controls everything there's an issue. The 400 wealthiest people in America have more money than the bottom 150 million people. That's a problem. If you take the 150 million people on the low-end scale of income and you combine their wealth and what they make—the 400 wealthiest American have more money than them. You can say Capitalism or these types of things but it's getting morally wrong. It's morally wrong when people are starving and losing their homes and they're just getting tossed around by these assholes in Washington that are bought and paid for by the people who have all the money. It makes no sense to me. No one is saying the government needs to be out of control. But a lot of the huge corporations are out of control. It's time to reel them in on people's behalf. We can vote a congressman, or a senator or a president out, but we can't vote out a CEO when they have a monopoly.

And they have enough money to keep you at bay or make the rest of your life a legal hassle.

RR: Absolutely.

Do you believe in the proverbial deal with The Devil? The Legend of Faust? Robert Johnson at the crossroads? Neil Young's *Greendale* when The Devil cleans the painter's glasses and his work begins to sell?

RR: I think there's angels and devils in us. A common theme that runs through most religions is that we can attain heaven in ourselves or attain hell in ourselves. What reality is based on is soul or morals and what you choose to give the world and to take back. I believe making a deal with The Devil is selling out. The proverbial—in my case—I could make a lot of money if I make this shit music or huge awful songs that appeal to common denominators of people's ignorance. Or I could do something a little loftier with the creative process and show things a different way to make mankind better, but it might not sell at all. I think we get caught up in the literal instead of the metaphorical. We do it with the Bible sometimes, and we do it with religious documents. I truly believe these metaphorical sort of teachings have permeated history. We're all exposed to universal things. You get into trouble when you confuse the metaphorical with 'it happened just like this'. That's what I think.

I know you played dulcimer and guitar on Patti Smith's *Twelve* album. Besides The Crowes and Circle Sound have you played on anyone else's album lately?

RR: I produced and played on a young artist's album, and she's from Scotland. That album will come out in February. But no, I haven't played on anyone's records in a while.

I noticed you guys played the Gram Parsons song "She" last night. The Crowes always rendered a great version of that. I look forward to seeing y'all in a couple of weeks here in Atlanta and Athens.

RR: Yeah, we did. It should be cool down there. I'm looking forward to it.

Well, Godspeed out there Rich. Hopefully I'll see you in a couple of weeks.

RR: Okay James. Thanks a lot.

The Sounds of David Barbe

I MET DAVID BARBE in 1995 or 1996 through Bloodkin. I'd tag along with them to Barbe's studio, and watch how the entire recording process went down. I even recorded a spoken word session there in 2007. These days, Barbe serves as the music director of The University of Georgia's Terry College School of Music. We conducted this interview in the era when The Drive By Truckers' album, *Brighter Than Creation's Dark* and Bettye LaVette's *Scene of the Crime* were happening and Barbe produced both albums, which earned critical acclaim. He remains an undeniable pillar in the Athens music community.

David Barbe's studio magic renders him a highly sought after engineer. His musical expertise proves essential to some of the south's finest contemporary groups and artists such as, The Drive By Truckers, Vic Chesnutt, Kevn Kinney and Bloodkin to name a few. Barbe, an accomplished musician, can play various instruments and his golden ear provides a vital asset to the aforementioned artists.

Barbe earned his engineering break from John Keane (R.E.M., Widespread Panic) which eventually led to opening his own recording studio in Athens, Georgia, called Chase Park Transduction Studio. Barbe's sonic mojo can be heard on Drive By Truckers albums such as *Southern Rock Opera, Decoration Day, The Dirty South* and their latest, *Brighter Than Creation's Dark*, set for release on January 22—as well as Bettye LaVette's *Scene of the Crime*. And he produced Bloodkin's last five records. Barbe also recorded hundreds of other musicians including Michael Houser, Johnny Jenkins, Son Volt, Kevn Kinney, Amy Ray, Barbara Cue, Jack Logan,

Southern Bitch and Tishamingo. Barbe remains of pillar of the Athens music and baseball (that's another story) communities.

Bloodkin's, Daniel Hutchens, recently told me this about Barbe: "More than anything, once you get to know him, you'd just flat out trust him with your life. He's one of those rare characters who never seems to let you down. And he damn sure creates one beautifully rowdy rock n roll record right after another. He's got that feel, that touch, whatever it is, and he just keeps on delivering. For us down n dirty rock n rollers who still believe that this "rock band" thing can actually be an art form—he's the very best we've got these days. "

I've spent various times in Barbe's studio to witness his work first hand. He's an expert of the highest order. This interview provides clear insight into one of the south's finest sound wizards.

Your parents were musical. You grew up here in Atlanta.

DB: Both of my parents were musicians. They were in a big band together in the fifties. That's how they met. My dad played baritone saxophone and clarinet. My mom was the singer.

Obviously any musical inclination started at a very early age.

DB: When I was a kid what my parents did they wrote and produced jingles. So I could not actually tell you the first time I was in a recording studio but I've been in one my entire life.

Could you name some of the jingles your parents per-formed?

DB: Well, my mom is a native of Atlanta. My dad is a New Yorker. They moved to Atlanta in the early sixties. There wasn't a whole lot of jingle business going on. I don't think there was a lot of competition. So they did a lot of things. They did commercials for Coke and I think they might have done the first Braves commercials campaign when they first moved to Atlanta in the sixties. I have a pretty sizable CD set that my dad made me of their commercials. They were constantly busy for a long time. Then my mom she had a general voice talent so she did all kinds of things. My dad also played on pop records sessions. He played a lot of the pop music sessions in Atlanta with Joe South, Tommy Roe, Billy Joe Royal—he played in the horn section.

What was your first instrument? How old were you?

DB: The first instrument I've ever had any interest in was the drums. I got a tiny little drum kit for Christmas when I was probably about three or four years old. The first thing I ever took any lessons in was piano when I was about six. Then I went through from there. I played the piano a while and then I got interested in the drums and took drum lessons. I played drums in bands from the time I was probably 11 or 12 years old until I was in college. I picked up a ukulele so I got a guitar.

What was your early record collection? Beatles…

DB: Totally…the Beatles, by 1970 I was picking up real rock and roll records which were the same thing tons of other people were listening to—Beatles—Stones. It's funny, I'd get into some kind of music and when I was a little kid, I'd watch the Monkees, I had a couple Monkees records and listen to them over and over. When I saw *Yellow Submarine* I just went nuts for the Beatles records. I bought all of John and Paul's solo stuff too. When I got to be about 11 or 12 a kid at school turned me onto the Rolling Stones. Then I listened to that for a while. The Who, Bob Dylan, Jimi Hendrix, Led Zeppelin all the stuff that I think is still great today. I can't even remember really being wrapped up in a music that makes me cringe now.

Where did you go to high school?

DB: I went to Ridgeview High School. It's closed now. It was over near Northside Hospital. I went to elementary school at Christ King which is on Peachtree and West Wesley. I have a very white bread school history. I went to three schools. I went to one first through eighth grade. I went to one high school and then moved to Athens and went to the University of Georgia.

What was your first band in Athens?

DB: A band called The Legion. They were guys I went to high-school with. They needed a bass player. They had a session booked with songs to record but they had no bass player. They figured since I could play all this stuff that I do alright with a bass. I remember I was so nervous my hands were sweating. The first time I played bass was in the studio for these guys session. I must have been 18.

What were you looking for at that point? A band? Being a songwriter? Session guy?

DB: Songwriter all the way. Everything I did stemmed from that. I started writing songs and I grew apart from those guys musically. I got turned onto a bunch of cool music in Athens. I knocked around. Then I started Mercyland. I always played in bands—this is 1985—I was 21. The three of us had a plan to start a band. But I always played in bands as an outlet for song writing. The songs are what stimulated being in a band. Then when I got in a band it was a hell of a lotta fun. The brief history was we started Mercyland in 85. Our drummer quit in 87. Then The BBQ Killers asked me to be in their band for a few months. But I always thought they were better as a four piece instead of a five piece. They didn't need the extra person. I bowed out of that; my old buddy from cub scouts was playing in bands around Athens—he used to drum for the band Crack. But even since I was playing in The Legion—right around the time the most radical development in the history of musicians recording their own music was introduced to the public and that was the Fostex four track cassette. Once I got that thing I really got into recording. I always done it—I had a four track reel to reel in the basement that was my dad's. I still have it. It's down at the studio. I think there's something wrong with one of the motors but it hasn't turned on in 30 years. I was always recording—I remember borrowing the Glockenspiel from the high school band in high school to take it home and use it as an overdub. I recorded all my bands coming all the way through high school. When I got this little portable four track you could go to other bands' practice space and their shows and record. So, I got into that. I made this one thing with the BBQ Killers in my parents basement. I think the Christmas of 84 or 85 when my folks were out of town. So I had the band over to record, but I started recording bands other than my own on a four track.

When I was in Mercyland we'd go over to John Keane's and record. I had a good experience over there so I told the BBQ Killers why don't we go over there and I'd produce a proper studio recording even though I really didn't know what I was doing. John was the engineer and I was the producer. I did a lot of stuff with John like that. I always had four tracks that I would play for John when I'd show him what I wanted to do. I realize now everybody has PRO TOOLS and stuff at their house, but at the time it was kind of an unusual thing to do. John, over time, began to recognize I might have an aptitude to do this kind of thing. So after that I'd go around the studios with bands I liked and produced their records—The Killbillies, The BBQ Killers, Jack O Nut and others I know I'm leaving out. So I got adept at being in a studio. I didn't really know how the gear worked very well. John didn't show me a lot of technical stuff, but he done me a greater favor.

When Mercyland broke up John called me and said, 'You should learn to be an engineer, I think you'd be good at it.' That sounds good to me. I was John's assistant. The deal was I'd go there and be John's assistant for a little while, and if I'd go to this crash course in Ohio he attended that took about five weeks that when I came back I could come back and start recording bands. So I helped John out and I learned a lot of cool stuff. Billy Bragg was over there working at the time. Kelly Hogan. The Vigilantes of Love. It was interesting to watch other people come through there. So, then I went to the recording workshop for five weeks one summer. There's some of these courses that take years to get through at some places—but this one was serious hands-on activity. You do it for ten hours a day, just like being in a studio. It was great. When I came back John said, 'Pick a band and record a song so you can show me you know what to do.' So I got Liquor Cabinet to come over and record one song in John's studio. John gave me a key and an alarm code and told me I could record as much as I wanted to on weekends. He had Monday through Friday and I had Saturday and Sunday. I worked over at John's for a pretty good while. He gave me an opportunity which is the greatest gift. He saw something in me I don't think I recognized in myself. I knew if I got good at it we could keep his place booked all the time, which we did until it got too big for two of us. So, then I branched out and started freelancing around to other studios in Athens which at the time was Maxwell Sound—he's still in business—he doesn't really do rock bands, Full Moon Studio, Kelly Noonan's Suite 16, Scott Stuckey's studio on Boulevard—Sound Gallery. I was the first freelance engineer in Athens. The idea of a guy who went from studio to studio recording wasn't the way things worked. It was fun to work in all these different places and you get a feel for each place—a vibe, an atmosphere from room setup to equipment—you get a good idea of what works and what doesn't work. So after that I got my first call to go do something in Atlanta. It was for a band I recorded at Full Moon Studios. They peppered me with what kind of records I'd been listening to and we had enough of a crossover of things so they hired me to go to Atlanta. It was Bosstown which was owned by Bobby Brown, which is now Stankonia, but way before it was any of that it was Soundscape which was where the first Black Crowes record was cut. It's a great big, nice, studio. I went down and recorded this Fiddlehead single in Atlanta which served two benefits for me. Number one, it got me into Atlanta. Now I just don't work in Athens—I've expanded my circle a bit. It was a different scene, a different set of bands. I got so much work off that Fiddlehead single, which is a great sounding record. Their drummer plays with me now.

One always needs a good drummer around.

DB: Yeah, if you've got a great drummer, you're recording sounds a whole lot better. That's why I'm so picky about drummers because it's the foundation. If the drums don't sound right or played right nothing sounds good.

There's no microphone, technique or trick to make someone who doesn't know how to play sound good. I know you can PRO TOOL anything, but it doesn't feel the same. So, other Atlanta bands began calling me up. As an engineer I now had a justifiable reason to charge people. Y'know traditionally, the lines are blurred…traditionally the producer is the creative director who doesn't touch the equipment. The engineer is the equipment man, but nowadays those lines are blurred. I rarely do sessions where I am not the engineer now. I have to have my hands on that. So, by the mid-90s I had a circuit of about 20 studios between here and Atlanta which was great because the studio people let some other person come into their place. The other thing is they realize, 'Hey, this guy is bringing us work we wouldn't ordinarily get.' Once I started working at John's I stayed busy right away. I was playing in a band called Sugar and working at John's. By early 95, when I quit Sugar, I had a solid circuit I worked. I knew I wanted to build a studio one day, but I didn't want to make the common mistake of build-ing something important without the necessary experience to get it right. So I began amassing my arsenal of equipment. Then in 97 I got asked to go to rural Illinois to work on the Son Volt record. I went out and had to fly home—and have a grand opening of Chase Park Studios. Then get back on a plane and fly back to St. Louis and drive down into Illinois again and work on that Son Volt stuff some more. That's 97 and that's when we opened Chase Park.

That's about the time our paths intersect. I remember being over there with Danny and Eric (Bloodkin).

DB: Yeah, exactly. I remember recording Bloodkin there that summer. By the time we were building the studio I already worked in so many different places in Atlanta and Athens—I also made records in Massachusetts, Texas, England and Japan. I been in all kinds of studios—even with my parents. When we started to build the studio it dawned on me on how many places I'd been in. I had a much broader knowledge base than what I was aware of—so it was great when we built it because I knew what worked. In 1990, me and John Forbes, who recorded great bands in Atlanta and Chicago, we talked about building something. We go to music shops and look for equipment. Now, thinking back what the guy recommended to us in the music store I realized how screwed we would have been. We would have gotten loaded down with the same thing everyone else had when they start. Let's go buy a bunch of cheap, mediocre crap and good luck, hope it works. For me working in studios that already had equipment and being able to process it all and buy good equipment one piece at a time. I'd tell studios send me a copy of your microphone list, so I'd know what I needed or wanted.

Danny (Bloodkin guitarist/singer/songwriter) gave me a copy of this latest stuff they've recorded at your place. That's how you and I met—through Bloodkin. I was over there for New Year's.

DB: I went to see them last night. They were really good—William Tonks played with them. The highlight for me was a good version of "Calling Back" and "Morning Chrome" that kind of makes me think we might need to record that, it sounded good.

You've recorded—over all—about six or seven Bloodkin related projects. I think I first did some spoken word over there around 98 or 99.

DB: I think you're right. You know Tony Eubanks—he owned the High Hat Blues Club back then. At the end of 96 he hired me to record live bands there. I did 8-track recordings…simple stuff…early versions of the Drive by Truckers, Jack Logan, Liquor Cabinet, Six-String Drag, Hot Burritos, the Continentals, the Real McCoy's and Bloodkin. Of course, Danny and Eric have been here in Athens since the mid-80s and I can remember seeing them way back with Barry and Aaron. I always liked them and knew them peripherally but not very well. We had a lot of common ground, but it's funny—you never get to see these bands in your hometown when you're in a touring band. They came over and did some mixes and there was something about the guitars…I think I turned them up really loud but Danny and Eric really dug the guitar sound when I recorded them. The song they recorded was going on a compilation. Then Danny talked to me about making a record which turned out to be *Out of State Plates*. That was the summer of 97 and I just started Chase Park and I probably done three or four records in there by that point already. In the middle of the summer we started making the Bloodkin record. I knew it was a few days into it where it all really fell into place.

Bloodkin's music and my work style came together. That's the way it is with all the musicians with whom I work. There's that point where you get over the hump where you realize everybody's creativity locks into a flow of this confluent experience. I know that with Bloodkin it was "Something To Say" was the song we were tracking and listening back to that and realizing, 'yeah, we got it.' My contribution and their comfort level…that was the moment it all came together. With them—and there are a few others that are pretty lucky—to have some people I've made records with repeatedly through the years—Bloodkin, The Drive By Truckers, Dodd Ferrell—I've been doing for ten years. I just made this new record with The Drive-By Truckers and I think it's their best one. Patterson hung drywall in Chase Park when we built it the first time. I knew Patterson because he was the soundman at the High Hat when I recorded those shows. I was sitting up in the perch of a sound booth with him up there and we were always talking music. He was, at the time, a huge Bloodkin fan. Tony (Eubanks) and Patterson both were always talking about Bloodkin. Like I say, I knew Bloodkin and I liked them, but Patterson always talked them up—about what a great songwriter Danny was and what a great guitar player Eric was. It's funny, my relationship with both bands started around the same time.

The first thing the Truckers did at Chase Park were not with me. They had already done some recording with Andy Baker at his house, so when we built the studio they made their first album with Andy at Chase Park. Then *Pizza Deliverance* they recorded out of Patterson's house and then came to Chase Park and mixed it. The next thing they did was—they were working on the *Southern Rock Opera*, but they made a live album and I mixed that…

Alabama Ass Whuppin…

DB: That's right. And then, once again, they kinda—same thing with Bloodkin. I mixed some live stuff and I think they felt like I got it as far as musical common ground. I think a lot of people's fear when they get their stuff mixed by some studio guy that the vocals and the snare drum are going to be way too loud. So that went really well. We recorded the *Southern Rock Opera* and I mixed that as well—they recorded it themselves. At that point, obviously their career really takes off when the *Southern Rock Opera* hits and gets all this great press. They get signed and then they want to record. *Decoration Day* was me working with them pillar to post—that was done entirely at Chase Park. While we were still finishing the record they had some sort of… their A&R person changed at their label—former label now—and you know the deal with that. An A&R person signs somebody and you're their band, but if a new guy comes in—well the new guy might want to make his own mark and not want to inherit someone else's band. Face it, people have different musical tastes. So anyway, while they were making the record—it seems like there was some conflict of some sort that the record never really came out on New West. *The Dirty South* was after that. *The Dirty South* was done half at Chase Park and half at FAME Studios in Muscle Shoals.

Was that your first experience of going to the Muscle Shoals Studio? I'm partial to *The Dirty South*, but I haven't heard the new one yet.

DB: Wait until you hear it. I just can't pick favorites. *The Dirty South* is a great one—it's got a great feel. *Blessing and A Curse* was mostly recorded in North Carolina and mixed back at Chase Park. That was a different kind of record for them. They decided to try and instead of making a 70 minute big, dark record, they made a 45-minute record with shorter songs and did some things different ways. On this new Truckers record we were talking about making the new record, but then the Bettye LaVette record came up—so we did the Bettye record in February 2001, and the mixes, because

Bettye's in New Jersey, the label is in Los Angeles and me and Patterson are in Athens. Mixing went back and forth—I'd do something, email somebody a file—we'd talk about it, and then I'd do some more. I did that pretty much last spring. Then the Truckers latest—*Brighter Than Creation's Dark* started in June. That's what I did in the summer of 2007, and we mastered it in New York September 24th and 25th. So, I basically worked on that for three and a half months and it comes out in about two weeks. This one has got it all…its 19 songs, 75 minutes with nine Patterson songs, seven Cooley songs and three Shonna songs. Everybody's stuff is great.

Now The Truckers have another Athens musician, John Neff, in the band who can play anything, especially the pedal steel.

DB: Yep, John's in the band. Spooner Oldham plays on the whole record. It's the Truckers' greatest record. I might be a little too close to it right now to say that—I guess ask me in ten years, but right now It feels terrific.

Talk about R.E.M. They really carved their own groove for a whole lotta other artsy, collegiate-type music back in the late 70's. You were working with them in your studio the day Danny, Eric, and I recorded our *Fandango Brothers* session in February 2007.

DB: I've worked on and off with R.E.M. several times over the years. As far back as the first two or three months I worked with John Keane. About a year and a half ago, I spent a few days with them recording a cover of John Lennon's "#9 Dream" for a benefit album for the people of Darfur, and then as you mentioned, last February I spent a few more days with them working on some demos for some new songs that were in the working stages of this new album they just finished that I think comes out in the spring.

Scene of the Crime **is a great record—the one you made in Muscle Shoals with Bettye LaVette and the Truckers were her backing band.**

DB: It was a great experience. We went to Muscle Shoals and into FAME studios.

You engineered the whole process.

DB: Well, yeah…sorta. The deal was, Andy Culkin who is the president of Anti-Records in California, wanted to have the Truckers backing Bettye LaVette on a record and that the record was going to be produced. He wanted it to be like a Drive By Truckers record, and they wanted Patterson to produce this record. Patterson—God bless him—said, 'Well, we don't make records without David Barbe'. First, they wanted Bettye to come to Athens, but we said, 'No, we want to go back to Muscle Shoals…to the scene of the crime'.

Where Bettye recorded a soul classic, but it never really came out?

DB: That's right. They said yeah we'd love to go down there. The Truckers said we want our guy with us when we do it because if you want it to sound like one of our records—we're all in this together. I mean there have been other things Patterson and I produced together because we have a good way of getting it done together. It ain't just me. I went down there with them and Bettye had picked out songs and so we worked through the things she wanted, and there was definitely some bumps in the road because it was a different kind of stuff that they would normally be playing. But once everybody figured out how to work together the results were great. She's tremendous. Everything was cut with her in the isolation booth, but everything else is bleeding into each other. A total live band recording…a large majority of the vocals on that were scratch vocals. The best takes by bands are when they are following her. She's singing the song. Bettye's the navigator…it all stems from following her and her voice. She's the conduit of it all. I also lucked out because I had a really great assistant. A guy named Ben Tanner—he's a young guy that works at FAME. He was a tireless invaluable guy. He knew the room, he knew the place. I realized I had totally different ways of doing things than most of the people who work there. He was pretty curious about what I was doing and he was eager to help any way he could. I took a ton of microphones down there. I recorded them with my own mics. I used their tape machine and console. It was a great experience.

So, the new Bloodkin album is finishing up next week.

DB: Right now I've got Bloodkin going on, which is my seventh—and I count the two Danny solo albums as part of the family. This is my seventh record with them. I'm in the middle of doing that—I love it—it's great. When I did this Bettye thing it was live and wide open—the Truckers record was the in the same manner and so was Bloodkin. I'm doing a Dodd Ferrell solo record where is backed with kind of my personal rhythm section—Kyle Spence and Jon Mills—that's a really great record. That's Dodd's best record by far. This is maybe my fifth one with him and it's easily his best one. I'm about to get some tracks from this New York band, The Young Lords, I'm going to mix and I'll probably do all that down here. It is my preference when I can to stay here and work, but I'm not against going to other places, but I can do things in Athens that are so much more affordable for people that are as good as or better that what they are going to get somewhere else. Let's face it, with most people, budget is a concern. So, we talked about going to Ardent to record the Truckers new record in the summer, and I'd love to go there—I've never worked there, but I always wanted to because I love all the albums made there. Super people. But when we started adding everything up—hotel rooms, traveling back and forth… they would spend $15,000 just eating and sleeping. We talked about going to Southern Tracks in Atlanta—I love the place and I love the results—a lot of great music, but three times more expensive. If they had U2's recording budget, I'd say hell yeah, let's go…but we don't. In January, I'm focused on Dodd Ferrell, Bloodkin, the Critical Darlings—another Athens band, the Young Lords and I'm in the process of slowly, but surely making another David Barbe record.

Yeah, I mean you play and write your own music. Your first solo record— *Comet of the Season*—**came out in 2001.**

DB: I'm just too busy making other people's music to do my own. You just can't listen to Bloodkin for ten hours a day and then come home and starting writing songs or recording—it doesn't work. To me it's a feel. I've worked on my own stuff over the holidays a little bit. I'll get that done soon.

Well, I'll see ya soon and we can continue into the next phase.

DB: Let me know when you want some more.

Sheet Iron Roof Chronicles:
The Mark Neill Interview

Mark Neill is old school—from his analog recordings to his hair wax. Born in Georgia, he moved to San Diego and lived there many years. Neill returned to Georgia a short while after this interview. He won the Black Keys a Grammy for their Brothers album. He later recorded the fi ve spoken word pieces included with my fiction collection, The Local Stranger.

RAISED IN SOUTH GEORGIA, Mark Neill exists as one of this generation's preeminent producer/sound engineers. He grew up in Hahira, Georgia. He lived on a farm in an area called Snake Nation. Neill cut his musical teeth on Sun and Chess Records. His first recording studio was his tobacco barn. He began playing bass in Quartets during his early teens. Neill played a vital role in the Valdosta music scene in the late 70s before he moved to California.

Neill's twenty five years in the art of sound design ranks him as a sought-after tone guru, especially after the inimitable sound and earning a GRAMMY for producing The Black Keys' latest CD, *Brothers* that Neill recorded at Muscle Shoals Sound on Jackson Highway in Muscle Shoals, Alabama. Neill has lived in San Diego for many years now, but after the Brothers-Muscle Shoals sessions, Neill intends to return to his Soil of the South Studio back to his Georgia hometown soon.

Neill's expertise at building studios began many years ago with his Three Track Shack Studios where the great Ricky Nelson recorded as well as designing London's Toe Rag Studios and building The Black Keys' Dan

Auerbach's home studio. Neill also co-recorded and mixed Auerbach's successful solo album *Keep It Hid* in 2009.

Neill once said: "My dream is that one day American Southern music will be recognized for its importance to the development of American culture." His understanding of how culture, the South and music all intertwine into a social fabric renders him a hero. In this extensive interview we discuss Neill's south Georgia up-bringing, his musical influences, old bands, the art of recording, his California endeavors, his friendship with luminary Jim Dickinson, the Black Keys Brothers album in Muscle Shoals, his current projects and his pending move back to Georgia.

James Calemine: You were from right outside of Valdosta, Georgia, right?

Mark Neill: Yeah, I grew up in Hahira, Georgia. We lived out on a farm. We lived in an area called Snake Nation.

Were your folks musical?

MN: No. My father is a professional race car driver.

I suppose those early Sun Records were a heavy influence on you.

MN: That happened because my parents and uncles and aunts had 45 rpm records. I was a toddler in the early 60s. I was a little kid—two years old and rolling around—this was way before the Beatles. They all listened to R&B like John Lee Hooker, Muddy Waters and all that stuff. The problem was with the Jimmy Reed LPs. When the LPs came out of those in the late 50s they bought LPs and put all the 45s in a box. My parents were young. My mom basically had me as a teenager. So they were still young when I was two. I got the box of 45s. I got a picture of me at two-years-old with a stack of 45s and a little record player. They were my toys.

When did you start picking up instruments?

MN: Right away—from the age of about 7 on I would tinker away on anything I could borrow. I did take violin lessons. Back then schools had programs for music. My kids unfortunately have a very limited version of that now. Back then schools had orchestras and bands. Then I went to tuba, but I always plucked around on guitars, but nobody really had them. Poor people didn't have Gibson guitars leaning on the walls.

Would it be safe to say guitar was the first instrument you became efficient on?

MN: I would say it was bass first because the gospel quartets in the south in the late 60s and 70s that was big business down there. These quartets were big. In the early 70s everyone started having their young ones play bass, and steel guitar with the old folks singing and that was the thing to have your family onstage. The Harmony Quartet in Tifton, Georgia, their kids I guess didn't want to play, so they hired some 13-year old to play bass, and that was me. I was sort of the surrogate stand in for one of those kids.

Did you tinker on piano?

MN: I can't really play piano. I know where the notes are, but I can't really play piano.

So, you're buying records all along.

MN: Yeah, all you had to do was go to Thrift stores and garage sales and you could get 45s for days.

I'm sure the Beatles, Stones and Dylan began to creep into your musical interests after cutting your teeth on Sun and Chess Records.

MN: Yeah, well the Beatles were great. I remember my mom being young and screaming at the TV because the Beatles were on Ed Sullivan. It was funny. I remember my mom and my aunt dancing to the Beatles' first record, which was a VJ record, called *Introducing the Beatles*, or something. It wasn't even the Capitol record yet. I think my mom and my aunt split the cost of the record.

I know you were playing in bands already, but did you do any DJ-ing in Georgia? I want to make sure I have my facts straight.

MN: I never was a DJ, but I messed around a couple of radio stations and learned how to do it. There was a station called WAFT radio, which was a gospel station in that county. I used to go over there because I knew the Tidwells, and I'd just go hang out and watch, which was great and I just absorbed it. I got my FCC license by the time I was 14. I was trained to operate what was essentially a 50s radio station—WVLD—by Ron Irwin. It has the same RCA console and AMPEX tape machine as Sun Studios.

How did your session with Ricky Nelson happen?

MN: That was a complete accident. My friend Pat Woodward, an upright bass player, he used to play with Billy Zoom and everybody in town. He was the only legitimate guy who could play that style. We'd become friends through Billy who I'd pretty much known him since 79. Pat just got the job as Ricky's bass player, and he told Ricky about the place, and Ricky flipped and said 'That's a dream come true.' So, that's how it happened. Pat brought him over.

That was at your Three Track Shack Studio, right?

MN: Yeah, I called it the Three Track Shack was because the multi-track was just a half an inch and three tracks. We didn't have an official walk-in business. It was just our project studio—kind of like Dickinson's Zebra Ranch. It was our own personal thing.

Let me ask you this, I know a lot of musicians keep recorders around them so they preserve songs and remember riffs, but when did you take the actual recording process so seriously?

MN: It's funny, before I could play bass and guitar very well I was literally building hi fi 's out of tubes because you could get them cheap. I'd modify amps, speakers and boxes—taking something off one turntable and putting it on another. It was all mono. There was no stereo and I would just mess around. My next move was to get a reel to reel. I did and it was an AMPEX—it was a good two-track AMPEX machine. It had belonged to a school system. I got it and started messing with it by that time I could play anything on guitar I had a way to record it. Then George Eager—he has a missionary thing in Valdosta called The Mailbox Club, and he gave me a machine called a Woolensack, which was another machine that was small that the school sys-tem used. That's what they recorded Arthur Alexander's fi rst two records on. I had no idea until Rick Hall or somebody told me that. It was a half-track machine with quarter-inch tape and it ran seven and a half IPS and it was for school systems. It was a little machine that had a weird sound. I used to bounce between that and the AMPEX.

I know you're playing and listening to music constantly, but for you building a recording studio became the goal. And soon that became a business.

MN: Well, the sticky point is I didn't charge anybody for anything until 12 years ago. You have to understand, before that in project studios bands were in developmental deals. They would record demos with me, put out a 45 or an EP and that's the way the 80s played. If you get signed to a major label then you can pay me for the time we spent in here. Of course, that never hap-pened…(laughs)

What was the first studio you operated?

MN: The first one was my tobacco barn in Georgia, but the first official studio that had an air-conditioner was in north Hollywood.

Tell me about leaving Georgia for California. For a South Georgia fellow, that's like going to Japan.

MN: It really is. In 1978 there was a thriving art scene of music—we didn't call it New Wave yet—we didn't know what it was. It was this weird stuff filtering in from New York believe it or not and it was coming in very slowly—the Velvet Underground and just a handful of people like The Modern Lovers…I think the record was called Modern World. That record was iconic. Peter Ivers and the Blue Communion with Yolanda Bavin was an insane record. It was a jazz set up and every single acoustic instrument had a pick up on it through a distorted amp. So, Peter Ivers played the harmonica sometimes the chromatic harp—it was all distorted, the drums were distorted, the bass was distorted. It was like the Modern Jazz quartet with pick-ups. There was this chick singing and she was great, and that record was really iconic. Don Fleming bought it at Woolworth's. What was happening in the deep south you had one thing that went down in a club or frat house, and that was "Play Freebird!"

Tom Petty once said something to the effect that if you were from Florida and didn't play Lynyrd Skynyrd you had to go out West.

MN: It was insane. All we wanted to play was "Only The Lonely", "Mustang Sally" and anything cool, but they didn't want to hear it. They didn't even like the good Marshall Tucker stuff. It was rough. People have this romantic vision about southern boogie rock and all these incredible bands—but I don't have that romantic vision. It was like the dregs of Woodstock. It was awful. We just rebuilt. We saw some precedent from New York City. Some of it was Television and Patti Smith was doing some crazy poetry stuff. It was starting to come down to the south because Valdosta was a college town. Back then around town it was me, Don Fleming, Tom Smith and Bruce Joiner. Those four people were involved in a vague alliance in music down there. Bruce and me went out to San Diego in 1979. Don Fleming was still in the Air Force, so he was stationed up there by D.C. and Tom Smith went to Athens, Georgia. In my opinion Tom defined the Athens influence. A lot of that stuff that went on in Athens during the 1980s is like mimeographed its crazy. Tom was the Lou Reed of Valdosta. Valdosta—believe it or not—was smoking hot in 1978 for indie music. Nobody was in competition with each other. Nobody was mean. Everybody could form a band for some gigs. It was pretty easy going.

In 1979, the four of us left Valdosta. It was a sad thing because we didn't know what we had. When we came out to San Diego there was actually a music scene here. Not now, but there was then. When we got out here we were really fascinated by the fact that people loved to document stuff. They had their indie music rags and there must have been four or five of them when we got here in 79. It was nutty, but the music and bands they were covering were weak. These bands were doing Elvis Costello covers. We just scratched our heads and said 'What?' It was bizarre. Bruce and me were living in my 60 Bel Air—we were homeless. People would say 'What are y'all doing out here?' We'd say we're going to get signed to Warner Brothers'. They'd just roll their eyes. We didn't know San Diego was a vortex and you couldn't get signed here. We were corresponding with Warner Brothers in New York. We didn't have any fear. We didn't know better.

How long did it take before you began to miss the South?

MN: One and a half years.

Not long.

MN: No, I remember it. We knew what we had going on in the south was a lot better than what we had going on out here. Seven and a half years we were in California.

Before you returned to Georgia, what kind of bands were you recording in California?

MN: I pretty much defined the Garage-Psych and Rockabilly market here. The records I made were the first Paladins record. *The Forbidden Pigs. Telltale Hearts. Nashville Ramblers.* The list goes on. There were tons of these bands like this—usually it was two songs. By 1987 I was ready to fly the coop. I couldn't take it anymore. The only thing I could produce and record out here were these kind of insincere retro—I call it—where people are just trying to dress-up old school and had vintage instruments, but they really didn't want to do their homework or learn to play. They just didn't want to know. They wanted to be able to say, 'Yeah, I recorded with Mark Neill and put out a record on that label.' They just wanted a trophy for their mantle.

They weren't about the future, which is very heartbreaking. When you do something on spec as an artist development deal all they've ever paid for is a reel of tape or two. It's a heartbreak to know these people are going to get day jobs and never even pursue it.

There's no concern for the craft itself.

MN: None. In fact, Jim Dickinson was great. We'd talk for hours and he'd say, 'Those are Near Records'. I said, 'Man I've got a whole decade of Near Records!' and he laughed and said so do I.' (Laughs)

So, you moved back to Valdosta. I lived there about five months during the time you moved back. I remember your band The Unknowns from back then.

MN: Yes, well what I did when I built the studio in Valdosta—it was a larger room than what I had in California. It was invitation only. I was able to do a lot more projects that you, Jim Dickinson or me would not consider 'Near Records'. If people came to Georgia from California or New York to record, they were serious. They weren't kidding around. They were in it for the long haul and they wanted to get it right. That's why *On The Go* by Big Sandy is kind of iconic. It was the first and last time those guys made a complete live record with that kind of energy level. That record in particular shaped rockabilly in the 90s, which was good for me because I was able to open doors and charge money. If it wasn't for that Big Sandy *On The Go* record I wouldn't have been able to open the doors and charge people for studio production. There was no more of that I'll pretend to record your record if you pretend to pay me. Valdosta put an end to those days.

We stayed there until the late 90s. To be honest, I probably blew it by moving back here to California because we were doing very well. Our band was doing very well in the area. Unfortunately, we were convinced we could do that out here again. The plan was to come out here, set the recording equipment in a room and make records out here for a while, and then go back to Georgia. I was meeting with clients who wanted me to come out here. Just like The Black Keys wanted me to go to Muscle Shoals. I had clients saying, 'It would be a lot better if you were out here.' We packed up and came back to California and we kind of got stuck. I got married, we had children and the family tree develops. I'm coming back to the South because I love it, and I want my kids to experience it.

How did you first meet Jim Dickinson?

MN: Well, it's weird. I always admired Jim because Jim Dickinson is an enigma. His persona comes through. He spoke to me in articles he did all the way back to the 70s. He'd be interviewed off and on and you'd hear quotes. People would always quote Jim. The book Jim Dickinson wrote really ought to come out because it's fantastic. His quotes, I swear was like having a conversation with a relative. Just his turns of phrase and opinions about the way human nature and music—it was like I knew him. I didn't know why I thought that. Maybe it's just the way he talks. I'm familiar with that vernacular. His quotes were just action packed. One quote from Jim Dickinson carries a lot of weight. Finally a friend of mine, Philip, recorded a record with Jim and told me I should talk to him. That we'd really get along. I'd never met him, and I was a little hesitant because I had this image of him and I didn't want to be disappointed, but once we met it was a pure pleasure. That was years ago. What's funny about Jim—he utterly hated the kind of music I liked (laughs), but he loved what I was doing with it. Mostly…

Explain the difference between the analog and digital influence on the recording process. You're a master of sound, so talk a little about how this affects what every-one hears.

MN: It's very simple. In 1979, we got ushered into 24-track recording studios. Let me say one name—that was prevalent at the time: MCI— they were a company in Ft. Lauderdale that made very affordable 24-track tape machines, consoles, 2-tracks. They were affiliated with companies like Express Sound who made independent studios that were all similar. So you go into a stu-dio say in Georgia like Capricorn or FAME in Muscle Shoals out here in California at Western Audio and they were almost the same exact room. They had this same Yamaha grand piano—they all had the same drum booth. Everywhere you went in the country—it was the same studio. Generic. The problem is we could never get a kick drum sound like we did on The Black Keys' *Brothers*. That same Gretsch drum set had the same heads it had back then. You could never get that sound on a 24-track that we did on this latest Black Keys record or other records I've made like that. It would never sound like that.

Back then we would play those drums in a room and we'd come back in and it sounded like Fleetwood Mac or the Talking Heads. We couldn't figure it out. We'd make all our demos in the band house—my house. It was similar to what Dan Auerbach has now for his home studio. Little PA mixers and AMPEX machines and some decent microphones. We couldn't release those records because they were mono. We'd put these demos on a chrome cassette at every San Diego and LA studio and they would press play and it would literally blow a hole in the back wall. They'd ask how'd I get that kick drum sound? That guitar sound? I'd say a Shure 57 (laughs). They'd say we can't get that sound here. We don't even know what you're doing! I'd say I'm not doing anything and that's the point. Fast forward to now, and everyone's blaming Pro Tools. Hey man, it's just bad taste. So, to put a fine point on analog versus digital—nothing ruins a good record like bad taste. Nothing fixes a bad mix like a great song.

Earlier you mentioned you built Dan Auerbach's home studio and co-recorded his solo effort *Keep It Hid*.

MN: Well, let me back up. One of the things that happens to a person in South Georgia or the deep south is they overthink everything (laughs). That's why the Muscle Shoals rhythm section is probably better than they needed to be in 1965. I mean, what was acceptable in New York or Los Angeles for a soul record that would have been in the mind of Rick Hall? Those guys over thought everything. That's what I did. I built my studio—I focused on the acoustics—mathematical acoustics. Jim Dickinson and I have the same problem where we see numbers backwards. I've always had that problem. What I would do is—me and Dave Doyle my bass player since 79—would sit down at a counter at a restaurant with these books on sound, a pocket calculator and we'd push the paper back and forth to make sure it was right. He was great at math. I decided many years ago that you couldn't have a studio unless it was acoustically designed with the Rule of 18. The Golden Section. This deep math goes all the way back before Babylon. Solomon's math. The Golden Section is the math of the universe. Acoustics apply to this and you have to design rooms using these non-divisible formulas. If you don't, these rooms sound like metal barrels or empty bedrooms. I was convinced most people who were serious about making records had done their rooms this way. I was mostly wrong. I got good at walking into a room, no matter what it sounded like, and make it sound the way you wanted it to. I already versed myself so deeply with the section formulas. I could make a small room sound like a big church. In turn, I could make a large room sound tight by working with diffusion so you could work without baffles in the room and still get a really clean sound on the microphones. So, I designed my studio and Toe Rag Studios and my studio as clones of each other as an experiment. Liam Watson—who owns Toe Rag—thought it was a great idea and that's what he wanted to do. It's all done on the Golden Section. Many years later when Dan Auerbach of the Black Keys visited my studio, and he loved it. He asked me how much it would cost to build the same studio in his home. I told him how much it would cost and he said that was really expensive. I said I understood, but you have to do it right or you're wasting your money. You might as well leave it the way it is and record in your basement. If you don't do it all the way—it won't work.

You actually have to finish the job and do all of it. That means floating the floor, internal dimensional structure, floating the walls and isolating things so that don't make noise out in the neighborhood. Even the way microphones and everything hooks up as a system. It has a design. It's all based on common practice since 1958. That's how Dan Auerbach's studio was designed. Dan came into my room and he loved it. He'd visited Toe Rag Studios and loved that too.

That brings us up to you engineering The Black Keys' *Brothers* album in Muscle Shoals. It's a great album and it's getting a lot of attention. You contributed in a big way to that…

MN: Well, thank you man. Let me explain, I'm going to quote Jim Dickinson a lot because you interviewed Jim. This is what I loved about Jim. I used to feel very guilty about playing my record collection to people like Dan. I used to feel guilty about saying, 'Hey—we really ought to use my Gretsch drums on this. I used to feel bad about saying give me your guitar I want to show you another way to play that chord pattern—it's fuller down here.' I felt bad about that for years. Jim liberated my thinking on that. He said, 'All Bets are Off'. Record production is everything. You have to do it all. You just can't do one thing. You've got to do everything. You can't do too much at once. You gotta be pretty vague and pretty quiet about how you do it because it's nefarious. The craft is nefarious.

Dickinson said if it feels right and you feel like it's got to be done, don't be afraid to put cream in somebody's coffee if they ask for it black and it helps them sing better. Don't be ashamed to say put that cigarette down you're going to do another take. The problem with The Black Keys record in Muscle Shoals for me was halfway through that situation—the process of making that record was everybody was thrilled with the soul music and heavy dark results. The other half of the process something turned. The worm turned in the middle of the process. We were almost done and the scary thing is the demos that we have—those songs we did here at Soil of the South Studios—was a completely different record in and of itself. I'll be honest—the direction on that was killer too. I mean these guys are super talented.

People don't understand what it takes or the price you have to pay to make great art. You guys were in Muscle Shoals for a couple of weeks, right?

MN: Yeah, about ten days.

I remember you saying a lot of electric and paranormal activity went on in the Muscle Shoals studio.

MN; Yeah, a lot. I knew it was going to happen because it happened in my cinder block studio in Valdosta. It was the same thing down there. I would have to run them out sometimes it would get so thick in there. I never said there were ghosts there. What if it was just electromagnetic residue? I never said it was anybody's spirit. Who knows?

I'm sure recording at one of the studios were some of America's greatest soul music retains its own mojo.

MN: Yes, absolutely. Jim Dickinson had just passed when we started the first song and I don't know—I think Jim has gone to be with the Lord and I believe that—but something like an energy was there. It could have been what's left behind when you go—who knows? But whatever it is there was a ton of strange physical things that went on while we were there. Dan has to wear glasses. He didn't wear them while playing, but people who could see that were inside that room saw it. It happened. Even if you couldn't see it you knew something was happening. You could feel it.

You're well versed in all the classic sounds and auras of Ardent, Sun, Capricorn, STAX, Muscle Shoals and be-yond. The right producer procures and utilizes all the visible and invisible elements to create a timeless sound that crosses generations to exist in the here and now. Brothers stands as testimony to that fact.

MN: The vibe in that Muscle Shoals room was heavier than a Pentecostal snake-handling service. It was nuts. Those songs Dan and Pat played… "Everlasting Light" or "Next Girl" something stuck to that tape. If you hear these Muscle Shoals songs they sound totally haunted, different, greasy and crazy compared to the stuff recorded at Dan's.

I love the R & B stuff, but "Next Girl", "Go Getter" and "Sinister Kid" rank as my favorites.

MN: The Black Keys songs are amazing. I'm pretty sure the people who were there with me all agree whether you like what I do or not it was an essential factor to what was going on in Muscle Shoals. My part of it all was flavor enhancer. There was some hard work going on there, which is a great back story and adds sparkle to an album that is already brilliant.

What are you working on right now?

MN: I just finished that *Hacienda* record, which is the band Dan took out on the road for *Keep It Hid.* They recorded that in Akron, and then I get a phone call in the middle of this *Brothers* thing and they wanted me to finish it up, mix it and add my sound design. So, I did that. Of course, it was a pleasure because the way his studio is set up and the way he is doing things now it was very fun to make that record for those guys. That record just came out, it's called *Big Red & Barbacoa.* I got a lot of people kicking the tires because of this Black Keys record.

When are you moving back to Georgia?

MN: I don't know. I see an exodus of people moving back to the South. I've been broadcasting that I've wanted to come back and I think this Muscle Shoals thing is the first fish. I reeled it in. After Muscle Shoals, I really want to return to the South. The musicians in the south are peerless. I mean— just to be honest—I don't even consider myself as some smokin red-hot player, but out here in San Diego I'm a very distinctive player. In South Georgia, people still think I'm this kid bass player. I go home and folks say 'Hey Mark, we always loved your bass playing. It was such an inspiration.' I don't mind being brought down a few pegs when I go home.

The Bloom of Underhill Rose

I met Underhill Rose in 2012 on St. Simons Island. They were playing a gig, and I obtained the first copy of their new release Something Real *for this article. Eleanor Underhill wrote a blurb for my book* The Local Stranger. *These days, they operate as a duo—just Molly Rose and Eleanor Underhill. I see them playing the Grand Ole Opry one day.*

"I've been told I've got a restless soul
How much dirt do I need to dig through
Before I hit the gold
I tried to be good
I try to do what I should
I try to walk that line
But that's not really my style
I need something to hold onto
I need something to get me through
Something real..."

—"Something Real"

IT SEEMS TO ME if you're an artist you should know your craft well enough that you've studied those who came long before you. Too many groups out there today playing music don't do their homework regarding the long line of American music traditions—much less express their own originality. The young Asheville, North Carolina, group, Underhill Rose, capture a rare spirit of inspiration when they sing and play that encapsulates tones, themes and stories of old-time music into their own patch-work quilt songs.

Underhill Rose conjures their rare inspiration through musicianship, eschewing the industry's standard practice of capitalizing on their good looks by wearing hot pants and tank tops without bras. No sexual pandering from this gang. Song craft stands as their main concern. Their voices linger in the imagination long after the song is heard. Their new CD, *Something Real*, contains bona fide proof of their raw skill.

Dear reader, you should seek out this group because they are an honest, hardworking gifted trio with no egos. This is not the age of the Rock Star. It is the age of artists who are real people... no gimmicks...no unreal images... no pretense. However, to follow such a long line of tradition—it's never easy. As Bob Dylan once said, "Anyone who wants to be a songwriter should listen to as much folk music as they can, study the form and structure of stuff that has been around for 100 years." I discovered Underhill Rose last summer and was blown away by their sheer graceful talent. Now, a year later we sat down on a beautiful Friday May afternoon for an interview. A light breeze circulated the sweet smell of wood smoke in the air. The girls were already eating when I arrived. I sat down next to them and said, "I brought a gift for y'all, because I know it's always good to have new music out on the road." I gave them a copy of Dust-To-Digital's *Art of Field Recording Volume 2*. I chose to give them this rare box set because their music falls into those old American folk traditions. I champion Underhill Rose because they retain the potential of tapping into the deep reservoir of America's songwriting and storytelling treasure trove—in the here and now....and beyond. "Well, we brought a gift for you also," said Molly Rose. "You are the very first person to get an actual hard copy of our new CD," she said with an intimidating smile, handing me a copy of *Something Real.* "The very fi rst person," she reiterated. "I also wanted to tell you how much I enjoyed your Bloodkin article. You wrote that really well being right there in the middle of all that rock & roll madness." We sat down at a picnic table and the interview began.

This Asheville, North Carolina trio includes Eleanor Underhill, Molly Rose, and Salley Williamson. Eleanor hails from North Carolina. She plays banjo, harmonica, guitar, piano and a little trombone. She's the main song-writer of the band. She's also an accomplished artist, and contributed illustrations for her father's two books, *How To Make A Joint Stool From A Tree* and *The Woodwright's Guide—Working with Wedge and Edge*. Molly comes from Douglasville, Georgia. She grew up in a musical family. She's a fine guitarist with an unforgettable golden voice.

Salley, the newest member, comes from South Carolina—near the Edisto River. She's performed with Doc Watson and The Carolina Chocolate Drops in the past. "I got really lucky with that," Salley said, "We were right there with Doc Watson and the Chocolate Drops at this show. My bass teacher was very instrumental in that. He wanted to play mandolin. So, I took over on the bass."

Underhill Rose formed in North Carolina during 2009. Since their inception, they've shared the stage with Jim Lauderdale, Kevn Kinney, Col. Bruce Hampton, Jon Fishman, Blackberry Smoke, Papa Mali and they performed at Warren Haynes' Christmas Jam. In May 2011, the group released their self-titled debut CD that augmented folk, bluegrass and country into one Appalachian sound, which served as a template to their musical vision. *Something Real* indicates, as well as playing with the aforementioned groups, they are broadening their horizons while staying true to their earthbound, folk roots.

They are all educated, well-traveled, talented women who are gradually accumulating a dedicated following—for good reason. The new CD, *Something Real*, was recorded at Echo Mountain Recording Studio (a renovated church), and was produced by Cruz Contreras, frontman for the Black Lillies, one of Knoxville, Tennessee's Americana stalwarts. Underhill wrote seven new tunes with five featuring her sultry voice. Salley composed two numbers which are sung by Molly. R&B, soul and country seep into the mix on this new release providing excellent variation upon the folk foundation of the debut collection.

Musicians on *Something Real* include Matt Smith (dobro, pedal steel), Mike Rhodes (drums), Ryan Burns (organ), Rayna Gellert (fiddle, viola), Silas Durocher (electric guitar), Steve Burnside (accordion), Justin Ray (trumpet), and producer Contreras on guitar and Wurlitzer. *Something Real* was recorded in two five-day sessions. Most of these musicians will appear at the album release party at the Isis Theatre in Asheville on May 31.

Molly revealed the organic process of *Something Real*: "We did Kickstarter for this album. We were nervous about it. We set a goal and exceeded it. So we owe everything to our fan base, which also gives us creative freedom. I was really adamant about the first track on *Something Real* keeping in line with what we did on the first record. We wanted to ease the listener into this new stuff."

Eleanor finished Molly's thought by saying, "We have high hopes for this record. It's been two years since the first one—to the month." Salley inserted, "We wanted to keep this true to our live sound even when we play as a trio. In the studio we actually cut out certain instruments that we had already recorded just because we wanted to keep the songs true to the live sound."

I asked how many songs were recorded for the *Something Real* sessions, and Molly responded—"We wrote 13 songs, but we recorded 15. There were covers that didn't make it. One was a cover of Neil Young's "Love Is A Rose" (a favorite of mine), and the other song was written by a guy named Billy Ed Wheeler. He's from West Virginia. He just turned 80. He's the songwriter who wrote "Jackson" (Molly began to sing in her amazing voice at the picnic table..."We got married in a fever"...)

Molly elaborated about Wheeler, "He also happens to be a graduate of Warren Wilson College, and we met him at an event at Warren Wilson about two years ago. We went to his 80th birthday party, and we performed one of his songs. He's a prolific songwriter, but mountaintop removal is a very big issue to him. We feel the same way because we live in the mountains. The song we chose to cover of his was called 'The Coming of the Roads'. "It's basically about getting rid of the forest for the roads and the money."

It just so happens, Molly, Eleanor and Salley all cultivate gardens. "I used to just sell vegetables at the Farmer's Market before I got so busy with the band", Salley said. "On the new album, there are a lot of nature-based themes and elements in the songs like 'White Rose' for instance," mentioned Molly. Molly's woodcuts are even featured in the liner notes between the printed lyrics. Earthy gals, indeed. "White Rose" lyrics from *Something Real* illuminates their close-to-the-soil ethos:

> *"Walnut tree so steady and strong, growing in the night*
> *Reach, reach up to the sky to the falling light*
> *Vines, vines tangle your boughs, branches dark and dead*
> *Walnut tree so steady and strong, grow above my head*
> *Sing, sing little white bird*
> *Sing, sing little white bird, wintertime is calling..."*

I inquired on how the group writes songs, if it was a collaborative process, or each member brought a song to the group. Eleanor fielded that question with this insightful response: "We draw upon inspiration when it comes. We write individually and then usually bring a just-about-finished song to the band." Only the trio will play tonight, and Eleanor indicated, "I think you'll really be able to hear the core of what we are. We thought a lot about that when we went into the studio with this album.

"Initially, we wanted it to sound identical to what our live sound is, but with each song we realized it would do a little more justice in the studio setting to add a little drums or pedal steel or Wurlitzer. So, some bells and whistles came into play. Eventually one day we may travel with a full band, but right now as a trio—it's the core of who we are. I think people are really satisfied with that.

"Then we work out the harmony together," Eleanor mentioned. "Everyone plays what they feel. There's one song on the new album that we all wrote a verse called 'Never Gonna Work Out'. That's how it is for me and Molly." Molly finished the question by saying, "Salley wrote two songs on the new album. She brought lyrics to the group and then she and Eleanor figured out the instrumentation."

Their compositions are heartfelt, sparse and evoke emotive harmonizing like the Trio album by Emmylou Harris, Linda Ronstadt and Dolly Parton. Their musicianship can't be overlooked considering how their song craft and harmonizing create sheer beauty. Compositions on *Something Real* like "Helpless Wanderer", "Unused To You" and "Bare Little Rooms" illustrate how a little musical coloring accentuate the group's raw talent. The title track may rank as the strongest number on the record.

Although I believe their decision to limit *Something Real* to only originals indicates their belief in their own songwriting voices. The ladies love to bring their style to cover songs by artists as diverse as John Legend, The Beatles, Gillian Welch, Patty Griffin, Solomon Burke, Taj Mahal and Jamey Johnson. They also tap into the deep songbook of R&B classics. "We just love the songwriting process...so whatever strikes us as a great tune is what we cover," Eleanor told me. When Underhill Rose played a show at Palm Coast later that night in my hometown of St. Simons Island, Georgia. They played almost 40 songs to an ecstatic live audience.

Old time sonic qualities emanate from their melodic tunes as if they could have been recorded in 1913 or 2013. Molly played her new Martin guitar, Eleanor displayed deft banjo-picking skills and Salley's low-bottom standup bass provided a solid foundation—but hearing them harmonize together just resonates on a soulful level. In their first set, they played a mix of new and old material from the Underhill Rose songbook as well as several covers. They're all smiles during every song casting an incandescent glow.

During the set break, I was smoking a cigarette far away from the stage when Eleanor wandered over, sat down next to me. With an irresistible smile she gave me a chewable vitamin she obtained from the health food store I took them to earlier that day. Soon Molly and Salley also sat down with us to chat. As these three intelligent and spirited beauties sat around me, I could envision them playing the Grand Ole Opry.

The second set only verified my aforementioned beliefs. For the last tune of the evening, they dedicated Neil Young's "Love Is A Rose" to me. Musicians play their personalities—these are clearly, earthy girls playing organic music—no gimmicks, no tricks, no acts. You can tell that when you that when you watch their fingers and listen to their voices. Or just play the CD.

The new record, *Something Real*, is worth hearing. They rise above contemporary music business flash and filigree by focusing on song craft. The music of Underhill Rose retains elements of the Great American Songbook by incorporating timeless stories and songs from a long line of old traditions.

When beauty does correlate with talent—they call it art. I've seen this come to life in Underhill Rose.

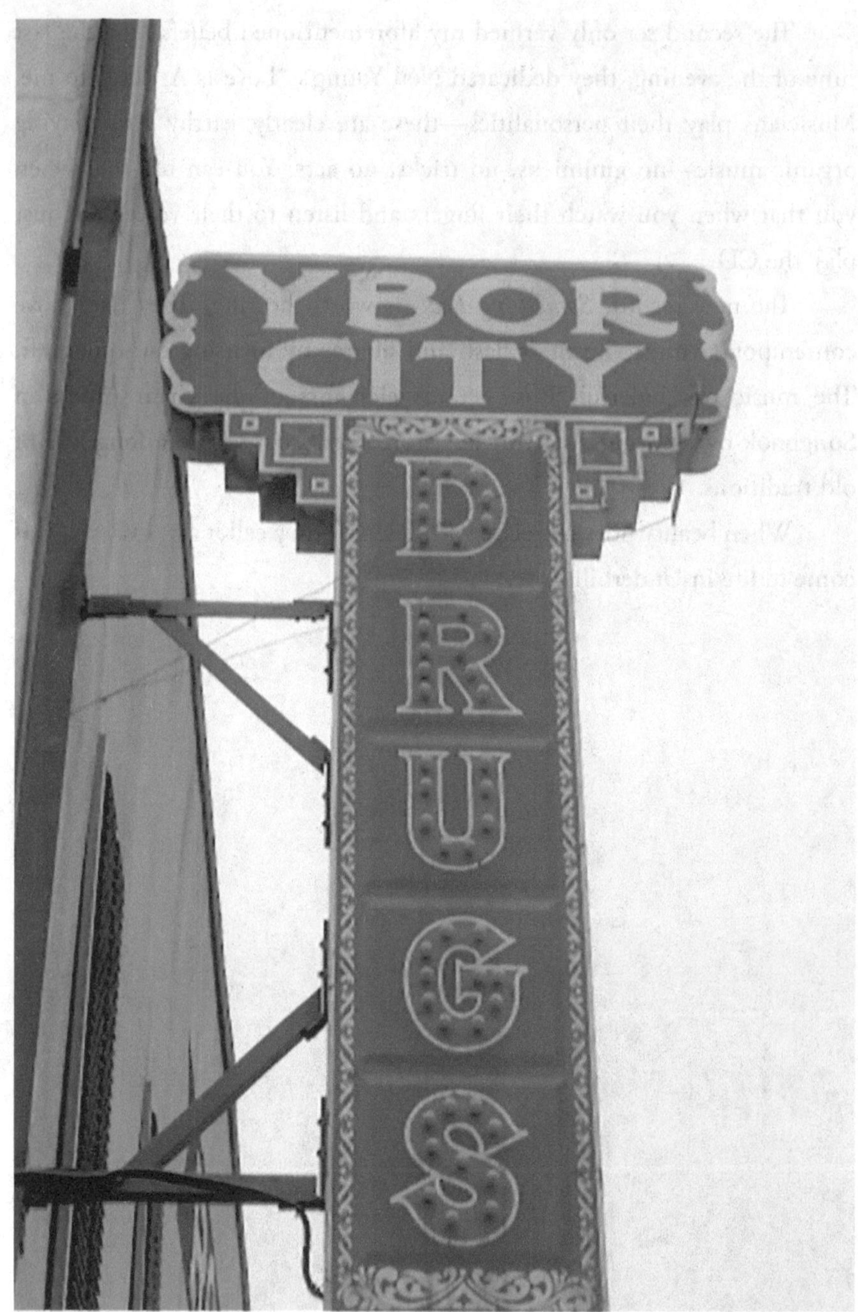

Ybor City Drugs

Essence of Light:
The Adam Smith Interview

> *I met Adam Smith in his hometown of Macon, GA., many years
> ago. We hit it off immediately. I don't think I've seen an in-depth
> interview like this before with Adam. On August 24, 2018, at the
> City Winery in Atlanta, Smith's photo show, 'See That My Grave
> Is Kept Clean' transpires.*

BORN IN MACON, GEORGIA, in 1975, Adam Smith's photography transcends his age. Smith attended college in Mississippi when he began to frequent the juke joint of bluesman Junior Kimbrough. After Kimbrough died, Smith raised money to place a headstone on the unmarked grave of the seminal bluesman. Adam Smith's soulful images speak for themselves.

Over the years Smith captured timeless images of Junior Kimbrough, R. L. Burnside, T-Model Ford, Jimbo Mathus, Grayson Capps, Precious Bryant, Abby Owens, Southern Bitch, The Whigs, The Sundogs, The Drive By Truckers, The North Mississippi Allstars, Don Chambers, Cary Hudson, Lucero, Bloodkin, Alvin Youngblood Hart, Widespread Panic, Dexateens, Centromatic, Beanland, Porter Wagoner, Frank Edwards, Jessie Mae Hemphill, Marty Stuart, Warren Haynes, Gregg Allman and many more.

Smith also provided artwork for labels such as Fat Possum Records, New West Records and Anti Records as well as periodicals such as *MOJO, Billboard, Paste, Living Blues* and *Hittin' The Note*. Smith even accompanied Annie Leibovitz on a photo shoot in the Mississippi Delta. He graduated from the University of Mississippi. He worked in Atlanta for years, and now lives in his hometown of Macon where he was named Photographer of the

Year in 2008. Smith's photographs were chosen for permanent display at The Georgia Music Hall of Fame.

A while back, Smith sent me a version of his unpublished book *Mornin' Ain't Come Yet: A Look Into the Music and Landscape of the Deep South*. It's a sight to behold. He's currently searching for a publisher for this inimitable collection. This book includes Smith's singular photographs along with written work by Larry Brown, Patterson Hood, Ben Nichols, Marty Stuart, Luther Dickinson, a poem by Daniel Hutchens and a few other surprises. Adam Smith's photos appeal to the senses.

This is what Patterson Hood of the Drive By Truckers had to say about Smith's work: "Adam Smith is a lightning capturer. He also seems to have the uncanny knack of clicking the camera at that exact moment the thunder strikes, the moment the magic occurs, when just one millisecond later would produce a fine picture but not the moment of alchemy that separates the great from the mundane."

Luther Dickinson (The North Mississippi Allstars & The Black Crowes) went on the record to reveal this about Smith: "Adam Smith captures the essence of the modern day south in all its extension cord run out of the bedroom window, Peavey powered backyard house party, midnight mosquito ridden fluorescent light glory. From the pool tables of back yard juke joints to the sleeping bag on the floor of a punk rock touring van, Adam Smith's photographs make you hold your nose, yearn for ear plugs and a semi-working window unit air conditioner. They don't call it the Dirty South for nothin'."

One cannot question the power his music photographs evoke, but to me the real spirit of his talent exists in his landscape photos such as a Highway 61 dirt crossroads, the Oliver Baptist Church, The Bluefront Cafe, railroad tracks and The Po Monkey Lounge in Merigold, Mississippi. These photographs capture a bygone era...a time that will not return, but the image is preserved. Stark beauty preserved on film. Without a story, song or photograph only the ashes of memory linger. Smith's work keeps memories alive.

Marty Stuart wrote this about the photographer: "Adam Smith is one of my all time favorite photographers. He shoots lean, neat and to the point. He understands the dance between music and photography and knows how to capture it. He eases up on a musical situation in the form of a ghost and his results are always timeless."

His personality, like his photos, represent no nonsense. He's a straight shooter. In this interview, Adam Smith discusses photography, his career, blues in the north Mississippi hill country, renown musicians he's worked with, his book *Mornin' Ain't Come Yet* and more.

James Calemine: You grew up in Macon, Georgia—a great music town.

Adam Smith: Yeah, I feel the great music was a little before my time. I grew up with my parents listening to a lot of that style of music. To tell you the truth, in high school was really into the Replacements. If you can believe it, I was a big Cure fan (laughs). I missed the whole Capricorn era since I was born in 1975.

When did you get your first camera?

AS: Well, I remember going to my parents mountain house up in Franklin, North Carolina, they were renovating. My father owned a business here in Macon that specialized in architectural woodworking. I left Ole Miss my freshman year and went up to Atlanta, to meet my parents in order to travel to this new house,and my father had an old Canon AE1. I literally picked it up and starting messing around with it. It was that weekend in the mountains that I gravitated towards it immediately. Like everybody, I started out (laughs) with babbling brooks, flowers and stuff like that. I went back to school, and a girl I was dating here had a sister that worked at a local camera shop—a real old shop for specialized photography, which is rare these days. Anyway, I got a heavy duty Canon AE1. It was a nice starter camera. They don't make metal heavy ones like that anymore. I got a job at Wolf Camera and really just started snapping pictures. It was horrible stuff, but I knew if I was going to do it right I had to learn everything. I wanted to master shutter speed, aperture and film speed. So, that's what I did. I went back to the University of Mississippi and tried to get in a photography class under a guy named Tom Rankin, but the class was full. I bugged him a little, and he ended up letting me into the Intro To Photography class. That's kind of where it all started learning the basics in Tom Rankin's class.

When did you first go out to shoot photographs at Junior Kimbrough's juke joint?

AS: I was into my sophomore year. Obviously, in college your whole musical tastes change. I started getting into Derek & The Dominos, The Band and Duane Allman. I remember hearing about Junior's juke joint. At one point I remember going out with some friends. It was only open on Sunday nights. We tried to find it one time, and we drove up and down this road, and unless you knew exactly where it was you'd drive by it ten times. It's literally a dark and gloomy place of the road in the middle of the night. I remember the first time we didn't have any luck finding the place. We tried to go a second time. I had my camera with me. I remember walking through the doors for the first time and seeing Junior in the corner of the juke joint playing, and just the atmosphere and the energy was overwhelming. I was taking the whole place in.

Obviously, being a white kid from Georgia walking into a place like this is a little daunting, but what I soon found out was that color doesn't matter out there. Everybody comes for the music. I was one of the only white people in there that night, and they were all like, 'Hey man, we're all glad you're out here. It's about celebrating life.' I was sitting on the couch, chillin' out takin' it all in, and a guy came up to me and said 'Hey man, you gotta get up. Junior's about to play.' He handed me a beer, and I remember they kind of set me in the front. Larry Brown described Junior's place best. I just remember people started dancing, and that style of hill country music is very...um, what's the word I'm looking for?

Hypnotic.

AS: Yes, hypnotic. The people would just lose themselves in the music. It's an amazing style. And up to that point in my life, I'd never heard anything like that. I thought I knew what blues was, but I'd never heard any raw energy like that before. Literally that night I had one of those come to Jesus moments when the energy and the power of the place was so overwhelming that I realized if I could ever capture the energy or the power that was coming out of that place that it was all I wanted to do. that moment will always stick out in my mind.

Ultimately, you were very instrumental in obtaining a headstone for Junior Kimbrough's grave, right?

AS: Yeah, I'd go back to Junior's and I was very lucky to be welcomed. There were few people Junior would get on a first name basis with, but he knew I came out there to take pictures. Junior and R.L. Burnside would hold court. I'd turn around and watch people dance. I'd seen other white people, tourists, want to take pictures and they would charge them $50 or $75 just to get in. That never happened to me. I'd like to say Junior could see in my eyes how much it all meant to me, and how respectful I was. We had an unspoken bond. He knew I was out there to document everything. He knew my heart was in the right place. When Junior passed away, and he was buried without a headstone...I thought that was crazy. So a friend of mine, Amos Harvey and I raised the money to get Junior a headstone for his grave. In certain circles there's always talk about the white kid goin' in there and just taking from them, but they don't know the full story. I was there to preserve things.

R.L. Burnside used to live out there right next to Junior and I got a bug to go out there. I started taking pictures and just hanging out with those guys. I met Paul Wine Jones and T-Model Ford. I'd call and make pilgrimages down to their house. You were lucky if you showed up and they were actually there, or you'd have to wait around. I just sat down with them and explained what I was trying to do. Most of those guys were all welcoming, and they would invite you in, and let you take pictures of them. That's what I started doing. I wanted to document everything that had to do with that music. Then I met the guys from Fat Possum Records. They did work with all those guys. They were the dirty little label that got these real deal Mississippi musicians. Matthew Johnson and Bruce Watson had a great marketing campaign. My friend Amos Harvey worked there, and they called me because they were doing Junior's *Meet Me In the City* album and they wanted my artwork. I was coming up in my career, and they wanted me to have the cover. That gave me a kick start. I continued on while I was at Ole Miss. I did everything I could possibly do to immerse myself in the scene.

Like I said, Junior died and we did the headstone thing. Then around 2000, when Junior's place burned down Amos Harvey and I got together again. They thought it might be arson, but nobody did anything about it. A lot of musicians lost their instruments out there and they lost income of coming out there to play. After Junior died, David and Kenny Kimbrough still went out there and played. When it burned down Amos Harvey and I did a huge benefit one night with many musicians who were there. It was a big jam in Oxford. Our goal was to raise money to rebuild and then we realized it would be impossible to recreate the place. So, the first part of the money was to buy back instruments for the musicians and give them some relief. I can't remember how much we raised—seven or eight thousand dollars. That was very important to me. I knew I was getting something because I took their pictures, but I wanted to give back to them, and the charity stuff helped me show them respect.

I could understand where that was an unforgettable education. Eventually you came across the rock & roll scene.

AS: Yeah, I apparently got on the radar with a lot of the right people. I got hired on by Annie Leibovitz around that time. Her people from New York got in touch with me that she was coming down south to do a book titled *American Music*. She wanted to do a blues part of it. I said okay, and they wanted a bunch of information, and I wondered if I gave them anything would I ever hear from them again. I called and told them I could put them in touch with all the people you'll need to know and when you go see them I'll line it up. I told them I would be the liaison between them and the musicians. I told them that would open more doors for them and the musicians would be more welcoming. People would come in and want something and they would never hear from them again. They ended up accepting my offer, and I basically produced the whole shoot for Annie.

Another big thing for me was these guys needed to be paid for their time because they didn't know Annie, and money talks. I knew she could afford it, and they were open to it. I lined up everything and it was a great experience. I remembered we finished that shoot and I was taking her to the airport, and she looked at me and said, which was completely true: 'Adam, we didn't see eye to eye on everything on this shoot, but I really respect your help.' I was very protective of those guys. When Annie got her photos, and left I would still be there. It ended up working really well. Annie is amazing to work with, but there were times I had to hold my ground. She was extremely moved by what I showed her down there. A couple of years ago, I got hired again. They did a shoot with the girl in Precious (Gabourey Sidibe) for Vanity Fair. Annie's book came out and I was hon-ored to have a working relationship with her.

I'm sure you picked up a few tricks of the trade from her.

AS: Oh yeah. She gave me a $3000 camera that I had been eyeing during the whole time she was here. She said, 'I want you to have this.' I think I was shaking when she gave it to me, and then she got on the plane. I lived in Mississippi for another year or so, and then I moved to Atlanta. They didn't have the real deal blues scene in Atlanta, and I was having withdrawal symptoms from it. I met Frank Edwards at the Northside Tavern in Atlanta.

That's where we first crossed paths, around some of those Music Maker blues musicians in Atlanta.

AS: That's right. I hooked up with Amos Harvey again who rediscovered and produced Precious Bryant. She put out a record on Terminus Records with Jeff Bransford. I went down and shot her and hung out with them. Then I did a Fat Possum session with a guy named Duck Holmes that Amos again produced. I did all the work for that. I was living in Atlanta for about a year working at the Atlanta College of Art managing their photography department, which was a good job. It kept me in the photography world and gave me access to top notch equipment. On Thanksgiving night, a friend called me and said I needed to check out a band. I was real close-minded at the time, and I thought if I hadn't heard of them, they can't be much. So I walked into The Earl in Atlanta and The Drive By Truckers were playing. That literally blew it all open. As a photographer, you always need new subject matter.

The Truckers did that for me—that low-lit gritty rock & roll, and it wasn't blues-infused. I was like, 'These fucking guys are amazing' the energy coming from the stage took me back to that night at Junior Kimbrough's. the hairs on the back of my neck stood up. It was one of the first night's Jason Isbell joined the band. I met their manager at the time—Dick Cooper—and he was a photographer himself. I introduced myself to them, and asked them to check out my work. My friend, Scott Munn, was managing The Truckers at the time, and I'd worked with Scott before and that's how I got in with The Truckers. Maybe two months later I got a call saying The Truckers wanted to do a shoot with me and we did it at the back of the Variety Playhouse in Atlanta. We did that first full-on shoot, and the love affair between me and The Truckers began. They are great guys, and I would bend over backwards for any of them. Patterson would do the same for me, but if you screw them, Patterson will put you under the bus.

You can't blame him.

AS: Not at all. I already knew Luther & Cody Dickinson of the North Mississippi Allstars. they were coming onto the scene. A lot of times when I was in Atlanta I wanted to show these bands support, especially if they came to Macon. I was always trying to lend a hand. I think Cody gave me a copy of Lucero's first album, which he produced. It was raw, but on the countryside. I'd never met Lucero, but I called them when they came to Atlanta. Lucero was on tour with the Allstars. Lucero's van was broken into and they lost all their cash. They didn't know they were going to make it to Atlanta. I called them and they literally came to my house. There's a knock at the door, and they're standing there. Ben Nichols says, 'Amos Harvey told us you wanted to shoot us. So we're here, but we don't have any money.' I was like, 'I don't care about your money, but I don't even know you motherfuckers (Laughs)! But we had that one night where we drank beers and really connected. I got them a gig at Smith's Olde Bar, and the folks at Smith's loved them. We got to be really good friends. So, I did that shoot with Lucero. Then I got them a couple of gigs at The Earl in Atlanta. so, it made me feel good to help them. I know you know just as much about this stuff.

How did you meet up with the great Marty Stuart?

AS: When Scott Munn left The Truckers he began working in Nashville. He worked with Marty Stuart. Marty wanted me to do the Porter Wagoner album. That was extremely important to me. It was interesting to cross over into the country scene, and I was paid well for it. It added a scary element when you have all that money on the table—you don't want to fuck it up. Every time I worked with Marty it turned out great, and he's a helluva photographer himself. He's got a book out of his own work. We've always gotten along really well. I've worked with Marty four or five times. Working with Porter Wagoner was amazing as well. I was really lucky to make impressions along the way.

The Last project I did with Marty was his *Ghost Train* album. He recorded it in Nashville at the old RCA/Victor studios where Elvis recorded. It was amazing, I got to work with Marty and Ralph Mooney and Marty ended up winning a grammy for that album for the song "Hummingbyrd". It was a great experience.

What's been going on with your most recent work?

AS: I've been staying busy with my core group of clients/bands, just trying to keep the light on, you know? Did an in-studio ses-sion with The Whigs recently as they were recording tracks for a new album, which was great because usually I am shooting those guys in a live setting, so the change of scenery made for some great shots. I like the studio work because you can catch the guys off-guard when they're not doing their rock star moves in the stage garb, just catching them as they really are, so to speak. Also, I don't smoke nearly as much in those settings, so that's a plus I suppose.

I did the album artwork for Fat Possum's Jim Mize release recently. It was a 7 inch. Bruce called me and said, 'You got anything down from the Mississippi Delta on the edgier side? YEP!' It came out great, they ended up using an image I called Delta Dogs for the front and back cover. It was 2 consecutive 6 x 7 film frames I shot several years ago and it worked out well. Always love when Fat Possum gives me a project.

And I'm headed to Athens this weekend to shoot the Truckers at the brand new Georgia Theatre, which is gorgeous, and I'm expecting some tremendous energy from both the band and the crowd just because it's such a festive occasion. And of course I want to see how they handle the new lighting, because to be honest I never liked the old place that much for shooting, just too dark to get anything worth a damn.

Let's talk about this book you're putting together called *Mornin' Ain't Come Yet.*

AS: For the last few months, my day-to-day focus has been putting together a book of my work, kind of a retrospective of my career at this point that I'm tentatively calling *Mornin' Ain't Come Yet: A Look into the Music and Landscape of the Deep South*. It's a story in pictures beginning with my work in north Mississippi with Junior Kimbrough and R.L. Burnside where I found that connection to the decaying juke joints and landscapes and the men and women that performed there. The story continues right on through the work I still do with bands like Lucero and the Truckers and other musicians that capture that same type of juke joint spirit—telling the truth, as they see it, every night, late into the night. A number of the folks that are featured in the book—Marty Stuart, Larry Brown, Patterson Hood, Luther Dickinson, Danny Hutchens—have contributed writing to help me tell the tale, and so far I'm really happy with the way it's coming out.

I've been shopping the first rough draft around the last month or so to some publishing houses, just looking for the right home, much in the way a band looks for the right label or distributor for their music. There's a certain type of person out there who can't wait to see and own a book like this, and I guess the trick is finding the publisher that knows how to reach that person time and time again, and of course believes in the work and how it should be presented and marketed. It's been a learning experience but so far, nothing but positives and good feedback. It's an exciting time for sure.

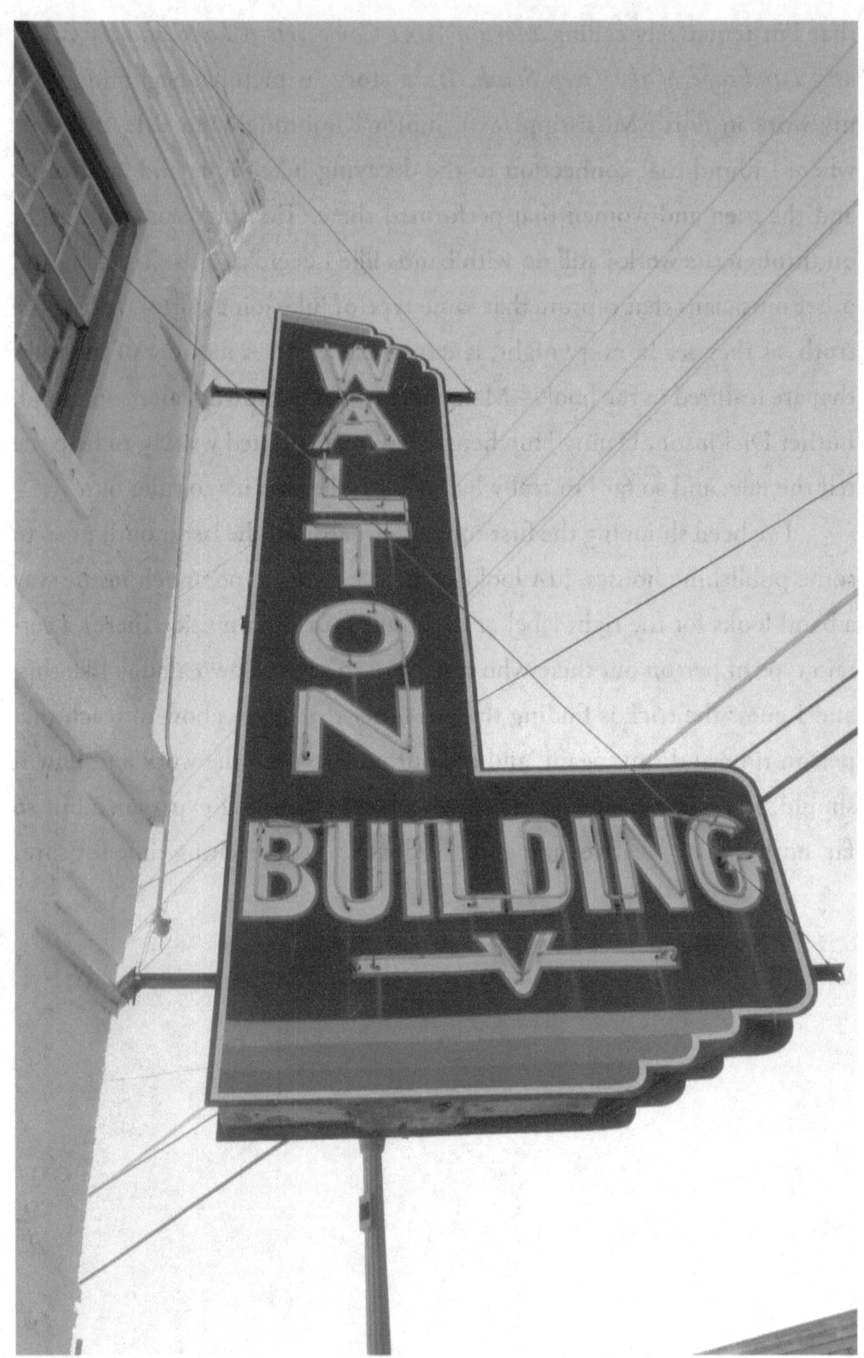

Walton Building

Cormac McCarthy's *Blood Meridian* Or the Evening Redness in the West

A CLASSIC VOLUME OF southern literature...

Blood Meridian or the *Evening Redness in the West* ranks as one of Cormac McCarthy's most violent, savage and philosophical novels. This story takes place on the Texas-Mexico border in the 1850s. These characters ride across the desert like a gang of Old Testament marauders.

Blood Meridian echoes Sam Peckinpah's murderous films such as *Ride The High Country, Bring Me The Head of Alfredo Garcia, The Wild Bunch* and *Straw Dogs* with a venomous riddle of violence. The main characters of this McCarthy novel, The Kid (a 14-year old Tennessean) and The Judge (perhaps Lucifer himself), propel this novel's ruthless balance between the mysterious tightrope between good and evil. Vivid pictures of grimness erupt on every page of this hypnotic book.

This mean, merciless story forces the reader to understand the deadly nature of how all territories are established. Every sentence in this book should be examined with wonder. Cormac McCarthy's writing can only be contested by William Faulkner or Flannery O'Connor. *Blood Meridian* endures time as one mean piece of art.

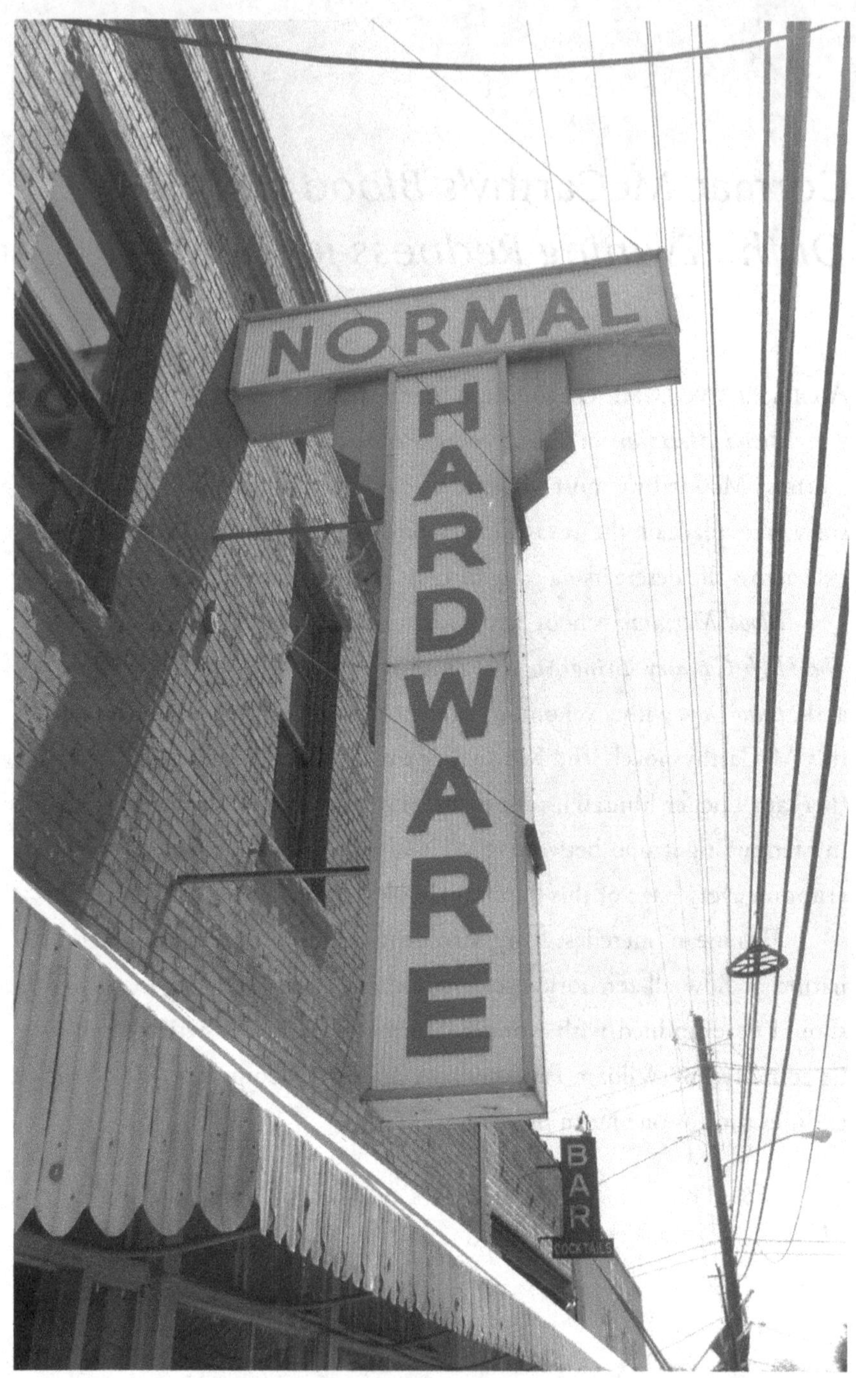

Normal Hardware

Down In The Groove with Widespread Panic's Todd Nance

Bloodkin's Daniel Hutchens told me this counted as one of the best music interviews he ever read. Perhaps he's biased because he's so close to me and Widespread Panic, but Todd did reveal some personal tribulation that comes along with Panic's high-powered glory in rock-n-roll. He provided a glimpse of the glory and cost it requires to be in a highly successful band. We conducted this Q & A right after I wrote Widespread Panic's induction into the Georgia Music Hall of Fame. Sadly, Todd's no longer a member of Widespread Panic. Ah, the strange changes time delivers.

"Either brace yourself for elimination / Or your heart must have the courage for the changing of the guard."

—Bob Dylan

FROM THE DRUMMER'S SEAT you can see everything. For example, three guitarists in front of you peering into the crowd, a keyboardist and percussionist positioned beside you—in another dimension a large audience watching you—with crew and loved ones nestled safe on the side stage behind powerful, state of the art amplifiers emitting electric sound waves through flesh, bone, concrete and steel. It's the best seat in the house. The drummer controls the pulse of the entire building.

Todd Nance has sat in that seat, serving as Widespread Panic's solid foundation, since the band's birth in 1986. Panic commands respect for creating their music, band and organization without submitting to fading trends or record company traps. Over the years, Widespread Panic has sold over 3 million records, performed with music's crème of the crop, released 18 different albums and remain one of the largest-drawing live bands in the last 20 years.

From 1986 to 2002, Panic cultivated a loyal following behind solid albums and incessant touring. After the death of the group's founding guitarist, Michael Houser, in August of 2002—from pancreatic cancer—the band entered a transitional phase while trying to maintain the vast inertia they built after many years of relentless playing. With the recent addition of Georgia guitarist Jimmy Herring, and a new album—*Free Somehow*—Widespread Panic enters a new era of momentum.

I met Todd Nance back in late 1992—or early 93—around the time Panic was recording *Everyday*. During this time, I was living with Daniel Hutchens and Eric Carter of Bloodkin in Athens, Georgia. Widespread officially recorded, at that point, one Bloodkin song on their second album they called *Mom's Kitchen*. These days, Panic covers at least 8 Bloodkin songs. Over the years, I met and kept time with various band members, family members, crew and staff members in the Panic community. Through time, I've spent various nights with Todd sitting at the kitchen table, listening to music, and on several occasions I've been invited to his home. I attended the bash celebration when he and Tammy got married. He's got an easy-going demeanor, but he's an astute musician, and one of his generation's greatest drummers. Plus, he has a built in shit detector.

Todd epitomizes the ultimate professional. In this interview, which doesn't feel like a Q & A, as much as a lucid conversation, Todd reveals insight into Panic's early days, recording on Capricorn Records, songwriting, Michael Houser, new guitarist Jimmy Herring, the new album *Free Somehow* along with a treasure trove of other priceless stories.

The Widespread Panic saga proves a venerable tale of artists who remained true to themselves and their music in a quicksand music industry. A few days after this interview, on February 16, Daniel Hutchens, Todd and I hung out at a friend (a noble and story-worthy individual in his own right) of Todd's with a beautiful pond in the backyard in the middle of 40 acres. When you read this interview, keep in mind, this is only the beginning of where I begin to tell their story…

We go back a ways and it's time to go on the record.

TN: Ah man, you're one of my favorite writers. Luckily, Ellie (WSP publicist) went to *Swampland* and read a lot of your stuff. Her comment was "his writing is very insightful." So I love to do this with you.

Well, thanks. Let's go all the way back. You're from Tennessee.

TN: I was born in Chattanooga, Tennessee in 1962. I lived there pretty much all my life. I left there in 1981 when I graduated from high school and I moved to Atlanta.

I remember you telling me years ago the first concert you ever attended was Lynyrd Skynyrd.

TN: Yeah, as a matter of fact when I was a seventh grader, I went to a private boarding school. It was a dorm with everything from seventh graders to seniors and not a whole lot of supervision. You learn quite a few survival skills being the youngest. Those motherfuckers could be cruel. It was intense and luckily they liked me and one of them turned me onto a lot of music. Of course, I had to endure a few beatings but I got exposed to a lot of music that year. We took a field trip—we were in Sweetwater, Tennessee, which is a town off I-75 between Knoxville and Nashville. We took a field trip and we went to the Coliseum in Knoxville and saw Skynyrd. I got separated from the crowd–it's like 1975—and I'm by myself, just watching it all come in. I started getting goosebumps. It had a huge effect on me. I knew then that that's what I wanted to do.

Were the drums your first instrument or was it something else?

TN: Guitar was my first instrument, but they said when I was a baby I used to beat on stuff. I'm a sucker for guitars—you know that—that's why I hang out with Danny and Eric. I love guitars. I love drums too—don't get me wrong, but guitar was my first love.

When did you get your first set of drums?

TN: Actually, I think it was Christmas of 1975. About twelve years old.

Well, if Skynyrd was your first concert, I'm sure you went out and bought those albums.

TN: The first records I've ever owned was when my parents gave me a stereo one year—this was like 73 or so and my uncle went and bought me two albums—The Beatles' *Abbey Road* and Eric Clapton's *461 Ocean Boulevard*. The first album I ever bought myself—not counting singles—was Lynyrd Skynyrd's *Second Helping*. I guess that was around 74-75.

When did you start playing in bands?

TN: Well, in middle school I learned how to read music—I became involved in organized music. I could read beats because as drummers you don't have to read the scales. I could…but basically you read the rhythm of it—but yeah, I could read music.

What was your first real group?

TN: A band called Just Us with Mikey Houser in Chattanooga. He and I met in 77 or 78.

He moved to Athens first, right?

TN: My birthday falls in November so I started school later that most people who were born in 62. He graduated high school in 1980 and he went off to the University of Georgia. I graduated high school in 1981 and moved to Atlanta. He and I didn't actually see each other—I saw him once in 81—and we didn't see each other again until 86. He was at Georgia and he called my mom one night and said they were looking for a drummer. It was February of 86—she gave him my number and he called me up in Atlanta and said 'Hey we got this group–come check it out.' So I drove over and said yes. And that was the beginning of Widespread Panic—twenty-two years ago. It was the same for everybody—that was their first band. That has a lot to do with why we're still around. We thought we had something together and we realized we had more together than we did individually.

Over the years—forget the music for a second—that's real brotherhood— all original guys in the band.

TN: Oh yeah, so taking a year off was great. We all went off and did something different. We got to be exposed to regular people and what it's like to be in most bands. When we came back together we really appreciated each other a lot more. We all have a lot of respect from each other—the dynamic in Panic is different than most bands. So, Mikey went to UGA in 1980—we didn't see each other until 86 so he and JB (John Bell, Panic guitarist) met each other in 83 or 84. They met briefly and exchanged some ideas and then they didn't see each other for a while and then they got back together and started playing a little but Mikey would write songs and JB would do them. They'd been together about a year and Dave (Schools) came down from Richmond, which was 84 or 85. So, they had this three-piece, and they didn't quite consider themselves a band yet. They went through different drummers.

The reason I fell into it so easy was because me and Mikey really learned music together—he taught me how to play guitar. His compositions made sense to me…where other people's made no sense at all… for good reason. They were getting frustrated and Mikey said, 'I know a dude.' Mikey and I had actually gotten into some trouble together back in Chattanooga and we weren't really allowed to hang out with each other. He called my Mom—he still had my number—and she gave him the number where I was in Atlanta. I was in Atlanta living in a condo and I couldn't play because it was too loud—I hadn't played in almost two years, and two weeks later, I'm playing a gig. That's when we became Widespread Panic. It was like February 6, and then Sunny came along a few months later—so we've had the whole band—with the exception of JoJo…

T-Lavitz played with y'all a bit.

TN: Yeah, he worked on an album with us-I guess it was *Mom's Kitchen* (Panic's second album)–but he played keyboards on the record and we were really blown away with the way keyboard sounded with our music. We asked him to go out with us so he was with us for about a year, but he wasn't the one but that was our introduction to keyboard players. In the meantime, we made friends with a band from Mississippi called Beanland and John (JoJo) Hermann was in that band. They had come to a point where they had to play covers or play their own music and then it was like—'Hey, why isn't anyone here anymore?' I think some of the guys were just content to play covers on the weekends. So that's when JoJo came in.

The band recorded many records at John Keane's—he's been an influence in the band.

TN: Yeah, especially over the years he was like the seventh member kind of thing. Even though we did our last two albums with another producer in a different studio—John Keane would be out on the road with us all the time. After George left he was very key in helping us throughout that tour. We know he has our best interests at hand. We might accuse him of being a little more clinical, but by having those two opposing forces you meet in the middle… usually in the right spot.

I remember when I went to school at Georgia you guys were playing the Phi Delta house every now and then.

TN: Oh yeah.

Widespread cultivated a loyal local following from the beginning and the fans are possessive. When I was 18 and from South Georgia, I was very possessive of Gram Parsons' music. Panic fans were the same way—especially because y'all were always playing.

TN: Exactly. We went through that—our first fans who were close friends of ours—when the shows began to be well-attended—selling out more and more, they began to get a little jealous because they felt like they were losing us to somebody. We've actually felt that sensation a few times over our career. It's a sharing kind of thing. I swear James, we didn't even own a guitar tuner for the first year. We were just struggling to get by—when we went to rehearsal we wouldn't practice songs we'd write new songs, which was great but the thing was I couldn't believe people would come pay to watch us. I remember the price went from a buck to two bucks. We flipped out and said there is now way in hell people will pay two bucks to see us play. They (management) were so mad at us because we said a buck fifty. But of course one-arm Steve at the door had to keep change and he was so pissed off at us over that (laughs). We were doing it for ourselves. You were involved in that same kind of group of things.

I remember when Dave (Schools) worked the door at the Uptown and you'd get a can of Fosters and just soak up the scenery.

TN: …(Laughs)… Hell yeah, the old oil can. They tried to hire me to enforce under age drinkers and I said "I ain't that guy." (collective laughter)

How did the first record deal go down?

TN: This guy we never met before introduced himself—Tinsley Ellis—and he told us he enjoyed it and he asked us if we wanted to jam later. We usually left our equipment in the place and come get it the next day. Then 'Crumpy' (Paul Edwards) came and we packed our shit up and set it back up at home at 3 in the morning and we started jamming with Tinsley. Tinsley and Bruce Hampton too—they both made Michael Rothschild aware of us (President of Landslide Records) and he started to come and see us and he saw something in it and he offered us a deal, on one condition, and that was that we stop playing "Knights In White Satin" (laughs). Then he said 'Have y'all ever heard of The Meters?' And we said no, and he turned us onto them. He was a big lover of music so we did our first record with him. Then Capricorn Records was reforming for our second record and Phillip Jr. used to be a Phi Delt and he was aware of the band. He used to get drunk and y'know 'My daddy owns....

But he made Big Phil aware of us. I don't think Big Phil thought we were going to be his cash cow, but for some reason he always let us do our thing. I can say this about Capricorn they gave us money to do our records and we'd go make 'em and that was it. They didn't try to manipulate us. We had a couple encounters with big labels that was a nightmare—they'd hear "Coconut" and just want a bunch of that—they didn't get it at all. We were confident enough in ourselves to turn those deals away and not just sign the first thing that came along. The band never second guessed ourselves, but I remember Warner/Chappell coming to us and we were starving to death and offered us a paltry sum for our publishing. We ate the breakfast first before we said no, and then probably said 'No, thank you'. But that would've been a nightmare. We would've signed away everything up to that point for thirty grand or whatever. We just wanted to be able to play music.

This is getting close to the time when our paths intersect because I was hanging out with Danny and Eric and by that time, Panic already recorded one of their songs.

TN: Exactly, Bloodkin's has been around as long as we have—longer even.

Almost thirty years.

TN: Way back...we met those guys and really admired them for their songs, and that was a band where it was your own little secret. Hell, you know that better than anyone. You remember White Buffalo...

Of course.

TN: Bands like that and the Athens music scene was very diverse—there was Porn Orchard…there was a diverse music scene going on. It takes a few years to build it up to where your can really start traveling and going on tour. A really cool radio station up in Chicago starting playing *Space Wrangler* from the get-go and they'd call and say 'When are you guys coming up here'? And we were like—'We can't get past Richmond yet…' But it took several years before we really toured. We'd leave on Wednesday and come home on Sunday. One thing that was really cool back then was—you mentioned the fraternities earlier—the fraternities let us play our own music which was something that was somewhat new, so we played the frat houses during the week to make money and buy equipment and then play the clubs and lose the money on the weekends.

But you never had to work jobs.

TN: That was the main thing, but I did work at Dial America (in Athens).

Yeah, me too. I got Danny a job there.

TN: JB and I also painted houses—it was bleak. Most bands don't make it through it, especially in college towns. You know summers are a little more active than they used to be, but you remember how dead summers could be in Athens. You just try to make it to September if you can. But it was never, 'I can't play because I got to work.' Mikey worked at Euro Wrap, and Dave used to deliver flowers, but it was understood when gigs came up we played the gigs.

When you recorded the second album and at that point the stakes are raised. Then you guys go to record at Johnny Sandlin's. He's an integral player in music history.

TN: Yeah, all of a sudden we were recording a lot in Decatur, Alabama, where Johnny Sandlin has a home studio, but we were also going to

Nashville to record in these brand new fucking state of the art studios. Gibson bringing these ten thousand dollar guitars by. Get your picture in *Spin Magazine* and all that shit. So, yeah, we're getting a little taste of it. Yeah, we wrote *Everyday* in Muscle Shoals. We had a shit load of songs written between our first album and second. The self titled one we called *Mom's Kitchen*. It was over two years between *Space Wrangler* and *Mom's Kitchen* so we had tons and tons of fucking songs. But Johnny was great—like you said—all the history. I remember sitting in the studio on the couch playing the same guitar Scott Boyer played on "Midnight Rider" for Gregg Allman's solo record. Stuff like that was so cool. I learned so much from Johnny Sandlin—I really did. It was a great experience working with him. We did the *Everyday* record with him over at Muscle Shoals. We were surrounded by the Muscle Shoals rhythm section at the time. You know Hood, Beckett, Johnson, Roger Hawkins. Hawkins was there most of the time. He used to call us the 'transition magicians'. I always like that compliment from him.

We made *Everyday* in late fall and we worked through Thanksgiving. I remember I was the last one to leave because I was the closest to home on Christmas Eve when we were mixing that. Capricorn put us in the studio earlier in the year and we weren't ready yet—they also sent the trucks to do some recording. We started getting big-time tools that are provided when they start spending the money. The cool thing about *Everyday* was when we were still playing clubs I would see that album you know how engineers use a CD if they know what it sounds like to tune the system up. I used to see that record there a lot which made me know that sonically it was a really good fucking album. That was JoJo's first record too. So, we were talking about Beanland coming to a crossroads in their career and we didn't want to break up a band but JoJo had been following us around—he was stalking us. He know exactly what was going on—he knew who the next keyboard player was going to be… and once we knew that we weren't destroying a band's future, we asked him to come with us. He's on *Everyday* which was another great thing that happened too was we had the GEEK sessions there. Y'know—that's when Danny and Eric came over to Johnny Sandlin's.

Johnny had this work ethic that he worked 18 hours a day until it made him sick. Then he'd have to rest for a couple of days. It was Danny, Eric, me, JoJo, Sunny, and Roger Hawkins—we all stayed at Muscle Shoals. We spent a whole day recording together.

Ain't Life Grand **was an interesting time during the underground downtown scene in Athens that was in full bloom during that period. I remember John Boy (Donley) singing "Airplane" in the Uptown.**

TN: Yeah, he always loved the pop songs. He definitely loved "Airplane".

Go back and talk about meeting Billy Bob Thornton. His film of Panic–Live at the *Georgia Theatre* was his directorial debut.

TN: Well, Phil Walden made that connection. Phil was managing Billy Bob…

And Jim Varney…

TN: Yeah Jim Varney was the reason Capricorn was resurrected because he was so successful. When Phil sold his contract to Disney that gave him the resources to start Capricorn up. Phil Walden introduced us to Billy Bob. He came to Athens. It was weird when we met him because he was wearing black boots, black jeans, black shirt, black duster, black hat, and we thought he was a pretty eccentric guy. He'd never directed anything at that point. He went, 'Hey I want to show you this character I've been working on' and he did Karl from *Slingblade*, 'I like french fried taters…' And we were like, 'yeah, whatever man' (collective laughter) He came back after we met and we shot *Live at the Georgia Theatre* and he brought the full production crew and everything. That was our first taste of an A.D… you know what an A.D is?

Absurd Dictator? (laughs)

TN: He's the hired asshole. The assistant director who yells at everybody so the director doesn't have to. That was our first taste of California folks. We did that which was like a performance video live—with interviews and stuff. You can still buy that…

You're still touring really heavy after *Ain't life Grand.*

TN: Yeah, we toured for four seasons. We take the winter off now, but back then we didn't. We toured winter, spring, summer, and fall.

The band stayed on the road.

TN: That's the reason I got married in December because it was the only fucking time I was home. When we would come home we'd go to John Keane's and record. We got to stay home and we were building a nice relationship with John. I remember one time I had a meeting with Rodney Mills and he looked at me. I played him our songs "Pigeons", I was super excited about the whole thing and he looked at me and was like, 'Do you guys want to make hits or what?' and I was like, 'I guess OR WHAT'. I didn't want to be like .38 Special and do the same fucking song every time. We realized early on that we were not going to play the game like everybody else does.

You guys have always operated outside of the industry.

TN: Exactly, I mean how it would be for a radio station to play your song 50 times that week and you come to town and don't play it because you played it last night. We couldn't rely on that method.

To me, it would get boring quick.

TN: James, I'm so spoiled I can't imagine what it would be like to play in a band and go out and play the same songs every night. I'd put a bullet in my brain. We are real fortunate that we get to mix it up but at the same time we're very responsible with that and making sure that it's something that's worthwhile. We do have enough songs. You could play three fucking shows and not repeat anything because you've got enough homers...you don't have one song as the closer you've got five, six, eight...

Or come up with one right on stage.

TN: Exactly. So, we didn't feel like we had to rely on two good songs to play every night.

By this point—I would think there's very little time for reflection.

TN: I never looked back, James, until Mikey passed.

The band is still gradually ascending. Next album—*Bombs and Butterflies*—there was a couple of years between albums.

TN: We'd stay on the road. We'd come home early December—January we'd be home and that's generally when we made the records. For us to make a record it didn't take long. It would take five or six days—a little overdub after that. We don't spend one month on one song. We've never had that luxury. I can't do more than two or three takes because I've got to get two or three songs a day. I'm not being pressured to do that but that is what it's going take to do that. But *Bombs and Butterflies* was a period when we all met our significant others and started having children. So, it went from the boys club to—y'know, the subject matter changes. I think that may have had something to do with it also.

Explain Panic's songwriter mode of operandi.

TN: Basically, well it had to change and that was the one thing. One of the dynamics too that I talked about before was when we all lived together we did everything together. I mean Mikey, if he had money, he would pay me to sit there and just play rhythm guitar with him for hours. Once we all separated from each other we didn't have that anymore so then what we started doing was we would make demos on our own and send them to each other and then fleshed out of that became the songs.

I have to say being behind the scenes at the 40 Watt that day in Athens when 100,000 people fi lled the streets of Athens to see Panic play…that was monumental. Of course Bloodkin and Government Mule played the after show party. That's like a record that many people in the streets for a show. That will be ten years ago this April. It doesn't seem like ten years, really.

TN: Yeah, that was pretty awesome.

I remember being in the back and all the TV cable wires are all over the floor… 20 different TVs—each showing a different view—newscasts—it was a scene. Danny, Eric, and I were just grinning at the screens they had set up inside, wondering how many people were really out there. That turned out to be *Light Fuse Get Away*.

TN: In my mind I was thinking maybe 30 or 40 thousand people I hoped would show up and it turned into exactly what we wanted. We'd get such a great feeling with a big night at the Uptown or the Georgia Theatre where you know everybody working as bartenders would be able to pay their bills. And all our friends are poor-ass bleeding heart social workers, artists, nurses, bartenders, and school teachers. You ever notice the occupation of the collection of people hanging around musicians, taking care of them? Just knowing that we could stimulate the businesses in town was our goal. We definitely had to fight off a lot of nay-sayers to do that, but as soon as we finished it all the naysayers come to us and say—'you want to do it again next year?' We had the mayor Gwen O'Looney, the president of SunTrust bank and the lady who owns Chick Piano—they were the three who really got behind us—everybody else…

Just waiting for the wreck to happen.

TN: Yeah, just so they could say I told you so. We just came back from our first overseas trip. We'd been over to Australia, New Zealand, and Europe. We'd only been home a matter of weeks for that big show. That was a big year for us. I remember being in fucking Australia laying on a road case after sound check listening to Bloodkin songs with a big tear in my eye thinking, 'I'm as far away from home that I could possibly be on the planet right now.' That was a very profound moment for me.

Til' The Medicine Takes **was a fine release. The last time I interviewed you was when the live record with the Dirty Dozen Brass Band,** *Another Joyous Occasion* **came out. I remember you telling me to tell Danny the next time I saw him to tell him that you got to meet Bob Dylan… they lined y'all all up.**

TN: You remember Jackie Jasper.

Oh yeah, she spent many nights over at our place.

TN: You know she loves Bob so much. I always promised her if I ever met him I would say 'Jackie says hey' to Bob. We played Alpine Valley. They removed everybody from backstage except us and lined us up—and Bob came down and we all shook hands with him, and I said 'Jackie says hey!'

But *Another Joyous Occasion* **was a solid release. The band sounded like you were from New Orleans.**

TN: *Another Joyous Occasion* was great because they really did turn us into another band. That always happens when we play with them. They liked us and they were into it. We got along real good. It was another step of experience playing with those guys.

It seemed the time right around *Don't Tell the Band* **things got a little crazy.**

TN: Yeah, things were getting nutso-folks. There were a few gut-wrenching days over at the studio. That's where JoJo really came in and really helped the band out by being another force and a songwriter to put in there. And with a keyboard things get a little more educated…or it should at least.

A little more complexity.

TN: Exactly. To me, that's what should happen. When you go from a bunch of knuckleheads strumming three chords to "In-A–Gadda-Da-Vida" to ragtime. JoJo was very deliberate and methodical the way he came into the band. He didn't try to come in and take over. If anything I thought it was kinda slow. We'd pick on him until he stopped referring to the band as you guys and referred to it as us. He was a big component in the album.

Til' The Medicine Takes **and** *Live at The Classic City* **were some sonically amazing recordings.**

TN: Yeah, by that time we became pretty good players, I remember it went from–when we fi rst started playing it was kind of watery. When we started getting our chops together we got tougher—muscular almost to the point where some of our more laid back fans were a little put off by it. About the time we were playing the Cotton Club—cause we could thump the shit out of it and we knew it, so we did. You worked out for a while and all of a sudden you got a gun (laughs) I remember vividly, people saying 'You guys sound so hard and aggressive'. And we were five guys in our mid–twenties, what do you expect?

This is difficult for me to bring up, but Mikey passing away, really. I can't imagine how difficult that was for his family and the band.

TN: Yeah, man. James, it was terrible. It was the saddest fucking thing I've ever had to go through in my life. You and I have both had to bury way more of our friends than we should for our age. Y'know what I'm saying?

But he was really the most laid back, clean living kind of guy.

TN: Yeah, lifestyle had nothing to do with it. You know, and people thought he sat down onstage because he was a junkie. If you can believe that. Now, we don't pay attention. We had his 40th birthday party. We tricked him in January with a surprise birthday party—Danny and Eric, Vic Chesnutt,

Jerry Joseph—all his favorite people. It was a beautiful fucking party: He'd already been diagnosed with pancreatitis. He had some difficulties on the road, but two months after the party he was diagnosed with pancreatic cancer. He passed away on August 10th that summer. So, it was real fast. He tried to do two tours with us between that and he didn't make it through the summer tour. Playing made him happy and being around his family. You can make a decision to tie up any loose ends or look for a miracle. Mikey was a science-minded person—he had a degree in chemistry—he saw the numbers, which were not very encouraging at all for pancreatic cancer. So, he decided to get his affairs in order and try to say goodbye to as many people as possible. Man, it was just the saddest fucking thing I ever went through. We were just stunned because—I swear to God, he died on a day that he knew we could not miss a show. I swear he did that on purpose. It was like 6 or 7 days and we were out in Colorado playing a big show—it was like 'what are you gonna do stay home, and die too?'

He was very adamant about us keep on going—so we did, but the next four years were rough.

It's so weird James, when you're on the road you're always moving away from your problems. Our light guy was murdered in Austin. He was missing when we had to leave town to go to the next shows…buddy, we were struggling. Then you have to take into account the fans out there, and people would come up and talk to me like he and I and Mikey had grown up together or something. Their intentions might have been good but that's fucking insulting. It's like they hear your mom dies and then they come over and talk to you like they're your brother. I did not handle that well at all. That's when I retreated from hanging out downtown. Everybody feels like they need to come up and tell me what they think about it. I don't need that. It was a weird thing that happened to me. It caused me anxiety. It was pure unadulterated sorrow.

We finished up. The year before we took a hiatus—we had two sold out shows at Madison Square Garden, and we said 'Okay, we basically got back on the horse. We've proved we're still able to do it, now let's go home and cry about this shit', which we did for over a year. That was great about that year because we all did side projects. When we came back, we all damn sure appreciated each other more. It's easy to forget how easy it is for me and Dave to play together. All you gotta do is try a little taste of the other side of the fence—and I'll be here waiting for you when I get back. You know, I played the Barbara Cue thing for eight years and made three albums. It was a few years before Mikey passed when that started. Some of the last stuff Mikey ever recorded on when he was sick. I'd take him over to David Barbe's with me and he had songs that he'd written he thought were too country for Panic—kinda like Danny with his solo stuff—and we recorded with Barbara Cue. He had some really cool songs. Danny talked about one song, and I agreed with him called "Bull Run". That was a cool experience because we did it in rehearsals and he tried to play as much as he could. Randall Bramblett and George were both there to fill in. At the dinner break I was telling his wife—I was taking him (Mikey) over to David Barbe's house because we were going to record over there. Some of the last stuff he did was with me and the Barbara Cue guys with David Barbe. I'm really glad that we did that.

When did the band begin to think along the lines of starting their own record company? It seems like a real headache.

TN: It's an overwhelming proposition. The first thing we did independently was *Another Joyous Occasion*, I believe. Then after that we met Sanctuary Records and they were really good to us in the same way that they would give us the money—a quarter of a million bucks—to record your album. I've been John's (Keane) studio before, working with other artists, and he'd be getting fucking emails from people at record companies putting in their two cents worth for the mixes. And it's like is that's the way it is? It's a fucking nightmare. Like I said, that's one thing we never had to deal with—we were on Capitol Records for a short time through Capricorn. They'd lost distributorship. I remember going to New York to the board room at Capitol Records and listening to somebody else tell us what they are going to do for us—or whatever, but our relationship with record companies were—we never took money from them. We were always self-sufficient. We didn't give away anything. You remember that guy that was with Bloodkin—he worked for Capricorn—he was going make them sign a management deal with them which guarantee him a salary per week, plus a percentage of the gigs. Of course, you know, they didn't do it and they weren't on Capricorn. Bands routinely get ripped off like that. I'm not saying we were more savvy but we never fell into those traps.

Time takes another turn on *Ball*.

TN: Yeah *Ball* was a toughie, but it was to find out if we could still do it or not. I never listen to any of these albums. One day I'll sit down and listen to them, but I never go back and listen to our music after I listen to the mixes. I don't even let my wife listen to it when I'm in the house. When I come off the road I make her take it all out of the stereo. You asked if we got reflective and I never took the blinders off until Mikey passed. Then I said 'next chapter'. I'd start looking around in our rehearsal space and seeing all this stuff we accumulated over the years from other bands and shows. But before… it was, 'what's your favorite show? The next one. Let's go.' People say, 'Don't you listen to your own shows?' No.

People don't really understand why you can't hear your own stuff. You play it, so you don't really need to hear it all the time.

TN: You can't enjoy it. Do you enjoy reading your own writing?

No, only years later when I forgot about it can I go back and read it—always in another era away from when it was written. The next story is always waiting to be told. Just like you're next gig…

TN: I can't even tell you what songs are on what albums for the most part.

You play them in a more abstract way than adhering to album sequence, or whatever.

TN: That's what I meant by being responsible for that by being able to have a different show every night we do know them enough. We can take a song I haven't played in years—if I hear it in my head, I don't forget. There's nothing Michael Houser ever played that I'll forget or forgotten. He could play a little ditty for me one time and I'd remember it for the rest of my life. You got to remember, he and I learned how to play music together. He used to give me guitar lessons over the phone. I'd tie the fucking phone to my head with a belt from a bathrobe. I'd sit there and play. I remember he taught me how to play "2112 Overture" by Rush like that. I can still play that motherfucker (laughs). But on *Ball* we didn't know what we were going do. We brought George (McConnell) over but we didn't know if we were going to try different guitarists or what. We got a couple contributions out of him there—it didn't seem to be broke in our minds. It was like JB said two or three years ago at rehearsal—'I couldn't make this band if I tried to get in it now'. I understood, because the thing was there's so much to learn. Like Jimmy Herring, he's such an accomplished and great player but he works so fucking hard. I swear James, he works like a fucking Trojan to learn this material. We don't have to sit around and play the same song five times, which we wouldn't do anyway. You remember when Bloodkin was auditioning drummers.

Oh Lord. People who didn't even own a drum kit showed up.

TN: That's why you have such contempt for the process…teaching someone to play a song you've played half your life. The shit just ain't fun. Also, Jimmy loved Led Zeppelin as much as I did. He grew up digging on the same stuff that we all did and he also wanted to be a contributor in songwriting. He never had the opportunity for it until now. One might think he writes that real music school kind of stuff, like coming up with a harder equation than the last one, but that's not how he writes. He writes melodic beautiful compositions and they feel good. He's not just technical and fancy for the sake of that. I feel like he's found what he's always been looking for.

When I went up to the *One For Woody* show Jimmy told me the story about the first time he played with the Allman Brothers. He said he was up onstage and Allen Woody got two inches from Jimmy's face and said 'Who the hell are you?'

TN: Well, to fill the story in—Dickey (Betts) got arrested that night. See, we were playing with them. So, Jimmy was called downstairs. The next thing you know, Warren is showing him how to play Allman Brothers stuff. That was his introduction to play with those guys.

The way Jimmy told it really embellished Woody's memory.

TN: And Woody could be a very imposing character. That was the night after *The Light Fuse Get Away* show we talked about when Mule played at the 40 Watt. So at that show in Athens, I'm backstage with my parents and Woody tried to pass a joint to my mom. (collective hilarious laughter). I was like, 'I'll take that.'

You had to run interference.

TN: I thought holy shit. I said 'Woody quit passing my mom pot.' I'll never forget that long as I live. But that Athens show—I remember people asking me what it was like playing for that many people and the more people there are the less you see them. I can remember, looking back at my mom and my brother sitting on a cooler—hoping we didn't run out of beer because my brother chastised the shit out of me one of the first times we headlined the Fox Theatre (in Atlanta) we ran out of beer. That was the thing, don't fuck up in front of mom, and don't run out of beer for my brother.

They wouldn't have made it out for a beer run that day.

TN: You got that right. Every beer in that town was gone that night.

Well, *Free Somehow* sounds awesome.

TN: You got it? Cool.

I already wrote the review. You and Dave have developed into a formidable rhythm section.

TN: Well, I appreciate that. We've played together for so long and stuff-we're good like that, but he'll go with me, or I'll set him up for the slam dunk. I'll set him up—he'll knock them down. The band trusts me—not to lead, but drive.

One of my favorite historic Bloodkin shows, was when you played drums with them at the High Hat in September of 96 for the release party, I believe.

TN: Yeah, one of my favorite things I've ever done is *Creeperweed*.

That night at Panic's practice space when they recorded "Mercy Train To Bogart" was classic. Remember I was sitting at the piano because no one was playing it?

TN: You, Guido, and Stigler were the only other people there.

Besides the musicians and the guy who recorded it…

TN: That was part of the Scooge Sessions. We were all playing acoustic instruments. I had a kick, a snare, a high hat. Danny was playing acoustic guitar. Chris was on acoustic bass and Eric was playing a dobro. We were all in doorways in this one room. It was like a hundred degrees. There was a bat flying around, cat shit in the fireplace. We played until we were too fucked up to play. But I love that fucking record.

Talk about how the band hooked up with Terry Manning.

TN: Dave did a record with Jerry Joseph—Stockholm Syndrome—and they recorded their album down there. It's not that we were unhappy with

John Keane—we made album after album there. The main thing we were getting tired of we'd be in town recording and word would get out, and it wasn't as homey-feeling as it used to be. It was probably good that we did take a break from each other because it made us appreciate each other again. But Terry heard something in the sound that he liked and thought he could make it even better. So we went down and it was an interesting relationship because he is one of those producers who is basically used to someone like Beyonce or Josh Duncan who go down there, get in a room and sing the same song and overdub for a month, but at the same time he did Led Zeppelin, Al Green, Tupac, ZZ Top, George Thorogood—I always gave him shit for that—the Talking Heads…his range is unbelievable. I'd written this one song and he goes 'Have you ever heard "Gallows Pole"'? I had to laugh to myself, and I said, 'Yeah, maybe once or twice'. He set the drums up the way he set Bonham's up—down at the end of the hall for a couple songs. He had a mandolin Jimmy Page left there. He had a guitar— it doesn't have documentation—but everyone is pretty much 100% sure that it was one of Robert Johnson's guitars. JB played it—they didn't even tune it–it was in tune with itself. Who knows what key it was in. We just bent the music to go with it. I think that was one of those special songs JB did in one take. We had a couple of them that were really cool moments. That was on *Earth to America*.

Recorded in the same place as *Free Somehow*, right?

TN: Right. The difference between *Earth To America* and *Free Somehow* we were still with Sanctuary Records when we did *Earth To America* so this last album was on our dime. It's pretty fucking expensive in the Bahamas. I mean, just shipping the gear down there. You have to take everything because you just can't run into a music store when you need something. And you can't overnight it through customs and all that stuff. Manning made it work. He found a common ground with everybody in the band. It was a good experience. We had some tense moments but compared to what most bands run into with producers, I have a feeling it was a cake-walk with us.

It'd hate to be in a band where everybody gets thrown out except the lead singer. That happened with the Neville Brothers. Willie Green—playing drums on *Yellow Moon* with that producer, oh shit…what's his name…

Daniel Lanois.

TN: That's right—Daniel Lanois.

He made another record we're both fond of—Willie Nelson's *Teatro*—

TN: Oh, I love *Teatro*. I didn't remember he was involved with that.

Lanois did great stuff with Emmylou. Dylan. Chris Whitley.

TN: I'm so glad Steve Earle quit writing fucking records about how much he hates Bush. Man, you know Jerry Joseph and Chris Whitley used to tour together. I never knew that and Jerry is a very close friend of ours. I love Chris Whitley. He died on my birthday—November 20. Danny's daughter and I have the same birthday. Yeah, I love Chris Whitley. I heard he hit the bottle heavy.

I think towards the end he started to come apart a little bit at his shows. Maybe he knew something was coming. How long did it take to record *Free Somehow* overall?

TN: Everything was done in two weeks. In two weeks we were out of there. We wrote *Free Somehow* in January of 07 and we recorded it in May of 07. We had about 22 songs. We came home, went straight on spring tour, came off spring tour in May, went straight to the Bahamas, recorded that record in two weeks. We came home, went on Summer tour—last year was busy as shit—wasn't home three months last year.

You'll hit the road again in April.

TN: April 1st I think.

What do you think—over all these years in the band—has been the hardest thing to learn?

TN: Well, basically, dealing with people who love what you do who might have a weird idea about things. It bothers me. I hear two things like 'Don't you feel under-appreciated?' I'm like, No, because drummers might not talk about me being the greatest drummer, but guitar players will. Y'know, Luther Dickinson came up to me and he was like 'Man, I just love your groove'. I either hear that or I was God and could do no wrong. Sometimes they give you too much credit and instead of saying thank you, I try to explain, 'You don't understand.' The hardest thing for me to learn was just take the compliment.

After a while you just take the insults and the praise with a grain of salt. You don't believe too much of either.

TN: Exactly. It's so weird. That's why I always love talking to you…when you write, you describe something. I've never heard you say, 'This band sounds like this group or that group. You write the story. I could never try to write like you. You're an artist.

Well, thanks. Coming from you, that's a high compliment. You should hear me play the drums. Some of this latest record ranks as some of the band's fi nest songs. The song "Free Somehow"–"Three Candles".

TN: Oh, that's so cool you say that.

"Up All Night" is a fine one. Ol' Jimmy Herring—he fits in really well. And he's coming in during a re-awakening of the band.

TN: Yeah, someone wrote that now is our kind of regeneration thing. Which is kind of fitting, with Mikey passing we were just trying to…

Maintain…hell, you've got a huge family to support.

TN: See, that's another thing too James. If I fuck up—I've got a condo out in Colorado when I go, I'm not going to ski because if I blow my knee out and can't play, I've got people depending on me. And it's not the ones that chose to be—it's their children.

You feel obligated.

TN: Not only that, but I'm going to make sure that they are going to have a good life if I have anything to do with it. They're going to be able to get the shoes or whatever. They're going to be taken care of.

Looking back—there have been so many—but what have been some of the high points—the low ones are obvious. I mean, meeting Bob Dylan is one.

TN: Yeah, that was a big one. For me, meeting Richie Hayward from Little Feat. I was scared to talk to him because I thought he might be an asshole. Mikey met him and talked to him and brought him over to me—so hanging out with him was cool. Playing with Carlos Santana. Playing with Steve Winwood. Jorma Kaukonen. Playing with Winwood was a big moment for me, I loved that. Other little things too y'know. The fact that we all still ride the same bus together. On days off we still hang out with each other—not as much as we used to, but we're still the same as it used to be.

Panic usually doesn't need opening bands.

TN: When you lease out the arena it's for so many hours and our show could possibly run for three and a half hours easily. So, the window of opportunity is usually the reason to have others out, and another reason is our fans aren't interested in seeing anyone else. It used to break our hearts to play with somebody—War is playing with us and the kids are like 'They're playing a Panic song!' We may have openers for a few shows here and there, but I don't know who it might be.

Well, at least you still have a good six weeks off.

TN: Let's see, we'll get together about a week before April. So, yeah, I got about six weeks.

What are you listening to these days?

TN: Pretty much the same old shit. I listen to alot of Athens bands. A lot of Vic Chesnutt. A lot of Bloodkin. A lot of Drive By Truckers. I like a band called Spoon. There's a band called Built to Spill I kinda like. You might want to check them out.

I did an interview with David Barbe a few weeks ago.

TN: Yeah, I read that actually.

Hell, I'm interviewing Jim Dickinson on Saturday.

TN: All right, man. That's big time. That should no doubt be an interesting read. Y'know old Luther's in The Black Crowes now.

Yeah, that's who put me in touch with Jim. I remember the first time I saw Luther and Cody was in 1990. They were playing as Jim Dickinson and The Hardly Can Playboys in Memphis.

TN: Luther and Cody are unbelievable musicians.

It should be interesting with Luther in The Black Crowes.

TN: He's got the temperament for it. He's a pretty laid back guy. I guess if you don't get involved in the arguments between the Robinson brothers he'll be ok.

Yeah, I can't picture Panic fist fighting during sound check or allowing the dirty laundry to fall out.

TN: Exactly. We don't air our dirty laundry in front of people. Y'know, now we've gone back and had some frank discussions and stuff like that but if

I'm mad at Dave, I'm not going to say something derogatory about him in front of fans or anything like that.

Talk about the Compass Pointe Horns who played on *Free Somehow*.

TN: Yeah, I think it's pretty much the same guys who played on *Earth To America*. I got to meet them once. We were there for two weeks and then we were on tour so pretty much the rest of the record Terry was responsible for and he would send us what he'd done, and we tell him what we liked and what we didn't. Jimmy Herring was like, 'What band at this level records and overdubs their record in two weeks.'

In the Bahamas (laughs).

TN: I've never even been to Nassau. I've been there four times and I've never even seen the town on that island.

It's not like you're in Atlanta or Nashville where you can get in the car and drive home—that's moving the whole operation.

TN: It really is–you got to get together a month or so before you go and really put together a list of what you need down there. You have to be self–sufficient. Like I said, if I don't have the right size drum head I can't send someone down to the local music store because you're in a third world country. The studio experience—it doesn't matter where they are—it's the same thing because you're always and basically inside the studio or on the way back to where you're gonna sleep. Everybody's like "Oh, tough life—recording in the Bahamas.' I never even stepped foot in the ocean (laughs) I got to go fishing one day though. We got to work, if we didn't we'd feel guilty. Like I said this last album was on our dime, so we were trying to be efficient as we could. Poor Sam (manager) was about to have a heart attack.

It has to make you feel good to know you've become a pillar in Athens' music community, right?

TN: The thing you gotta remember too—back in the day, you didn't have money for food, but you could get a free meal at The Taco Stand one day, or somebody would feed us over at Steve-a-reno's one day.

You've told me once before, in the early days, John Boy (Donley) supported the band in certain ways. I'm sure there was a network of people who assisted the band.

TN: People we knew downtown they gave a lot for us, but not the scene—the scene really overlooked us for a while. It was a show we did in 2000 when people bragged on us—that's an Athens band, which was weird—it doesn't bother me. One of the reasons was because we were never there anymore. We were always out on the road. We never felt like an Athens band for a few years, but that all changed too. A lot of people put a lot of effort into helping us out to get where we are and we don't forget that. A lot of bands just leave those people by the wayside. I know a couple of bands that have actually done that to the point where we've even hired some of those people they cast out. It just seems easier to be loyal.

Every so often we'll have to keep these dialogues going.

TN: You know, usually, Ellie may have told you this, but basically if I talk to a so-called music journalist for more than 20 minutes it's a rare thing. They don't do their homework. They don't know anything about the band. They ask stupid questions. It's rare to talk to someone like you who can actually write.

Hey, do you still have that beautiful hollow-body Gibson guitar? I remember one time, over at your house you had it out.

TN: Oh yeah—still got it.

I've got some great photos of you I've taken through the years. Some are from the New Year's show in Macon with you and John Boy.

TN: Holy shit. See, that's another angle you have on the band. You watched the development of it all. One thing I wish could happen, big time, is you could write a really definitive article about the band. You could talk to everyone in the band…you've got the angle and the ability.

It's interesting, because the older I get the more significance those early accomplishments, friendships, and connections of the past hold. Panic, no matter what people say, play the game by their own rules.

TN: We all stay involved with people who believed in us like the Michael Rothschilds… even the Phil Waldens. When we talk to people we see if they believe in this thing and make it want to happen. One of the things that turns this band up better than anything, we were in the Bahamas making the record and our management said you guys want to make a big deal out of your twenty year anniversary? And we said, 'No, let's wait until 25 years.' For a band to even consider that fact—most bands can't make five years, much less 25. We try to fi nd like-minded people, unfortunately there aren't many.

They are few and far between.

TN: They really are.

Having graduated from The University of Georgia, living with Bloodkin all those years and all the folks I've known, it's a pretty compelling story that all fits together. Even back then, Danny, Eric, and I went through some incredibly funny times, sad losses, weird shit and everlasting collaborations—and beyond that, it's like family because you realize how fragile it all is.

TN: I know Danny would never admit to it, but he's had to feel frustrated when kids ask him to play that Panic song that he fucking wrote. He's gotta feel a little of that why not me kind of thing, but at the same time you gotta be relentless about the whole thing. People always used to fucking ask me what is it with Bloodkin? I'm like, what do you want me to tell you? They write music, they love music, they love to play it, but maybe they didn't fall in with the right outside people. I'm not sure, but the thing about Panic, we're pretty tenacious as far as doing what we do. People ask, 'Did you ever plan this?' We just wanted to be able to play music and not…

Work a job…

TN: …not work a fucking day job… it's that simple.

It's harder to do than people think.

TN: They have no idea. I love my parents because they've seen the whole process from the days when we slept on the floor to now and what it's all come to. My parents knew it made me happy—they're proud as shit of me and the whole thing. All our parents are now, but it didn't start out that way….not at all.

I guess every parent fears their child selling their soul for Rock and Roll.

TN: Yeah, because you might have a better chance getting hit by lightning twice than you do making a career out of being a musician with a band. You can still be a musician, but to be able to live a nice life and be able to staff so many people that derive a living from what you do is rare. It takes a lot of stick–to-it-ness, a lot of fuck everybody else.

Consummate professionals I'd say. We should cook something up in the spring and streamline a story.

TN: You just call me. I'd really love to have a relationship between the band and you where you could speak for us. The other guys would be convinced of that. You could write a great history of Widespread Panic—maybe I shouldn't say that, but we went through a lot of shit together James.

Well, let's strike up the band.

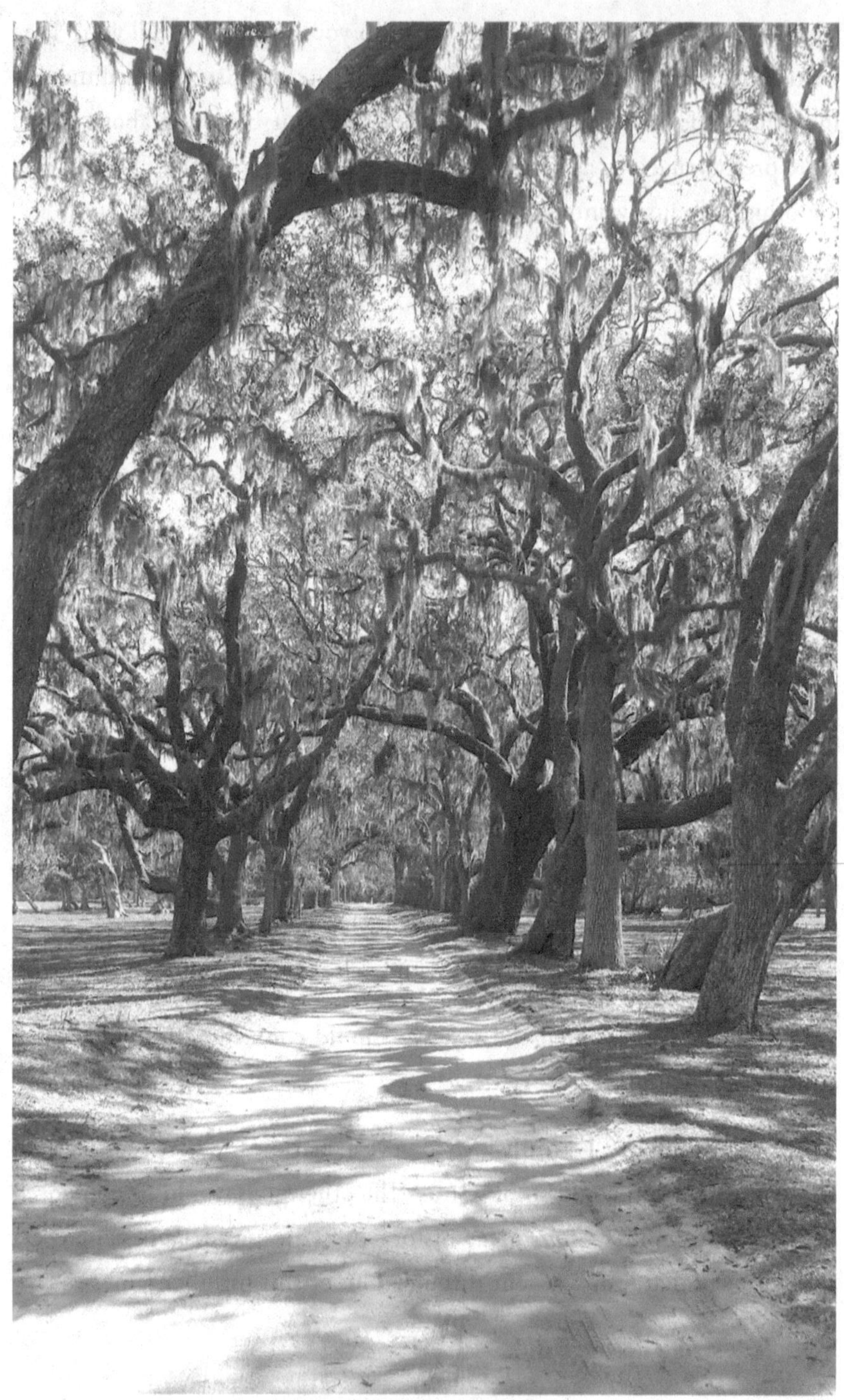

Cumberland Island

Barney Hoskyns' Biography
The Lowside of The Road:
A Life of Tom Waits

> *"Take an eye for an eye*
> *Tooth for a tooth*
> *Just like it says in the Bible*
> *Never leave a trace or forget a face*
> *Of any man at the table*
> *Any man at the table*
> *When the moon is a cold chiseled dagger*
> *Sharp enough to draw blood from a stone*
> *He rides through your dreams on a coach*
> *and horses and fence posts*
> *In the moonlight look like bones.*
>
> —Tom Waits "Black Wings"

BARNEY HOSKYNS' NEW TOM Waits biography—*Lowside of the Road*—was not an easy book to write. Waits, known for his privacy, conveyed to certain musician friends he requested they'd decline to go on the record for the book, making things difficult for the biographer. Nonetheless, Hoskyns wrote a fine portrait on one of America's finest songwriters.

In the book's prologue, Hoskyns writes about his dilemma: "At various points during my two years of researching Waits' life and work I had to stop and ask myself, 'Do I actually have the right to write a book about Tom Waits?' It's tough not to personalize the rebuffs, not just from the Waits camp but from certain acquaintances and collaborators. Tough, too, not to see their polite requests that such people not consort with me as covert censorship."

Hoskyns, a seasoned literary professional, has written for publications such as *MOJO, Melody Maker, New Musical Express, The Times, The Guardian, The Independent, The Observer, Arena, Harper's Bazaar, Interview, Spin, Rolling Stone* and co-founded the music site *Rock's Back Pages*. Hoskyns' other books include *Across the Great Divide: the Band and America, Say It One Time For The Brokenhearted, Hotel California: Singer-Songwriters* and *Cocaine Cowboys* in the *LA Canyons, Glam!, Beneath the Diamond Sky: Haight Ashbury 1965-1970* and *Waiting For the Sun: A Rock and Roll History of Los Angeles.*

Lowside of the Road traces Waits' childhood in San Diego, his parents' split, his fascination with music and the Beat Writers up through his early recordings and performances, relocation to Northern California, encounters, deals in the business and through Waits' latest tour behind *Orphans*. Hoskyns does manage to speak with Bones Howe who recorded Waits' earliest album and various other associates that had nothing to lose by telling the truth. He also interviewed Waits twice. Hoskyns covers Waits' career in movies—like *Ironweed, Shortcuts, Down By Law, Candy Mountain, Night On Earth* and *Dracula*, and how each era of his life was funneled into his music.

The book highlights Waits meeting his wife—at Francis Ford Coppola's Zoetrope studios—Kathleen Brennan, which marks a distinct change in direction and method to his music making. Hoskyns chronicles Waits' albums and professional maneuvers through the years with honest fact. Email including even Keith Richards backing out of an interview with Hoskyns, which may indicate Waits asked the Rolling Stone to not say a word. Here's an email exchange Hoskyns included in the book between he and Keith Richards' personal manager Jane Rose to indicate how the process transpired for Hoskyns.

"Thu, Feb 8, 2007, Dear Barney, Keith has asked me to check with Tom to confirm that this is authorized before doing any interview. Will get back to you once I speak to Tom or his representative." Later that day, Hoskyns received this electronic mail: "Dear Barney, Keith will not be able to do the interview. Another time, another situation. Kind Regards."

Richards played on various songs on *Rain Dogs* and *Bone Machine*, and indicates Waits' talent even interested one of the greatest rock and roll legends of all time, Keef.

Other close associates of Waits who refused to be interviewed for the book in included Jim Jarmusch, Prairie Sun Studio Founder Mark Rennick, musicians Smokey Hormel, Greg Cohen, Matt Brubeck, and Waits' old flame, Rickie Lee Jones. *Lowside* also contains rare photographs of Waits at different times throughout his prestigious career.

Hoskyns presents Waits' influences such as Dylan, Ray Charles, Son House, Charley Patton, Howlin Wolf, Sinatra, Kerouac, Bukowski and Waits' dislikes such as the California Laurel Canyon scene with his label-mates the Eagles.

Hoskyns does an excellent job of dissecting each Waits album by connecting musical lineages and influences to particular songs or eras. Also, Hoskyns does a fine job of presenting Waits' business deals, dilemmas and choices without judgement or scandalous innuendo. Even Waits' lawsuit against Frito Lay for using his style is elaborated on in the book.

Lowside also investigates Waits quitting drinking and how it influenced his work, which most might say it contributed to his prolific songwriting. Hoskyns writes of Waits collaborations with William Burroughs, Robert Wilson, Francis Ford Coppola, Jim Jarmusch and even Keith Richards in an indepth way. Hoskyns, despite all the resistance to Waits camp, has managed to portray and prove Waits as one of America's great songwriters.

Hoskyns does a fine job of documenting all of Waits' albums, especially *Swaordfishtrombones, Rain Dogs, Bone Machine, Black Rider, Mule Variations, Alice, Blood Money, Real Gone* and his latest work and tour from the *Orphans* CD. Hoskyns interviewed Waits on several occasions, and even Hoskyns admitted Waits could be quite evasive. Hoskyns also elaborates on other accomplished songwriters such as Rod Stewart, Bob Seger, The

Blind Boys of Alabama and Bruce Springsteen as well as many others covering Waits' songs. In this Interview Hoskyns provides insight to his journey about writing this interesting book about the reclusive Waits.

James Calemine: How did with you grapple with "Do I have a Right to write a book about Tom Waits?"

Barney Hoskyns: You resort to the old clichés about "public figures", for example, anyone's life is fair game if they stick their head above the parapet of fame. After I finished the book I thought of another tack: asking Tom Waits if he himself had ever read a biography of a living musician. I very much doubt the answer is no.

Most important thing to remember about Tom Waits?

BH: He's a fish in the jailhouse and all heart.

Elaborate and verify why Tom's an artist's artist...a songwriter's/songwriter.

BH: He's an artist's artist in that he's virtually never accommodated or second-guessed his market. He's a songwriter's songwriter in that several great writers have sung his songs.

His movie career augmented his musical persona. Did it help?

BH: I don't know if movies helped his career but they helped him develop new "characters" for his songs. They also, eventually, made him impatient with waiting around in movie trailers – and so got him properly back on track with his music.

Significance of Kathleen Brennan?

BH: Kathleen allegedly saved Waits' life. She also allegedly pushed him outside his comfort zone and helped him jettison his '70s props. It's unlikely there would have been a *Swordfishtrombones* without her. There certainly wouldn't have been a Waits homestead and progeny.

Artists such as Keith Richards admired & collaborated with Tom. Keith's email declining to go on the record indicates Tom's power of persuasion. Yes?

BH: It's possible that even Keith Richards is a little afraid of Tom Waits, whose bite can be worse than his bark. For me, the Waits' overstepped the mark by censoring the likes of Richards, who only wanted to say glowing things about him. I tried not to hold it against them.

Safe to say Waits is a master of controlling his environment?

BH: One spin on the Waits' modus operandi would be say that they are control freaks to a fault.

Most difficult part about writing this book? Waits' stone-walling?

BH: The hardest thing about writing a biography is leaving no stone un-turned. You get paranoid that you might miss the "key" to your subject.

If you could take only one Tom Waits CD on the road with you...what would it be?

BH: Probably *Mule Variations*. Maybe *Foreign Affairs*.

Any feedback from Waits or his people on *Lowside*?

BH: They would never stoop so low.

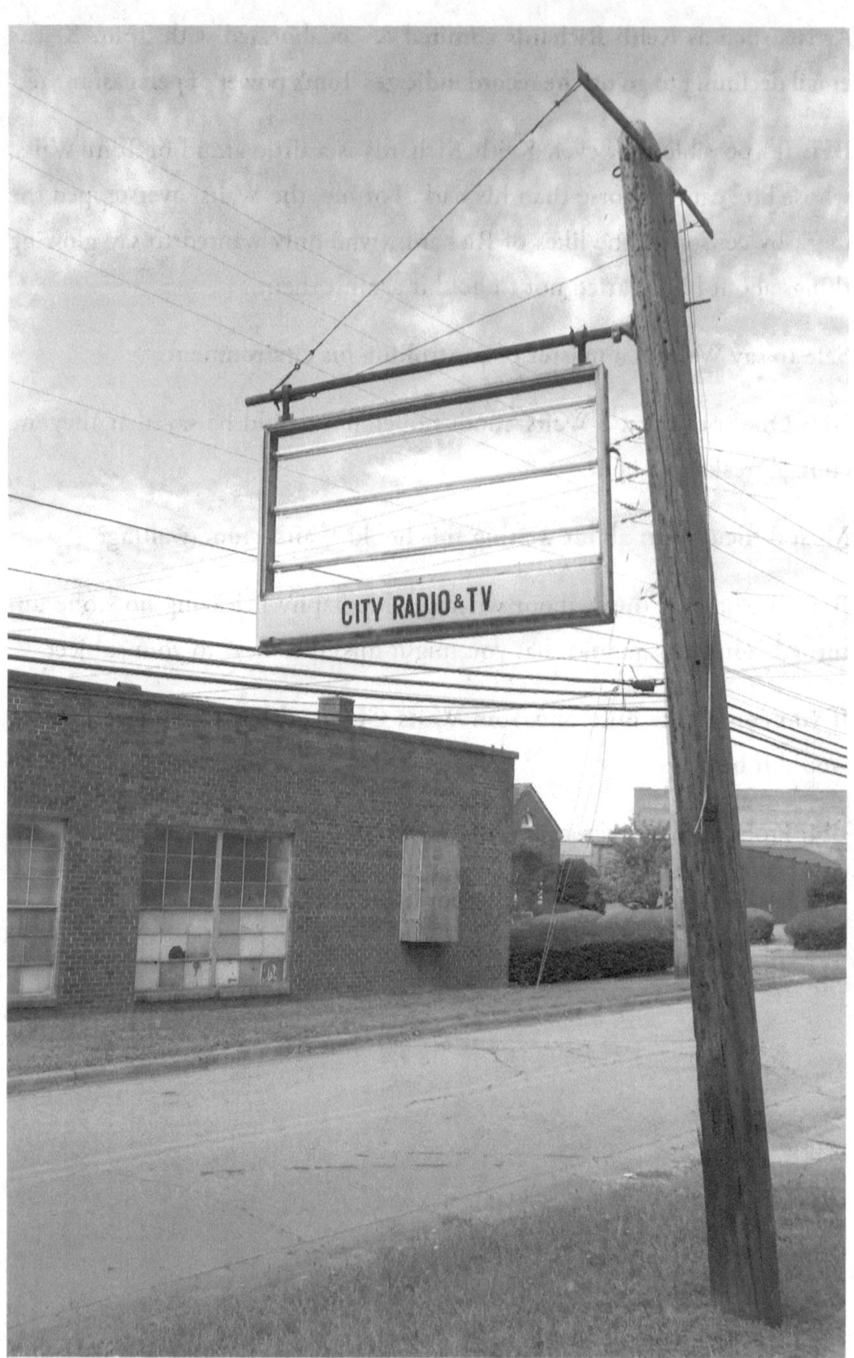

City Radio & TV

Janisse Ray: *Ecology of A Cracker Childhood*

—"Beulahland"

BORN IN 1962, JANISSE Ray grew up in the coastal plains of southern Georgia—near Baxley (Harry Crews' childhood home). Ray's book of poetry, *Naming The Unseen*, won the 1996 Merriam-Frontier Award from the University of Montana where she also earned a creative writing degree.

A naturalist, Ray has written essays and poems in a wide variety of newspapers, magazines and several books. Ray's book *Ecology of A Cracker Childhood* represents a fine example of inimitable southern literature. In Ecology, Ray writes about growing up in a junkyard along U.S. Highway 1, near the Okefenokee Swamp and the Florida stateline. Ray's childhood playground was the parameters of the brutal geography of where her father's junkyard was located.

Her stories about ways of life, hardship and the awesome ecosystem where they lived provides a rare glimpse into a way of life most people nowadays never even hear about. In every chapter Ray writes about facts indigenous to South Georgia, which even includes folklore, biology and comedic strands of storytelling that captures the reader's attention.

Chapters in the book include indelible descriptions of local pine farms, her family tree, black & white photos, her father's junkyard, origin of the term 'Cracker', poverty, poisonous snakes, salamanders, The Altamaha River, music, her mother, recipes, a plethora of birds, religious beliefs, wildflowers, local history and a variety of other unforgettable stories.

It's not a sad, boring or scientific story, but one of the human condition…and love. The way Janisse Ray writes in *Ecology of A Cracker Childhood* makes any native of the land beyond proud.

Soulful Sounds From A Delta Lady:
The Shannon McNally Interview

Shannon McNally recorded with Jim Dickinson on several projects. At the time of this interview, Jim was still alive and she began promoting Coldwater, which Dickinson recorded at his Zebra Ranch studio. I later encouraged her to write a story for Swampland, and she wrote about being a mother on the road. McNally's latest work, Black Irish, was released in 2017 and produced by Rodney Crowell.

BORN IN NEW YORK, Shannon McNally began singing in clubs at an early age. Her hypnotic voice proves unforgettable. Soon she fell in musical company with the likes of John Hiatt, Dr. John, Charlie Sexton and Jim Dickinson. Shannon now lives in Mississippi. With each year, her musical aptitude increases. She's now on the road with her band Hot Sauce, touring behind her newest studio album *Coldwater*.

In this interview we discuss her past, present and future musical on goings. She was in Texas when we conducted this interview last week. I look forward to our ongoing series with the soulful and graceful Shannon McNally.

Shannon McNally: Hey James! How are ya?

Mighty fine. You ready to go? You've worked with a lot of great artists, and I'll name just a few: John Hiatt, Dr. John, and Victoria Williams.

SM: Yeah, that Vic thing was a long time ago. I sang on a John Hiatt record.

You've worked with Charlie Sexton, and once again, he's back in Bob Dylan's band.

SM: I've done quite a bit with Charlie—aside from Dr. John—everyone else you mentioned I've done session work, but I've worked extensively with Charlie.

You sang on Jim Dickinson's *Killers From Space* record. Is that how your relationship with the Dickinsons started?

SM: No, that came afterwards. I had reached out to Jim to do the follow up to Geronimo just after Hurricane Katrina because we ended up in Oxford. Katrina put us there. So, I just sent him a letter to say hello and to see if we could work together in the future. I cut a whole record with Jim that didn't come out. It didn't make it through all the downsizing at EMI. So that was very disappointing of course. Then I did more sessions and various things as well as singing on his record. Last April we went back into Zebra Ranch and cut *Coldwater*.

You also sang on Luther Dickinson's tribute album to Jim *Onward and Upward*.

SM: Yes, the record they did for Jim's passing. Luther and I have written a song together called "If Ever I Loved You". It's going to be available some-time soon probably as a download on my site.

***Coldwater* is your fifth studio record. I know there's a live one and an EP.**

SM: Eight releases—*Coldwater* is my fifth full-length studio release. I had two records—one I did with Jim Dickinson and one with Dr. John—nei-ther one was released. I can't say if the one I did with Jim will see the light of day, but it's hard to say. The one with Dr. John I hope will come out. It was all Bobby Charles songs. It's hard to say, but I think they'll come out eventually. I hope so.

Coldwater was recorded at Zebra Ranch from March 16-April 10, 2009?

SM: Actually, it was a two-day record. We recorded on those two dates. It should have been a comma, not a dash between those two dates (in the liner notes).

It definitely contains the Jim Dickinson Zebra Ranch mojo.

SM: Yes, it does.

How long have you been together with Hot Sauce?

SM: Actually, the band on the record—we've been playing together for about three years. I just thought, 'I gotta get these guys on tape.' I didn't have a record label or anything and I was dealing with a limited budget, but I didn't quite know exactly…I knew I had to get the band recorded at that minute. I didn't really realize I was going to end up releasing it myself. I thought it was going to be a full record. When we were finished it sounded really good and I couldn't see any reason not to release it myself. Although I was daunted by the notion of doing…

You've got a lot of dates coming up.

SM: Yeah, we've got a lot of dates in Texas. We're in Texas now. We just did a week in Texas and we're about to do another week. We'll be in Austin tomorrow night—Tuesday night. And then we go to West Texas. We just did Houston, Dallas and a couple of shows in Austin. We hit the perimeter of SXSW. I did dive in a little to SXSW.

I'm sure you'll want to keep the pushing *Coldwater* for the rest of the year.

SM: Oh yeah. I do want to push it for the rest of the year because it's really kind of picking up steam. Nothing overwhelming, but it's moving along. Honestly, I was daunted at the idea of putting it out myself, but now I feel like I'm getting the hang out it. I'm just rolling with it. I would like to get in and cut another record.

I'm sure you've been writing songs through the process of *Coldwater* being packaged and everything.

SM: For sure. I would love to get in and do another one. Now it's a matter of time. I want to let this one run its course.

I think *Coldwater* is going to make the future easier on you.

SM: I think so. I've been looking at this as kind of…I'm out here in Texas, and we haven't been on the road as a band in a long time. I've been doing all these solo acoustic shows as much out of necessity as artistic vision. I've really liked being able to turn up the volume and I've been playing more lead guitar. I'm just really enjoying being in a band right now.

Anything else on your horizon folks need to know about?

SM: Right now we're just on the road getting back into the rock scene and the clubs—turning up the volume and waiting to see what happens. At this point I've sort of orchestrated what I can orchestrate and from here we'll see if it catches.

We'll always keep you in the rotation here at Swampland. You know I got Jim Dickinson to write a couple of articles for Swampland. I extend that invitation to you if you're willin'.

SM: Well, now that you say that James—I don't know if you have any need or interest for it, but put it in the back of your hat—I do a fair amount of writing and would you be interested in an article about what it's like to be a rock and roll mom? I do all of this with a baby on the road. It's pretty interesting. It's a boy's world out there, but there are some women out there doing it with a baby. I'd be happy to contribute if you think that would appeal to your readers. It adds a whole other dynamic to the road.

Well, I'm ready when you are.

SM: Good deal.

Ann Peebles: *Straight From the Heart*

RELEASED IN 1971, *STRAIGHT FROM THE HEART* counted as Ann Peebles' third album. Produced by Hi Records legend Willie Mitchell, *Straight From The Heart* generated four hits for Peebles.

Born in St. Louis, Missouri, Peebles began singing in the church with her family when she was a child. In 1968, Peebles was discovered by Hi Records' George "Bowlegs" Miller. Soon Peebles began writing and singing tunes for the legendary Memphis label. Peebles later cited her musical influences as Muddy Waters, Sam Cooke, Mahalia Jackson and Aretha Franklin. *Straight From The Heart* features the Hi Records Rhythm Section that included Howard Grimes (drums), Leroy Hodges (bass), Charles Hodges (organ & piano), Teenie Hodges (guitar), Wayne Jackson (trumpet), Andrew Love (tenor), James Mitchell (bass) and Jack Hale (trombone).

The album opens with the funk gem written by Wayne Jackson titled "Slipped, Tripped And Fell In Love". Co-written with her husband Don Bryant "Trouble, Heartaches & Sadness" showcases the golden voice of Ann Peebles. Peebles collaborated with R&B vocalist Denise LaSalle on the sultry "What You Laid On Me".

One of the most moving tracks on this album serves as Peebles' cover of the Bettye Crutcher song "How Strong Is A Woman". The lyric "I heard a woman say she could do anything any man can / But I'm here to tell you that woman who said it didn't have herself a man" drives a stake through the heart of the women's liberation.

"Somebody's On Your Case" revolves around a cheating lover that evokes universal truths. The standard cover "I Feel Like Breaking Up Somebody's Home" charted in the R & B Top 20. The venom of this song resonates on various soulful levels. The original composition, "I've Been There Before", weaves another story of lost love. "I Pity The Fool" sends out a message to a poisonous ex-lover.

"99 Pounds" captures the essence of Ann Peebles. Written by Don Bryant, Peebles sings "99 pounds of natural born goodness/99 pounds of soul" with such conviction you know she's singing about herself. Good things come in small packages, indeed.

"I Take What I Want" closes *Straight From the Heart* with such a soulful sass that just this song pays for the price of the album. *Straight From The Heart* contains musical evidence of why Ann Peebles existed as the original funk soul sister.

Jonathan Wilson Interview:
A Southern Son Out West

In 2017, Wilson toured with Pink Floyd's Roger Waters. On March 2, 2018, Wilson released another new album, titled Rare Birds. This interview transpired around 2007-2008.

> *"Are you satisfied?*
> *Are you occupied?*
> *Do you have enough time*
> *To reflect in your mind?*
> *As your life moves on*
> *Towards some Avalon*
> *Just remember your beauty*
> *Was almost undefined."*

—Jonathan Wilson, "Dreaming"

BORN IN SPINDALE, NORTH Carolina, in 1977, Jonathan Wilson ranks as one of the modern day South's most talented musicians. He can play a plethora of instruments, but these days other musicians seek him out for his emotive six-string talents.

Wilson grew up in a strong Baptist family of musicians. His grandfather was a preacher, and his father was a bandleader, which proves where Wilson's musical inclinations originated. In 1995 he started a band called Muscadine. The band proved a force on the Charlotte music scene. Once the band broke up, Wilson moved to California, Georgia and New York City where he continued recording and writing songs.

Wilson's solo album, *Frankie Ray*, ranks as a classic collection of quiet, indelible compositions. His music contains an inimitable sound that belongs to only him. On *Frankie Ray*, Wilson played every instrument on the record such as guitars, electric bass, acoustic bass, moog, mandolin, banjo, drums, pedal steel, lap steel, baritone uke, mellotron, theremin and percussion. Wilson emerges as a true original. A couple of years ago, The Black Crowes' Chris Robinson and Wilson struck up a friendship that centered on Wednesday night jam sessions at Wilson's house. Robinson and Wilson began playing gigs together and they immediately developed a serious musical brotherhood.

These Wednesday night jam sessions in Laurel Canyon serve as the fulcrum of a blooming music scene in California that operates around the talent of southern musicians. This contemporary music scene mirrors an influence that Gram Parsons, Leon Russell, Gregg Allman, Delaney Bramlett, and Tom Petty pioneered decades before by pollinating California with seeds of southern music.

Wilson's soulful playing found him collaborating with Robinson, Gary Louris, Vetiver, The Grateful Dead's Phil Lesh, Elvis Costello, Jonathan Rice, Jenny Lewis, Susanna Hoffs, and many other talented folks. Wilson prepares to release his next solo album, *Gentle Spirit*, in the coming months with most of the aforementioned musicians making appearances on his new disc. Wilson also plays on Elvis Costello's new record *Momofuku*. In June, Wilson returns to his native south for some upcoming shows, and this writer respectfully suggests readers seek out Wilson's work...

In this interview, Wilson discusses his southern musical up-bringing through the development and progression of his career up to his current plans, which make him a busy man these days. His original musical talents prove even more influential once you discover his down-to-earth-openness. Seek out this talented southern son's work. You've not heard the last of him...

JW: Hey man! What's happening?

Not much. It's raining here in Atlanta.

JW: Yeah? In the Hollywood Hills it's hot. It was a hot one today brother.

When's the last time you've been to your old stomping grounds in North Carolina?

JW: I always go for the holiday vibe. That was probably the last time. I'm about to go back down there on June 1st.

You just got off the road, right?

JW: I was on a little tour I was doing with this band called Vetiver. They're from North Carolina for the most part. They're from Richmond, Chapel Hill—around there.

Talk about the band Vetiver.

JW: Vetiver is simply one of America's best bands, and some of the most vital and timeless music being made. Andy Cabic's understanding and deep knowledge of great songs and dynamic music is astounding, it does not surprise me that he cut his teeth in North Carolina, he has a way of giving himself to a song, every moment in his performance is focused, and it's an inspiration. He is one of a few friends that makes the hair on my arms stand up a few times during his shows, and on record.

It is also par for the course that he is one of the most humble sweet fellas you will ever meet, completely devoid of ego, and is an open antennae into the world of genuine communication and art, and Otto, Sanders and Brent Dunn are some of the grooviest most amazing musicians walking the planet right now, they embody the adage, "You gotta know the rules before you can break the rules". These guys have done their homework, and they know more records than anyone I know, except maybe Chris Robinson! All of that would mean nothing, but they apply and respect all of the influences that are floating out there in the cosmos, and it's in their songs…I hope we do many more shows together and communicate all of this to the listeners that are in need of the real.

You were born in Spindale, North Carolina in 1977, right?

JW: Yeah.

You come from a very musical family.

JW: Yeah, well it was one of those things where I was basically coming into all the stuff you would expect like growing up Baptist in North Carolina. My grandfather was a preacher. So, I was always getting into that type of vibe. When I would go back to my house, my dad's got a band. So when all those dudes would come up to hang out—one of the guys would be gone or couldn't come up—so I would jump around on all the instruments.

You were the utility guy.

JW: Yeah, totally. All the time. I didn't even think about it. You just thought that was what you did. Now when I look back and I was playing with those guys and I realized how good they were. You're from down there—you understand the vibe of how some of those guys can really pick. It really wasn't until I spread out or moved out West and up to NYC, and started seeing all these Yankee vibrations and the West Coasters that I started seeing a lot of young people that really didn't understand any of the old school shit.

You play all sorts of instruments very well.

JW: Yeah, somewhat. That's not my main thing. Most of the time—these days people sort of get me involved with something for my lead guitar stuff. That's sort of turned out to be my thing…which is cool.

You formed the band Muscadine with your old buddy Benji Hughes.

JW: That's right.

Did you gig around North Carolina a good bit? How did things develop?

JW: Well, the band started there. We did lots of shows in Charlotte, which was our hometown. Somehow we got involved with—well, one of the guys there that wrote for the paper there was one of our biggest fans. He also wrote for *Billboard* so he put us in there all the time. That got some shit happening with our gigs. It was a good band. Then we got our own self-produced thing, and we did it for $13,000 and we turned around and sold that for $280,000, which was cool at the time. Those were back in the days when bands would get big deals and shit. That was a huge deal. It was one of those deals that you hear about we got into when we were just young-sters. Being there in that town we were like the only band with that type of thing happening. Of course, we thought we were hot shit (laughs). It kinda turned out to be a good thing that band. We only did one thing for them, and then we put it out a little six song thing. It was good that the band didn't turn into a one-hit band. Then it would be—nowadays—'Oh, you're the guy from Third Eye Blind' or something, which would kind of be a drag. We did that, and we sort of broke that up in 1999.

Then you moved to California.

JW: Yeah, I came out here and I moved to Topanga and lived in the last real hippie shit there—which is gone now. That was some awesome shit. We're talking like 2000-2003, something like that. Then they kicked everybody out. There were 55 homes down in this little enclave—there were sculp-tures, painters—Moms, Dads, kids—everybody's down there. But basically somebody passed by it and said 'They gotta go.' People built their own fucking houses—just tons of shit down there that was just cool. Once that occurred I kinda got soured on the vibe. Then I moved down your way and went in business with this dude in Alpharetta (suburb of Atlanta). That was fun. But he got mixed up with the wrong thing down there and he got murdered, which was pretty fucked up. And that was the end of that. Then I moved to New York City. That was where I started my solo stuff.

I love *Frankie Ray*. That's been one of my favorites for over a year.

JW: Ah, man. Thank you.

I heard about you through Chris Robinson of the Black Crowes. So, I sought out your record. You play every instrument on *Frankie Ray*.

JW: Yeah, that was sort of a concept thing that I had fallen for this stranger. It was a girl I'd seen and thought she was the most spectacular thing I have ever seen. I talked to her two times. I rushed home and cut two tracks. I'd written the fi rst song. If you listen to the whole CD, there's a Beatles song that's like the last thing on there.

Past "Masters In China", past the reprise right?

JW: Yeah, it's past that—it's a bit of a hidden track. I had done those first two songs and I wasn't even thinking about it. I just did those two songs. I wasn't thinking about turning it into a whole fucking album. So then, six months later I was out at this place and there she was. I walked up to her (laughs) and she was like, 'Who the fuck are you?' I was like 'I've got some-thing for you'. She told me her parents were splitting up and she told me this stuff super fast, and that her dad was thinking about her mom. That's why I'd done that song. So I was telling her that, and she didn't understand, she was like 'Okay dude.' So, that was it. Then I was fucked up. I went and wrote tons of songs. There were about ten other songs that didn't even end up on there.

That was just done at a time where I could just spend thousands of hours on a project. That's what it is. I think there's only a certain amount of times especially when families get involved…kids and stuff…so that was done at the right time. That album ended up being I can say there's not one thing on there I wish something was this way or that way.

Frankie Ray got your name out there. You're a good enough player to sit in with all kinds of folks, but you played gigs behind *Frankie Ray*, right?

JW: Yeah, some. I signed up with some people called Koch. Basically, at the time it seemed like the right thing to do because they were going to sign me and give me my own imprint so I could sign 15 bands during the whole thing which would have been from 2006-2009 or something like that. So, at the time nobody was beating down my door. I was like 'Yeah, this seems kind of cool.' So, I signed up with them and it turned out to be that they did what typically people sometimes do with bands was they kept putting it back. They've got all this shit about to happen so they say we'll put this out in the spring of 2009, or whatever.

Then the artist is so far past the timepiece in which he's written in, it's so far gone he's not as enthusiastic about it.

JW: Exactly. That's the worst thing that can happen to someone. I've experienced it. To make your stuff and for it not to be able to come out right on time…Then you start thinking should I get into some other shit or should I just hang out with this sound or what should I do. That was kind of rough man. Finally, they put me off so long—like 15 months or something, that I said, 'No, this is a bad idea.' It came out on iTunes, but that's about it.

Let's see, this copy I have of *Frankie Ray* is on Pretty and Black.

JW: Is that the one with all the artwork?

Yeah, lyrics, the pictures—one of two crows in a tree—picture of the studio.

JW: Yeah, good. That's one that I did. Oh yeah. Ah, I see (Chris) Robinson is calling in now…it's okay. I'll call him back.

Well, speaking of crows in trees, serendipity and Chris Robinson—you guys formed a strong musical bond. How did you meet up with him?

JW: Well, he basically came to town. I guess we met on his birthday—December 20, 2006, and he was playing a show. So we did a show out at this old roadhouse that's in Joshua Tree. Somebody told him you should give this guy a call. He gave me a call and we practiced down the street from here in this fucking awesome spot. I went down there and we got into some songs and it was on from then on. Both of us—like the way we do harmonies and stuff that was our bond. We didn't even have to say anything. We turned into homies right off the bat. He's such an awesome guy. Since I've been friends with him I've just been turned onto stuff. That's been really fun. Then we started doing these things at my house.

Yeah, that was a birthday gig too. That was our birthdays in 2007. Our birthdays are basically the same time. His is December 20. My birthday is December 30. He's a one of a kind guy. It's funny, ten times I've walked down the street or gone in a bank and somebody thinks I'm him. It's not really because we look alike. We do to an extent, but I think it's more of the things we're interested in.

Chris played a big role in Gary Louris' record y'all played on, *Vagabonds*.

JW: Oh yeah. Chris is the one who put the band together for that. It turned out to be a really fun thing. Chris did a second thing with Gary and Marc (Olson).

The Jayhawks.

JW: That album—for me—that's the one. I didn't play on it—that was just those guys. It's so fucking good. I think it comes out sometime in the fall.

That Laurel Canyon scene, to me, seems like the second coming of southern musicians moving out west—pollinating California with a southern seed. Gram Parsons and Leon Russell moved to California. You and Chris represent the second generation of southerners to move out west.

JW: Totally.

Even Adam MacDougall (Black Crowes new keyboardist) played on the Louris' record—he's also part of that Canyon scene.

JW: Adam's insane. That dude is actually the one of us who is a prodigy. That's definitely the vibe. The house that I got here—I bought Leon Russell's mixing board that's here. Those are our dudes. They understand. We understand.

In California country, you even began playing with The Grateful Dead's Phil Lesh.

JW: Yeah, man. That was fun. The thing about Phil—lots, not lots, but people get to go out when Phil's on the road. He always has people helping him, but being in the studio—that's some other shit.

Real music mafia.

JW: (laughs) Yeah. Some people think about it like, 'Oh, that's just some other thing I did. He was cool—but he's not so cool now. Just the way people think.

Sometimes even the most music loving people have really shallow perspectives.

JW: That's right. There's something about Phil in the way that occurred at the right time that was such an inspiration. Just to see the way he came into the studio just fucking all business man. He turned up his amp to about fucking nine, and just went boom! That's why he's Phil. That was fun.

Talk about working with Elvis Costello.

JW: Basically I'm playing and singing on his latest record which came out on April 22. He took us down to do the big opening for the album, which was in Memphis. So we got up with him there—things went so well that he said why don't y'all hop on the bus? So we went and played the next night with him at the Ryman. That was amazing. We played about six songs with the band. I just talked with him this afternoon and he's going to be in town and he's doing a big show here on May the 25th. That should be an awesome show. Elvis is the same type of deal. He's just an inspiration. He's the same way—he's balls out man. He sings his fucking ass off onstage.

You play a lot with Jonathan Rice. How'd you meet him?

JW: Well, I met him here in L.A. through his girlfriend who is in that band Rilo Kiley. It was the same type of deal—they called me and I came in and played with all them in the studio. It turned into some other stuff too.

Tell me about your new album you just recorded.

JW: I'm talking to some labels now. There's been some I thought where it was going to happen, but it didn't—that's okay. I want to do it with these people Vanguard because they've done tons of awesome shit. That may happen, but the album is called *Gentle Spirit* with 16 tracks.

Who plays on it?

JW: It's got most of everybody—Chris Robinson, Adam MacDougall, Gary Louris—he sings a little bit—and some old school guys like Barry Goldberg.

That's a link between the past and the future; he's played with Bob Dylan, Duane Allman, and Eddie Hinton.

JW: He's played with everybody. He lives down the street from here. Through the things I've been doing here on Wednesday nights has been totally off the hook, and that just begins to spread. We've been doing it about 2 times every six weeks. For a while there was one every week at the house here. We've had tons of folks here. That's what really opened things up here in town.

I plan on writing an article about southern music infiltrating the California music scene. You're really the nucleus of that scene now.

JW: Yeah.

Discuss your approach to songwriting and sonic qualities you employ.

JW: The songwriting process to me is usually akin to painting, or visualizing to fruition, and nothing is more gratifying than starting with something and seeing it through the recording process and mixing, every step is shaping the fi nal tune. So I leave parts of a song purposely unfinished to insure an element of chance in the process. Most all of my songs start on an acoustic guitar or piano, I have yet to be able to compose or record riff based tunes, or studio wizardry that cannot be stripped down and played on my porch.

I pull many sonic ideas and guitar sounds and moods from Psych bands I love, The Apryl Fool, JK and Co., Mcphee, the list goes on, but I still find myself writing a song first, and composing interludes and free sections later, while recording. My song-writing influences are vast, but lately JJ Cale, John Prine, Gary Higgins, Andy Cabic, Skip Spence, Canned Heat, and of course Lennon and Neil Young, these songwriters do it for me.

Lennon and Neil Young always have since I was a boy, and as much as one would like to pick and choose who truly influences you by citing esoteric rare elite musicians, I feel who you are influenced by and who you want to be infl uenced by are usually 2 different entities. Some people are intrinsically influenced by the likes of the Pet Shop Boys, whether they like it or not. I have the advantage (or Curse) of being able to lay down all of the instruments myself in the studio, which while it is hard work to preplan parts and sections that a band would organically do and each man would split the load, it does offer great satisfaction when you see a song reach fruition, alone, with your vision being committed to tape one building block at a time, it's a grand process, and fulfilling, although the technical aspects and setups, engineering stuff is getting to be a drag the older I get. I'm on the hunt for the perfect engineer who I can be one hundred percent creative around, but then again just having a presence in the room changes the level of concentration that I can achieve in solitude, so I may be stuck with myself forever.

Frankie Ray was done alone, however *Gentle Spirit* is the first recording I've done with a band helping and many guest musicians, and that was a joy also. As long as I can have plenty of alone time to place parts, experiment and sonically comb, I'm cool.

All of this is leading up to a live record we make in two days days I guess!

Your site, The Songs of Jonathan Wilson contains some of your photos.

JW: Oh yeah. Nothing's been done on that thing for a long ass time. You know what I've been thinking about doing? I've got so many besides I've done in all these other studios. I'm thinking about putting some songs up on there just so everyone can have it.

Some of the other songs mixed with the *Frankie Ray* songs on your MySpace page are great.

JW: Yeah, that's some different stuff. I think there's some current material on there—one song is on the upcoming disc.

I'd like to get you to contribute to *Swampland*—put up some of your photos and have you write something. Jim Dickinson recently contributed.

JW: Yeah, that would be cool. I'll tell Chris I was on the phone with you today, and you're the dude. You know, I read your Mudcrutch thing and I was just at their gig the other night. That was a good show. Far out. I want you to send me your address so when I get the album done—I'll send you a copy. You know, I really like Jim Lauderdale.

His new record *Honey Songs* is great. So, let's do this again before too long. I'll be in touch when I get this interview worked up…keep you in the rotation.

JW: James just give me a call anytime This all sounds cool.

Thanks for taking the time to talk. I'll be in touch.

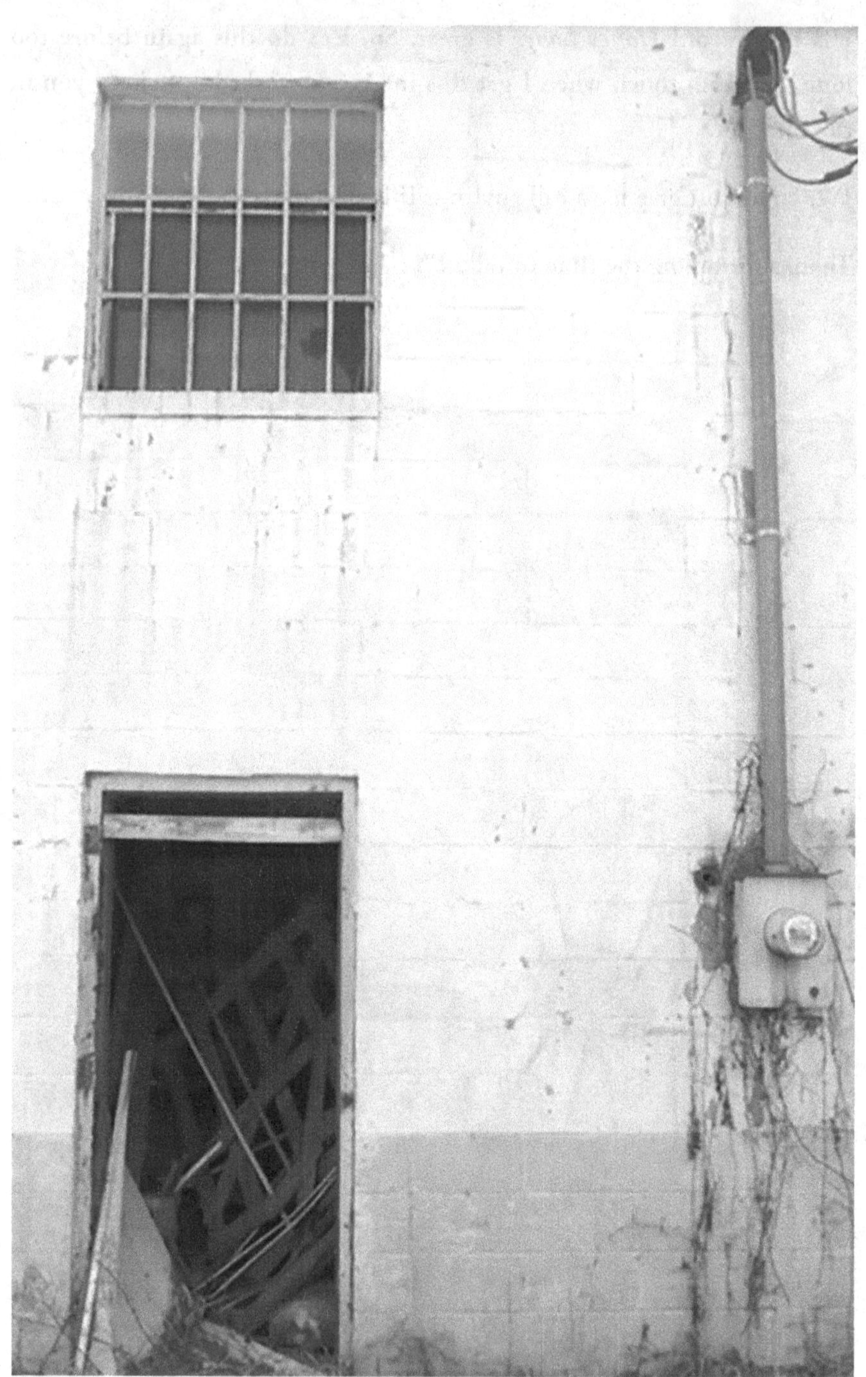

Somewhere In Jackson County

Ken Nordine: *Devout Catalyst*

IN 1991, KEN NORDINE recorded a spoken word album, *Devout Catalyst*, at the Grateful Dead studio—Club Front—in San Francisco. Nordine began his career in the 1940s by recording radio voice-overs and commercials. Later Nordine hosted a program on NPR as well as various other sonic endeavors. In 1958, Dot Records released Nordine's first influential "Word Jazz" album. Ken Nordine is a world to be explored. He's still out there performing his word jazz at 97.

Jerry Garcia and Tom Waits recorded with Nordine on *Devout Catalyst*. Garcia, David Grisman, Howard Levy, Jim Kerwin and Joe Craven served as the musicians on this timeless collection. Official Grateful Dead biographer Dennis McNally wrote that *Devout Catalyst* contained "No-retakes, no touchups—voice meets fingers, word meets jazz." Nordine still exists as one of America's most influential voices.

In a 1992 interview, Jerry Garcia said this about Nordine's influence: "You gotta go back to 17-year-old me growing up in the bay area. When I heard Ken's first Word Jazz albums, it was like a religious experience. It was not only a completely different way of thinking, but a fantastic combination of words and music...it wasn't songs. It wasn't poetry or songs exactly—it was a wonderfully peculiar kind of thing you thought only you think about. A lot of these things were formative and brought a significant sense of where my own aesthetics came from in those recordings..."

"*Devout Catalyst* commences with "I Love A Groove". Nordine explained this track in the liner notes as "...is grooving what comes naturally when the groove begins to happen inside your metabolic rate, anybody does it." "Mr. Slick" begins with the lines: "Mr. Slick is smooth as a snake sliding through a bellyache", as Garcia and Grisman weave serpentine notes that leave strange patterns in the sand. Who else better to play on an improvisation album than Jerry Garcia?

Nordine described "Inside Of Is" as: "A half real, half unreal bar called the Bubble where I've spent a lot of liquid, maybe you've been there, it's a place where forgiveness erases the awful things you said or did the night before."

Garcia's acoustic guitar and Grisman's mandolin contribute to the "shaggy doggerel" of "Aging Young Rebel". "Quatrains of Thought" emits an outer space jazz quality to Nordine's clever vocal inflections and delivery. "Spread Eagle" sounds like a story told by a family member on the front porch with two friends playing a subtle acoustic soundtrack in the background.

"A Thousand Bing Bangs" is a dialogue with Tom Waits where they trade verbal choruses as Garcia's signature guitar tone floats around the words. Nordine explains to Waits a screenplay no one wants to make on "The Movie", which turns out to be a humorous conversation colored by Garcia's acoustic meandering. The final number, "Last Will", Nordine reveals "is a non legal document wherein the aforementioned allegedly gives away all his whims and notions."

Devout Catalyst ranks as one of the most essential spoken word albums in the last 30 years...and beyond.

Blind Willie McTell:
Atlanta Twelve String

PERPAPS THE MOST GIFTED of all blues artists, Blind Willie McTell ranks as a seminal figure in American music. Born in Thomson, Georgia, in May of 1898 (some say 1901); McTell's visual handicap befell him at an early age. Well educated, he mastered Braille and often traveled alone while memorizing streets in every city he visited. In his early years, McTell trekked through Georgia developing his own indelible acoustic and 12-string guitar style and brilliant lyricism that transformed him into a timeless songsmith.

Throughout his lifetime, McTell recorded under various pseudonyms. As a black, blind musician in the social climate of America during this time render McTell's achievements even more amazing. He performed for both black and white audiences at county fairs, carnivals, minstrel shows, dances, parties, street corners, auctions, on trains, and in barbecue dens.

His travels led him to New York, New Orleans, Michigan, Florida, California, North Carolina and many other untraceable destinations. McTell recorded 120 songs in 14 separate recording sessions. McTell's deep christian sentiment—as well as his sharp wit—echoes throughout his work. Any of his songs remain worth exploration and committing to memory such as "Statesboro Blues", "Your Southern Can Is Mine", and "Savannah Mama".

McTell's album, *Atlanta Twelve String*, contains some of his greatest songs (and sound quality) like "Broke Down Engine", "Little Delia", "Dyin' Crapshooter's Blues", "You Got To Die", and "Ain't It Grand To Live A Christian". Examination of McTell's lyrics on "Dyin' Crapshooters Blues" proves his command over language and songcraft. "Send poker players to the graveyard / Dig my grave with the ace of spades / I want twelve police in my funeral march / Playing blackjack leading the parade / I want the judge who jailed me fourteen times / Pair of dice in my shoes / Let a deck of cards be my tombstone / I got the dyin' crapshooters blues." Every line commands examination and wonder...

This album captures the rare spirit and pure talent of Blind Willie McTell.

On the Road:
Email Dispatches from Appalachia

Another dispatch to Paste magazine's Travel section.
By James Calemine | February 23, 2016 | 12:45pm

From: James Calemine
To: Paste Travel
Day: Tuesday, 10:48 PM
Subject: From The Coast To The Mountains

We drove six hours from the Georgia's Golden Isles Sea Islands to Asheville, NC. It's a scenic journey—from a barrier island to the Appalachian trail. From swamp and ocean to mountains and valleys as the road rolls along like a cinematic reel of changing landscape. We arrived in Asheville around 7:30 PM.

Heather booked us at Hotel Indigo on Haywood Street. The bliss of the Blue Ridge Mountains unfolded around us. Our room provided a majestic skyline view of Asheville. First stop: Ben's Tune Up, a hip brewery that an eclectic mix of food. We had the butternut squash hummus appetizer. The Firecracker Chicken main came on a bed of rice and vegetables. Heather had the scrumptious black bean burger. We washed it down with zingy lemon-ginger sake. During the continually changing music series, Ben's hosts musicians like Underhill Rose, Savannah Smith and the Gypsy Swingers. On this night, Woody Wood & The Asheville Family Band rendered their gritty, honky-tonk repertory.

Day: Wednesday, 9:38 AM

Subject: Morning in the AVL

The streets of Asheville were empty and quiet this morning. We ate breakfast at the 'farm-to-table' establishment Early Girl Eatery located on Wall Street. Open since 2001, the joint has big floor-to-ceiling windows which spew the bright morning light. I devoured multi-grain pancakes. Heather chose the shrimp and grits. After two cups of strong coffee we left and started to wander. Asheville's architecture and avenues evoke a blend of cul-tures, which is why the town was once dubbed "The Paris of the South."

We visited the great indie bookstore and cafe Malaprops. I picked up a copy of Elmore Leonard's *Cuba Libre*. On the way out of Asheville, we drove by the landmark Basilica of Saint Lawrence that was opened in 1905. I could stay in Asheville for some time. But, we were bound for the great Smoky Mountains on Highway 40.

Day: Wednesday, 1:14 PM

Subject: Into The Great Smoky Mountains

It's a scenic seventy-mile drive from Asheville to the Great Smoky Mountains National Park. The Appalachian highways move through carved mountains and huge walls of stone. Signs line the interstate warning of fall-ing rocks. The colors of the mountains and the bare trees spread across open vistas and clear panoramas. The air smelled different. We drove though the national park and to Gatlinburg, Tennessee. Gatlinburg is like Disney World for adults. But, we felt tired and decided to stay the night at Baymont Inn, located in the heart of town and on the Little Pigeon River.

We ate tacos and drank a couple of beers at Loco Burro, Fresh Mex Cantina. It's hard not to admire the regional beauty sitting on the roof-top bar here ... though there is, admittedly, a loud and rowdy vibe at this joint. It's a cross between a cruise ship and a sports bar. As we sipped our Heinekens, I sifted through the photos I'd snapped of barns, motel signs, old gas stations and local antique stores nestled in this Appalachian heaven.

Day: Thursday, 11:23 PM
Subject: Welcome To Pigeon Forge

We woke and drove a short distance to Pigeon Forge. Dolly Parton created a thriving economy here based on Dollywood. In fact, Dolly is now creating a documentary with Peter Greenberg about Tennessee. Pigeon Forge revolves around a plethora of shops, restaurants, bars and diversions for tourists and many of the establishments nestled in these environs were engineered by the Great Dolly.

We browsed through boot, hat, tobacco and clothing shops. We visited the high-ceiling Smoky Mountain Brewery, where I tried several of the local brews such as Thunder Road Pilsner and Black Bear Ale. Each beer is brewed in East Tennessee. These local beers are concocted without chemical preservatives, additives or pasteurization. Tennessee takes its beer seriously.

Heads blurry and tired of the tourist traffic we checked in at the Arbors at Island Landing Hotel. In the evening, we enjoyed dinner at the Pottery House Cafe and Grille. This restaurant was once the home of founding potter Douglas Ferguson. The original stone floors and fireplace provide a warmth this time of year. There is a pond out back. I ate the Old Mill Grill Chicken Breast. Heather ordered black bean spring rolls. Just the fresh bread at the Pottery House is worth the visit.

Stuffed and exhausted, we slept by the hotel fireplace. The next morning we knew it was time to come down off the mountain … and get back into the grind. I'm already looking forward to my next trip back to Appalachia.

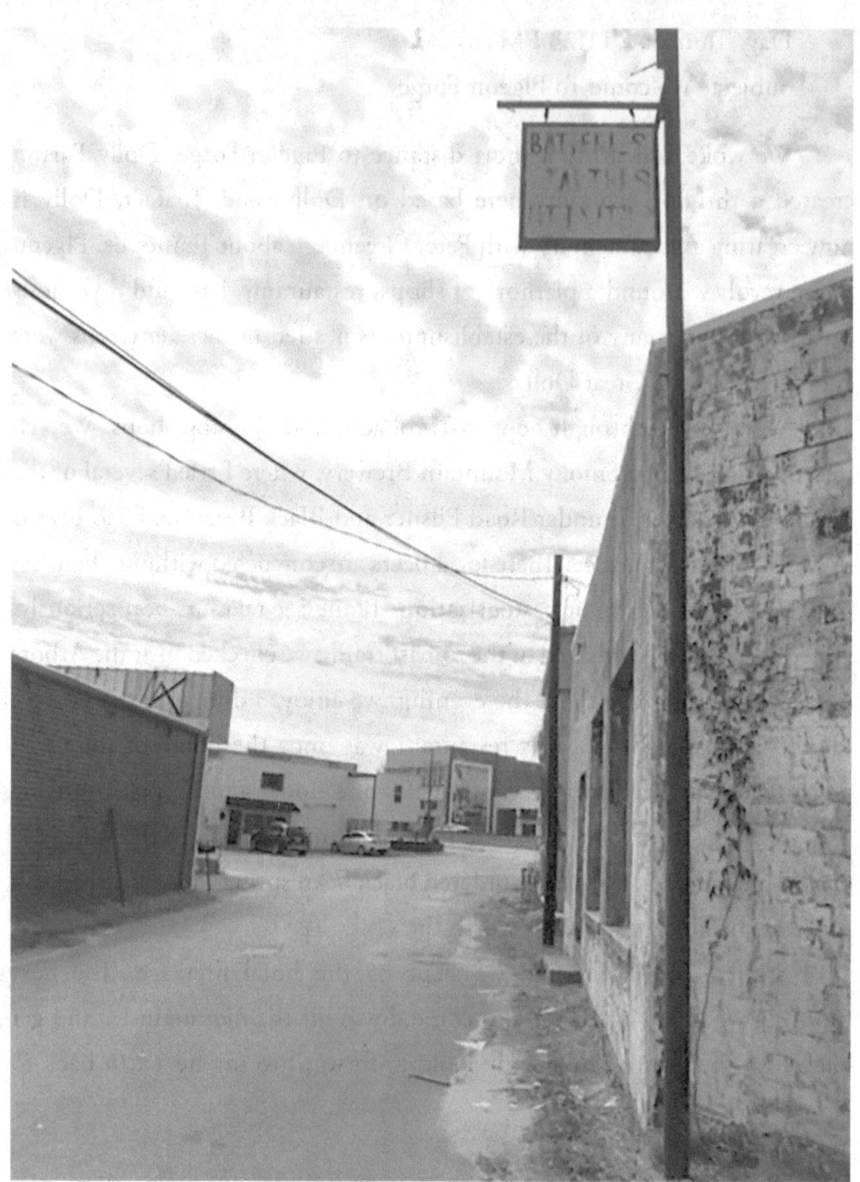

Dark End of the Street

Automatic Y'all:
Weaver D's Guide to the Soul
By: Dexter Weaver

PUBLISHED IN 1999 BY the University of Georgia's Hill Street Press, Dexter Weaver's book *Automatic Y'all* contains stories and recipes revolving around the Athens, Georgia, soul food joint Weaver D's. Weaver grew up in Athens. In *Automatic Y'all* he reveals how cooking became his life, and eventually how his restaurant slogan became the title for one of R.E.M's greatest selling albums.

Each chapter begins with a slogan of Weaver's like, "In the ghetto, your notebook is your treasure chest" or "Greens are good for you, but it's the drippings that make you want to eat em'. Taste life!" Dexter began preaching in 1976, and there are powerful biblical convictions through these pages that resonate with the reader.

Weaver D's eatery has served as a main cultural staple in Athens since 1986. Dexter Weaver's motto, "Automatic For The People", caught the local band R.E.M's eye, and they asked permission to use the title to an album that ended up as a Grammy-nominated album of the same name in 1992. Warner Brothers shipped Weaver D's special peanuts all over the world for promotion of the album.

The soul food guru outlines his religious upbringing and humble intentions along with advice and insight on what it takes to make people coming back to his place. He's a great guy, always has been. When I attended The University of Georgia, I sometimes ate there every day of the week.

The book contains rare photographs, culinary insight and over 50 recipes that prove worth the time to inspect and try to replicate in one's own kitchen. His cooking philosophy always ran parallel with his strong spiritual convictions, which seems to explain why his food is so soulful. The chicken has always been out of sight, and his greens are my all-time favorite, but also dishes like sweet potato soufflé, broccoli with cheese, potato salad and fried squash rank as delectable. My old friends Widespread Panic once issued a statement regarding Weaver D's that still resonates: "We've eaten at Weaver D's a lot over the years. It's just good home cooking and you can always count on Weaver to make you happy."

Immortal Blues — In Memoriam:
Chris Whitley 1960-2005

I wrote this the day Chris Whitley died—November 20, 2005. I believe An Honest Tune magazine published it. I remembered sitting in my wood-floored office staring at the computer screen when I heard he passed away of lung cancer. I became a Whitley fan in 1990 when I heard his debut album Living With The Law. His blues-based, soulful songs resonated around his stellar steel playing. He counts as an American bluesman. After watching Whitley perform live, Bob Dylan commented Whitley gave him chills. Whitley's music should be sought out—it's timeless. When he died, I felt like I lost a friend.

> *There's a dirt floor*
> *Underneath here*
> *To receive us*
> *When changes fail*
> *May this shovel*
> *Loose your trouble*
> *Lay them*
> *Far Away*

—"Dirt Floor"

AT 45, CHRIS WHITLEY died of lung cancer on November 20, 2005, in Houston, Texas. Whitley learned of his fatal illness only five weeks before his death. Few contemporary songwriters possessed the rare talent of performing alone onstage with an ability to inspire an audience like Chris Whitley

Born in Houston on August 31, 1960, Whitley moved around a lot as a youth. When he heard Johnny Winter's "Dallas", Whitley became a devout bottleneck slide player. Often armed with his National Steel guitar, Whitley commanded respect from even the most hard boiled guitarist. Quitting school at 17, he played on the streets of New York for years until he moved to Belgium, married, and became a father.

In 1990, Whitley met Daniel Lanois who recorded with Bob Dylan, Willie Nelson, Emmylou Harris, and U2. Lanois scored Whitley a deal with Columbia Records. Lanois' protégé, Malcolm Burn, produced Whitley's classic debut released in 1991, *Living With the Law*. Recorded in Lanois' New Orleans mansion, *Living With the Law* contains Whitley classics such as "Big Sky Country", "Poison Girl", "Dust Radio", and "Phone Call From Leavenworth". The *Thelma & Louise* soundtrack included Whitley's song "Kick the Stones", allowing him to gain national exposure. *Living With the Law* reached #36 on the Heatseekers chart. Later in the year he opened for Tom Petty. Soon Whitley became known as a modern day, cutthroat bluesman.

Four turbulent years later, Whitley released his sophomore CD, *Din of Ecstasy*. This collection aimed for a darker, electric, more spontaneous sound featuring gritty songs like "Guns & Dolls", "Narcotic Prayer", and "New Machine".

In 1997, Whitley released *Terra Incognita*, a CD recorded at the Teatro Theater in Oxnard, California where Daniel Lanois recorded Willie Nelson's landmark *Teatro* album. *Incognita* followed in the musical footsteps of Din's electric sludge, but distinguished a sharper focus. For the *Terra Incognita* tour, Whitley employed a band. Rare live gigs with a group allowed Whitley to loosen up a bit musically which made for unforgettable performances. However, he never stopped performing solo shows.

Whitley's underrated songwriting skills remained the backbone of his talent. His lyrics covered a wide scope of emotion from "psychosexual" to Zen lullabies which proved a serious combination augmented by his guitar prowess. His soulful lyrics fit each riff, like "Three o'clock this morning / I thought I saw Jesus coming down / He came through the concrete baby / He came through the wall without no sound / Now I mean concrete walls that ain't no clay / I closed my eyes and watched him slip away."

In 1998, Whitley released his solo masterpiece, *Dirt Floor*. Recorded during one day in a rural Vermont cabin, Whitley played banjo, guitar, and his trademark foot-stomp on these quiet songs that represent some of his strongest material.

Whitley's first live CD, recorded two nights in Chicago, *Live At Martyrs*, reiterated his sound never strayed from earthy folk, country-blues, and mercurial rock. On this disc, "Home Is Where You Get Across" epitomizes Whitley's talent. The same year, 2000, Whitley recorded a CD of cover songs titled *Perfect Day*. Billy Martin and Chris Wood of Medeski, Martin, and Wood, accompanied Whitley on these sparse tunes. The way Whitley renders Dylan's "Spanish Harlem Incident", Willie Dixon's "Spoonful", and Robert Johnson's "Stones In My Passway" the compositions almost sound like his own.

In 2001, Whitley recorded his next studio effort on ATO Records titled *Rocket House*. He experimented with hip-hop ingredients on this release which procured strong tunes like "To Joy (Revolution of the Innocents)" and the proverbial "Say Goodbye". Whitley operated on some subterranean level during this point in his career, uninterested in following atypical steps in the music business.

Hotel Vast Horizon, Whitley's seventh studio release employed a European sonic atmosphere. Whitley began living in Dresden Germany during this period. Each CD sounded different. He never attempted to duplicate his previous work for commercial appeal.

Whitley's 2004 War *Crime Blues* found him alone with his guitar. This collection proved, once again, Whitley's vocal talent and incandescent bottleneck sound. These songs carry a political overtone, unlike most of Whitley's work.

The same year, *Weed*, an acoustic collection of his old tunes like "Bordertown", "I Forget You Every Day", and "Weightless", hit the streets. This era of Whitley's career exposed his deep roots in American blues.

In early 2005 Whitley's eleventh CD, *Soft Dangerous Shores*, was released. Old friend Malcolm Burn produced this edgy collection of dark, electric songs that evoke a spooky musical landscape. Whitley experienced some problems touring this past summer, which in hindsight now seem apparent from terminal health reasons. Nonetheless, Whitley wrote and recorded another album in 2005 he called *Reiter In* for release in 2006, which will prove an essential chapter in the prolific catalogue of his work.

In October of 2005, Whitley cancelled tour dates without an explanation. A month later he died. Chris Whitley leaves behind a daughter, brother, fiancé, ex-wife, and father.

Great artists take a little piece of you with them when they die. Often through the years I'd play some Chris Whitley on a mean, depressing night looking forward to the next opportunity to see him live. I remember when he toured with a band behind the *Terra Incognita* CD. Before the Atlanta show they ate outside at an Italian restaurant called Pasta de Pulcinella's. Chris sat at the table wearing his finger picks hours before the show—ready to play. Seeing him live always proved amazing.

Now I play his music and it's hard to believe he's gone. Even for those who never knew him, Chris Whitley's death feels like the loss of an old friend.

Marc Ford's *Southern Harmony*

In my humble opinion, Marc Ford contends as one of the world's best guitarists. Yet, he's no one trick pony. He's demonstrated his songwriting skills on each solo release. I became familiar with Ford when he joined The Black Crowes in 1992. Years later, we became good friends. I first met him in 2002, and we kept in touch through the years. We conducted various interviews through the years. This counted as the first interview in 2007 he conducted after quitting The Black Crowes in the fall of 2006. Ford had just released second solo album, Weary and Wired. I wrote the official bio for Ford's 2016 release, The Vulture. In early 2017, Ford performed many sold out shows with ex-Black Crowes Rich Robinson in a group called the Magpie Salute. As I write this introduction, the Magpie Salute is recording for their 2018 double-album release.

> *"It's too soon to tell the difference*
> *Read that page another day*
> *It's not clear the lines you're crossing*
> *Just wake up and walk away."*

—Marc Ford

MARC FORD'S MUSICAL LEGEND continues gaining momentum. Best known for his guitar virtuosity in the Black Crowes—where he helped develop the band's sound—Ford just released his second solo CD, *Weary and Wired*. Born in Los Angeles, California, in 1966, Ford's love for southern roots and blues music resonates through his own unmistakable tone. His old band, Burning Tree, now serves as Ford's back-up band on the diverse *Weary and Wired.*

Ford joined the Black Crowes in the winter of 1991. He played on three vital studio albums with the group and performed hundreds of shows during their musical peak before departing in the summer of 1997. From there, Ford played and collaborated with Federale, The Original Harmony Ridge Creekdippers, Gov't Mule, Blue Floyd and Ben Harper. In 2002, Ford released his first solo record, *It's About Time*, which highlighted his skilled songwriting ability.

Around this time I met Marc for the first time. We hung out on several occasions and I interviewed him for *Hittin' The Note* magazine. Ford joined Ben Harper's band in 2003. Ford played on Harper's GRAMMY-winning album, *There Will Be A Light*, which featured the Blind Boys of Alabama. Ford eventually won a NAACP award for this record—an honor bestowed on few Caucasians. The great songwriter Johnny Neel once told me, "Marc Ford is a genius. He has the best guitar sound I've ever heard." Ford's soulful guitar mastery transcends all barriers…musical or social.

In February of 2005, Ford rejoined the Black Crowes. The *All Join Hands* tour proved a formidable affirmation of the Black Crowes' majestic power with Ford in the band. Ford's performances with the Crowes can be heard on a plethora of *Instant Live* recordings. The Crowes were back on top with Ford. However, two days before the Crowes were to hit the road for the fall leg of their 2006 tour Ford faxed the band indicating he quit over concerns for his sobriety. Sometimes the volatility of greatness wears on everyone's nerves, and one can only hope one day Marc will play with the band again. However, due to contractual obligations, Marc cannot discuss personal matters concerning the Crowes. A month after he left the Crowes, Ford began recording *Weary and Wired*, which comprises Muddy Dutton and Doni Gray—Ford's old Burning Tree cohorts—as the backing band.

In this interview—which Marc arranged on April 13, his 41st birth-day—he discusses his early musical aptitudes, *Weary and Wired*, old romps, his son Elijah—another guitar wizard in his band, southern music and a few hilarious surprises. This timeless conversation provides insight into one of the world's greatest guitar players.

Well happy birthday man. I appreciate you doing this interview on your birthday.

MF: Thanks very much, James.

Remember our last interview was down here in Atlanta at that practice space? *It's About Time* **was out. I stood alone in that little room with the band blaring that night.**

MF: Yeah, yeah—I do remember that.

That's where you were telling me about getting your first guitar at the swap meet at 10…you've come a long way since then. How many guitars do you have?

MF: Right. I don't know. There's probably five or six here at home. Always a dozen around…but someone is holding them for me…I just got one the other day, a Trussart—a James Trussart. I had a few in the shop that were here in town. There's a peripheral Spanish guitar…an acoustic here or there…I picked up a couple of Reverend Guitars recently. Reverend's a company that the guy who started it—what he had in mind was he was gonna make the modern Silvertone—a cheapie, but quirky enough to use. They're really cool guitars.

What's the main acoustic you always resort to?

MF: Well, that's not here. It's a Martin D-18. Don't have that here.

Let's break Q&A tradition and skip around a bit. The other night you told me you were going to record some songs, so even with a new CD, perhaps another brewing? That's the spirit.

MF: Well, I've just been writing so much lately. I'm trying to get it down. I—what I was trying to do, maybe—a friend of mine, John, has got this old four-track in the back of his house—like reel to reel. He's done his garage up real cool and it sounds great in there. So I wanted to demo some songs real quick—just roll it. I did a couple and he said 'Man you gotta do a record by your-self'. He said we'll do it here, but we haven't been able to get our schedules together. Even if I just peddled it over the Internet.

You've got some tour dates coming up, right?

MF: May is filling up. We had plans to go to Europe for six weeks or so at the end of May all through June and into July, but there was too many American dates and offers coming in so we told the guy in Europe 'Look, you're not filling in the dates…dates are coming in here…we're gonna take these', I think what we're gonna hit a couple of important festivals in Europe and then come back and to the States real hard and then in the fall go back to Europe properly—with a better set up after having done the festivals.

So playing with Burning Tree again is almost like coming full circle. Now, we'll travel back in time—you got your first guitar when you were ten. The neck was screwed up, right? You couldn't play past a certain fret.

MF: Yeah, this old guy was selling a bunch of crap guitars. The neck was so warped you couldn't get past the third fret…every note was the same after that because it was actually bent backwards. There was a big lump in the middle of it. I didn't have any business being up there anyway.

The deed was done. So you hit the LA music scene, what 16-17?

MF: 15. I was getting rides from Mom to clubs. I'd get a ride home.

When did you meet up with the Burning Tree guys?

MF: Oh gosh, around 17-18. Y'know, you start playing all the same clubs and everyone is keeping an eye on the competition. They're competition until you get to know them then, of course, you want to play together. You know what? I know Doni first because that was through a friend in high school. He was through a friend in high school. He was three years above me—we got together through someone—and they were already in a band together. I went to go sit in with that band. I didn't realize it was this big audition. So I just bought a guitar and an amp a couple of pedals and went nuts on 'em. They were like wow!

What did you lock onto early as a guitar player? Y'know writers have their Hemingways, Faulkners…

MF: Well, the early, early stuff I heard was Mom and Dad's 45s of Chuck Berry, Smokey Robinson.

Eventually rock and roll infected you.

MF: Yeah, I didn't really get that until I was in High School. I had a big Elton John phase before that. The first thing I wanted to have—I told my Mom—I saw *Yellow Brick Road*, and I'm thinking to myself—now after hearing it again recently—that is not what a nine year old should be listening to. I begged my Mom for it she got it for me. It's a heavy record.

I thought the same thing years later when I realized I bought Aerosmith's *Draw the Line* when it came out. Strange record for a fifth grader.

MF: You know, that's good you owned that James, because they scared me back then actually. They scared me. It took me a long time to get to Aerosmith. I was kinda clueless, sorta secretly listening to Elton John records, and hanging out with guys listening to Judas Priest, Deep Purple—who I loved for a minute. Then a friend of mine—we ran together—the whole time it was like, I gotta get this one record. To be honest with you, where I grew up I didn't have a whole lot of exposure to music…or different types. It was very bland-white-suburb. The Beatles were about as far as it got. I had *Sgt. Peppers*. Until this friend of mine pulled me aside and we have a little smoke out session—just particularly for this thing he's gonna turn me onto.

Holy Hell…here we go.

MF: (Laughs) Yeah…yeah…(laughs) so I didn't know that, but he's like I gotta play you something. His Mom's boyfriend—this was the guy in the '70s who had the latest super stereo for high fidelity—massive speakers. So he sits me down between these two giant speakers—'Just lay back' he says-and, we're blowed—and he says, 'Listen to this.'I can hear this hiss and I know it's gonna be so loud and on comes "Machine Gun." I was blown outta my head, and from there I took a hard left.

Did you have a Stratocaster at that point?

MF: Oh yeah. I always loved Stratocasters, but I never heard no sound like that coming out of one (laughs). I went immediately back to the house, pulled the amp out and turned it loud as it would go, and stood in front of it—what it did—that was my direct line to the blues. Ever since then I was drawn to roots music. Whatever it be gospel, country, blues-Delta or Chicago…the birth of rock and roll happened in the south.

Music is the south's greatest contribution.

MF: Absolutely.

So you met "Muddy" Dutton from Burning Tree soon after that?

MF: Yeah, couple years later. I was in the ninth grade when my friend hit me with Jimi Hendrix. High School was when I started slinging dime bags out of the back of my car, working in pizza joints…then I got into Jeff Beck…I had younger brothers that were much younger than me—so I was kinda on my own.

The Roving Gambler.

MF: That's right. And the guitar just meant trouble for everybody (laughs).

Listening to those Burning Tree releases—your sound and tone were already defined at 23.

MF: Yeah, 23. I just had my first kid. Well, yeah your sound is in you. If you're playing from an emotional place and you're willing to open yourself up enough to be like this channel, really, then your sound is there already. As I sat there doing my damndest to play what these guys do that I wish… ah, 'I just can't get it—why doesn't it sound like that?' I'm struggling, but little did I know, the whole time it was there. It just hadn't developed. I was obsessive. I hated my life. So I stayed in my room and played my guitar for a very long time. I just felt completely crazy and it was very difficult to be social so I went and sat with my guitar for hours and hours every day.

That's what it takes.

MF: Yeah, I was in a very sort of fantastical dream world with my guitar and my records.

Didn't Booker T. Jones play on that first Burning Tree record?

MF: Yeah, man. Are you kidding me? STAX records? Damn.

I just got the new STAX box set.

MF: How is it? I bet it's great.

Incredible, so is that STAX-WATTS stuff.

MF: Oh yeah, that stuff is heavy. Booker T showed up with a little sack lunch. He had a hearing-aid in. I'm thinking, 'Damn, that's Booker T—he looks like a regular dude!' He sits down; he didn't say too much—very pleasant. He said 'Let me hear the track once.' Literally, he made one pass and said 'Okay, next song.' He did two songs and he was gone. I was sitting behind the board just watching. I was still trying to get over Booker T was playing on my songs. You know, I played with Steve Cropper at a festival in Copenhagen with Blue Floyd. They met us there—and Blue Floyd was backing the band. I sat there and watched Cropper and my jaw was on the floor because I didn't really appreciate what he did as a guitar player. Forget the writing for a minute, which was phenomenal. But his rhythm is just driving the whole thing-just pumping. So bad. I'd been listening to a lot of Ann Peebles, Al Green and The Hodges Brothers. You know Cropper's over there-there's nobody else that can make that sound.

James Burton told me Ricky Nelson didn't want him to play on other people's records because people identified Ricky Nelson's music with James Burton's sound.

MF: Right. Yeah, I know some other people that did that.

Yes, you would know something about that, but the *Burning Tree* was a great first record. Y'all hit the road hard behind that release.

MF: We thought so. Yeah, we went straight to England behind that just because the record company didn't know what to do with it in the States. 'We love it,' they said, 'But we don't know what to do with it.'

Well, 1989 was not a good year for bluesy, rock bands.

MF: Yeah, groups like Poison were the thing. We didn't fit. So what do we do? Send us overseas! It kinda worked out. Just the part that you're from another country, people are curious.

Europeans are very appreciative of American blues.

MF: They really are—I'm already getting so many emails through the website from Europeans saying thank you for that record. Now that it's out here people are starting to dig it. It's like they've been waiting for this one.

I heard a live show of yours from last April-the 26th, I think—that version of "Smoke Signals" was interstellar space—great stuff.

MF: Yeah, someone mentioned something about that show to me the other day. This person was comparing it to something though. Now with the

Internet you are under relentless scrutiny—you can't just try something out because people just start scandalizing.

Before the Internet, you didn't really know what the band looked like until you got there—all you had was the albums.

MF: And eight out of ten shows most likely sounded horrible because they were so high. By the time I get home from the gig it's already out and people are downloading it. You can't really create any kind of mystique or mystery, it's what's it's come to…but if I was a kid, I'd be on there too. He did what? (laughs)

So, of course, I'm hesitant to ask you anything about The Black Crowes considering the latest developments, but your history with the band remains intertwined. I saw your first show with the Crowes at the 40 Watt in Athens (Georgia)in March of 92—under the name of the Roach Clips. But it wasn't until the April 92 NORMAL show in Piedmont Park did I realize the band really transformed into something else.

MF: At that point they'd been on the road touring for 18 months and they were in the zone. I'd been keeping busy touring, and it was a very exciting time with the Crowes. A lot of excitement going on. It's unfortunate, I'm under a contract.

How long will all this last?

MF: Y'know, I don't know. Perpetuity. (pause)

You mean forever?

MF: Forever in the universe (laughs).

Really?

MF: Yeah, man. In 2005-2006 the Crowes hit the road hard—criss-crossing the States, Canada, Europe—a lot of miles on buses and planes.

Yeah, well y'know that's like our old days. We ran hard. We were in that bus a long time together through blizzards, storms-we attacked it pretty good. We were all fresh and excited and ready to go. 2005 was easy. It was great for me. I had a great time. It was a good atmosphere and I was enjoying playing again with them. Things change. I can talk about my own experience, but I can't tell stories about what anyone else did or the business side of things. No one can tell me I can't talk about things I did. I got a message from a lawyer saying 'Heard you did an interview—we just want to remind you about this gag order' (laughs).

Great bands contain a certain intensity that becomes hard to maintain.

MF: People get real. People have to keep in mind this is all a big smoke and mirrors trip. Even though you may be pouring out your heart in a song or something, you're still onstage entertaining. What happens in the psyche and the ego when you're in front of so many people all the time just telling you, you're wonderful and you don't get 'You're an asshole, take the trash out,' people get weird. It's hard to keep a check on yourself sometimes unless you have some perspective on it.

Living in a tube for eight months doesn't help.

MF: Yeah, you don't have any perspective at all that's sane. It's a lot of moving. You're moving constantly. You're moving when you're sleeping on the bus-it's rocking. When you're sitting still—you're moving-it's constant fl ow. I tell people—the only way I can describe it—coming off the road—it's first three days for me is bewildering. It's like being on a boat all day. When you get back on land, you still feel like you're on the boat. It takes a minute to stop twirling. You think you have to be somewhere. It's routine at one point and then it's bewildering—non-stop. (Laughs)

Did you really not know how to play slide guitar until you joined the Crowes?

MF: No, I'd pick up the odd beer bottle or lighter once in awhile; but no, not until then. I wasn't exposed to a lot of music when I was young out here in L.A. Chris and Rich had a great record collection. I spent a lot of time in

Atlanta working there. I really have to like the place. I love the south…it does get a little hot (laughs) but it just suited my personality and my pace. The music is so indigenous to where it's played. I think that's why my connection with southern music is so powerful—like it's been inside of me forever.

Why didn't Tom Petty ever invite the Crowes to play when y'all opened for them on the tour? I love Mike Campbell's playing.

MF: Umm…well, because they have their show worked out pretty well. They're not as free and loose as they like to appear. It was the same gig every night. They're all great guys—the band is superb, I enjoyed watching them, but there's no interaction or variety. They're not out there to jam. He's a songwriter and they're his band, and that's it. It's old school—got a gig to do—we're going to do the gig, and jam for the rest of the day after sound check.

You've played with some real heavies. When you were with the Crowes— who were opening for the Stones—you hung out and played guitars with Ronnie and Keith. I remember you saying Ronnie's room was the place to be, but the only rule was you had to be out by 8AM.

MF: Yeah, that was his wife Jo—'Okay boys, it's 8AM'—she'd come out from the bedroom—it's 8AM, see you tomorrow!' (laughs) We'd have to stagger back to our rooms. 'Oh, alright…' Ironically, sitting with The Stones in a hotel room with them that first night I had a moment where I kinda left the room and was talking with myself—I was there—but in my head I was like 'Look at these shrivelled up old, teenagers—you know what I mean? And they're goofin' around and being dumbasses just like we do on the bus playing, and it's all fun and Yuks. Then I start thinking, so this is it…there it is…it's what you dreamed of—are you getting what you want? I was like 'Holy shit; you're kidding me—what a drag.' It was unbelievable, but then again I thought—I don't know if perpetual adolescence is really what I want now. I just realized that where I was—was at the top, and I'm peakin' over the mountain. And I thought this isn't really what I'm looking for, I don't think. I think that was the moment I started to deflate. Now what? Rock and Roll wasn't the answer, but I guess I wasn't asking the right questions. Or I was looking in the wrong places because cause rock and roll can produce some great fun and release, but you're not gonna get the meaning of the universe in a rock and roll song.

You should slip a few lines of lyrics from *Weary and Wired* on your website. Some of them are obscured quite well.

MF: People say that a lot to me, but I just say pay more attention. Put it on again. Listen harder. I thought about it actually. I thought about it for a minute-should I put it on there, but it sorta takes away from it.

Spoken like a true guitar player.

MF: And plus, for me I think there's a deep down insecurity about words—I don't read very well, and I wasn't good in school—I could pull it off and razzle dazzle you and get by. I don't think I have a grasp of language really that well to demand people pay attention.

Tell the story about hanging out with Neil Young.

MF: Yeah, yeah. I got to hang out at his ranch one day when we did the Bridge School thing. When I went to soundcheck—Jay the keyboard player is Elliot Roberts' (Neil Young's manager) step son since he was two, so he was used to Stephen Stills stopping by the house. He tells a great story of Steve Stills coming in his room one day goin' 'Whatcha listening to?' He was listening to a Neil Young record, and Stills was like 'Ah, man…lemme show ya'. He takes the record off and begins to give a guitar lesson in his bedroom. Anyway, he takes me over to Neil's ranch for sound check and we just spend the day trippin' around, coming up on these guest houses and walking in and sitting down, grab a coke.

Neil's driving?

MF: We were walking. Neil sits on top on these rolling hills in northern California. It's a working cow ranch so you see these Black Angus running around. We're walking along and we come up on another house, and it's his soundman that lives there. You walk a little farther and Ben Keith's house is there. Neil has all these people living on his property. It's so bizarre. You walk a little father and you're in these big Redwoods. There are people all over the place working. The guy that's in Neil's car barn—that's his gig. His job is to keep Neil's old Lincolns in shape.

Did you get to play any?

MF: No, we didn't get to play. On Friday night he threw a barbecue at his house and invited the band and the crews over to have 'hot meat' over at his house. So, I was sitting with Jay and he comes down and we have dinner with Neil. Of course, I saw Neil earlier in the barn playing with his train, which I think I walked into his own personal space. He's like 'Who's there!?' I said, 'I'm sorry. Whoa. (Laughs) I shouldn't be here—I'm gonna leave now.'(Laughs)

I've heard it, but I cannot decipher who's playing the guitars that night in Florida when the Crowes and the Allman Brothers were in the studio together?

MF: Ah, the guitars—I think it was me and Warren. Dickey or Rich weren't there. It was me, Chris (Robinson), Johnny Colt, Gregg, and Allen Woody. I just saw a picture from that night the other day. Duane Betts was there. That night Gregg was…

I remember on the tape he said, you upstarts play too loud!

MF: Yeah, he was drunk as hell and all sassy and he ran the band out of rehearsal earlier, so they all split. We were jammin' and I was playing through Dickey's amp loud as hell, and he was like 'Turn that down! I can't stand you guitar players playing so loud.' By the end of the night—he was like 'You're my brother. I dig you.' (laughs). It was hilarious. There were a few hangers-on, probably the dope man was around somewhere. The fire department came at one point and we had to shut it down because there was so much smoke being blown in the place that the fire department came. (laughs)

Listening to that stuff with Duane in Muscle Shoals sounds incandescent.

MF: Yeah, that stuff with Aretha. Ronnie Hawkins. Muscle Shoals, man-Eddie Hinton, are you kidding me? I'm a huge Eddie Hinton fan.

Eddie Hinton seems to personify the underdog. All the heavies know he's a star, but he remains obscure.

MF: It's a blues story. The blues is still around. Its face changes, but it's still running deep in people. Also, people kinda buy into it—your singing and, you're trying to get people to listen. It's a down and out place to begin with and people buy into that and they stay there because they think they deserve it.

Or they have to.

MF: Yeah, exactly. Like if I don't stay here, miserable, I won't be singing to truth. But your truth doesn't have to be miserable .

It was great you won that NAACP award with Ben Harper.

MF: Yeah, they had a problem with giving me one. I was like, 'Shit, I'm playin' y'all's music for 20 years—'It's about time I get something for it' (laughs). It's in a box somewhere. We're moving. So I haven't seen it around. I wanted to weld it on the front of my car like a hood ornament (laughs). It's huge—it's holding up a globe—NAACP. That's right-That's right. I feel good about that-it's very validating.

There Will Be A Light **was a fine record.**

MF: We did it so quickly. We sat down and arranged the tunes and recorded the tracks in two separate sessions sitting there face to face. It was me, Jay, Juan and Ben pretty much working out the arrangements. Then other people would come and go. It was five songs each day. That's the way I love making music. If you gotta think about it too much, it's not gonna come out right.

So your son Elijah is in your band. That must be an interesting and fun situation. Did he pick up the guitar early?

MF: Well, it wasn't too early. He was probably 13. He was kinda showing interest in it—picking it up around the house. I was about to leave on tour. I remember the day I was leaving. I had my bags packed. So, I go, 'Here, let me show you something.' So, I wrote out a little guitar neck—put the frets—these are the string names. You tune the guitar this way'. I put a couple of dots in them. 'Here's a D. Here's an A'. I get back a couple of months later and he's playing Eric Clapton! It's so easy for him. It was pretty easy for me too. It didn't take me much effort to get going. He just picked it up so quickly and he has such an amazing sense of time and sense of melody. I'm just blown away with the parts he comes up with.

He's going out on the road, right?

MF: Oh yeah.

He's already out of school?

MF: He took the test to get out of school a long time ago. When I left for rehearsals with the Crowes (February 2005) he'd been in a little trouble. I had to get him from school when he was suspended, so I was leaving for rehearsal and I said, 'You wanna go?' So he came with me for six weeks and watched that whole thing come together because it wasn't too long before that I started hearing Black Crowes records coming out of his bedroom. He comes out and he goes, 'Dad, the Black Crowes were cool!' (laughs) I go

'Yeah man, we were pretty cool.' In my mind, I just got done with that—not thinking that was 10 years ago. For him to come with me and see the Crowes' first rehearsal, to the warm up gigs, to the big opening, I think at that moment he was hooked. Now he comes back and tries to play with his little band and tells me that he's so frustrated, and I say, 'Elijah you are on a completely different level. You're not gonna get those guys to do what's gonna happen when you sit in with me.' I said 'You had it, tasted it, you've done it. Leave those guys alone'. I said, 'You got a problem. Just come with me, learn the ropes of the road a little bit, when you get back you can find a band or something. I'm kinda blown away at his talent. I can give him a record—the JBs—check this record out and he'll come back and point out the juiciest nugget. I'm like, 'Yeah, you got it.' (laughs)

Talk about producing records. You've been getting into that some.

MF: Yeah, in fact, speaking of the JBs, there's this woman named Betty Mae from Alabama who's out here—I was just producing six songs for this girl here in L.A. We got together and I heard her voice. She doesn't have a deal so she's paying for it herself. So I got hooked up with her through this studio. I mixed the record and I sat with her and the girl sings like Aretha and I was like 'Whoa that's a big voice for a little white girl.' So I knew exactly what we were doing. She wanted to do "Spirit in the Dark", she wanted to do "Losing You". All these great things, and I said this is my bag. I said I'm going to make a tight, funky, soul record. We did "How Strong Is A Woman" by Ann Peebles. I just walked up in the studio and he has it all set up—amps in the other room isolated—I said "No, no, no—take it all down and the amps we're listening to are the ones were recording. This room's too live. Bring in these baffles and tighten it up. Make it dry. Yeah, I really like producing a lot. It's like, after all these years of making records and touring—I outta be a doctor (laughs) but it can't prove anything that I'm even worth walking into a burger shop and get a job. So, where do I put all this stuff?

Sooner or later you have to turn it into breakfast food.

MF: Exactly. It's such a perfect environment for me because I get to play a little and you're right in the center of the whole thing. The concentration it takes to sustain 12 hour days hanging onto every sound. There's a training—I was talking to my wife because there will be music playing I'll just go, 'Ah, that's crap!' Let's get out of here. I can't even stand to listen to it.' She was like you're always complaining, and I thought, 'Why do I do that…' it's because I've trained my ear to listen so closely and zoom in on things people don't even know are there. Tiny syncopations—words—the whole package. If it isn't excellent I don't want to be there. It's insulting in a way. I've tuned myself to appreciate the finest. You can't drink ripple after high-dollar wine. Speaking of wine, Sir Paul McCartney—when I was with Ben Harper on some festivals—Sir Paul sent over a $500 bottle of wine. That was something else. We were in Europe at some festival. We were gonna do a few shows together. The first night we came over to do some stuff—he was all bouncy and silly, like he does and he sent over this wine. The way he travels it just unreal so that's the kind of wine he drinks with dinner. The stuff was an explosion in your head when you drink this stuff—unbelievable. It's a good Paul McCartney story, right?

What about Jason Isbell leaving the Truckers? Y'all played a show together a while back. When the Truckers opened for the Crowes last summer you guys got to hang out a bit…did either of y'all realize you'd be leaving the band?

MF: I hung out with him a lot on tour. We weren't sharing any of that with each other. To be honest with you, I didn't know I was leaving the Crowes until it was two days to go back out on tour and it just dawned on me, that I don't have a single need or want to even do it anymore. It's time to move on. It just started to feel old. I knew what I was gonna do if I started allowing myself to be in the situations that I didn't dig. You start getting into this victim trap—or I did. I started feeling that and I knew it was time to go—to take the reins and run.

Is it true that you recorded some of those new Crowes songs y'all played on the road in the studio?

MF: No, just the live stuff. We didn't go in and cut anything.

Just hittin' the road.

MF: Yeah, a little too long for my taste.

You and Rich always sounded great together.

MF: Yeah. Rich is an amazing player—an amazing player. That song "Sunday Buttermilk Waltz" at the Fillmore is pretty heavy. That was the first time me and Rich actually went out and performed by ourselves together. It was pretty intense. I love the Crowes music. I love playing the music. I didn't always appreciate what it took to play the music.

You left the Crowes in early September of '06. Did you go straight into studio and cut *Weary and Wired*?

MF: We went in—I did the record in November. We had four days booked. We cut all the music on the first three and a half days.

Who played the horns?

MF: I started—I got called by the house band leader on the Carson Daly show—Joe Firstman. He called me up to come do the show. Those horn players were there—we got friendly. They have this Sunday night jam—this jazzier thing—and I thought I could go out and (humour-filled insinu-ation) 'Get Funky' with this jazz thing (chuckles). So I started sitting in and learning quite a lot. One of the horn players told me everybody was learning. He said you may be learning chord changes, but we're learning the value of simplicity, and finding a riff to hang on, and running it into people's heads. They were like 'the only time people were dancing were when you were up there'.

Who's talking through the song "The Big Call Back?" Is it you?

MF: No, that's Mike Malone.

(In a fake hick drawl) Well, what in the world is that feller saying?

MF: (mischievous cackle) He was supposed to come do keyboards and he called way late. He goes, 'Aw man I fell out. I'm sorry. If you still want me to come down there call me. If not, I'm good like Wednesday or Saturday I could do something if you wanted me to.' So he leaves me this message—the way he's sort of half asleep and the rhythm in his talk—he's a funky white dude, but he plays the blues. It was just so musical the way he left it on my machine was hilarious. I played it for the guys, and I said put up a microphone and record this. So we recorded the message from my phone and just sort of dropped it over the track. It fit perfectly. We snipped it in spots, and let it come in and out. The way it works out if you can make out what he's saying it sounds like there's a guy that calls and says, 'I'm sorry I missed the thing, but I can still come if you want. Give me a call.' Then he hangs up, and then calls again saying 'I can do Saturday, Wednesday…' like the guy just won't stop calling.

You covered one of Ryan Bingham's songs. Who is he?

MF: He's a guy from West Texas. He's an amazing guy. He's like 24-25—sort of Townes—Steve Earle kinda guy. He's pure. I walked into the King King one night for no reason, it's like 12:30—there are seven people in there—no one's paying attention. Here's this skinny kid with a big hat and a guy behind him playing a kick-snare and a high hat and just floored me. I was looking around wondering if anybody was seeing this—thinking 'God, I hope nobody in L.A. has got hooks in him and going to ruin this.' So, I introduced myself and offered him some studio time. He came out with this record where this guy tried to Nashville him out—smooth out his sound—they took the story out of his voice. He hated it. They came to California on the flip of a quarter. Home or California? So they're just driving around with a little PA system and a couple of guitars and just playing anywhere and everywhere—just to make a buck and peddlin' these records. I go 'You know what, I listened to it and it doesn't represent you at all. It's like a whole another person. He's like, 'I know—I hate it.' So, I call up my buddy Anthony at the Compound, where I've been working when I make the Pawnshop Kings record, and I go, 'Look man you gotta do this favour for me. I said give me a day in the studio. You won't regret it. I said he's amazing and Anthony said, 'Okay—I'll do it.' I told him we were going to record for a day. By the time it was done, they were like, 'Wow, we've never got do record and have it sound the way we sound!' They were blown away. I said, 'Well let's get those tracks and we'll just fuck this record up. I stripped off everything—some of the tracks we just rebuilt entire tracks behind his vocals. We did it for free. A friend of his paid for a couple of days in the studio, so he puts it out saying, 'This is a record I can live with,' and I just heard Lost Highway wants to put it out. The deal is goin' down now. We're gonna go back in and record a couple more songs to sound out the record because I never really thought it was done.

It's a nice gesture to cover his song on your CD.

MF: Well, he's incredible, I love the guy—he's super amazing. He's just got soul.

"Featherweight Dream" is a great opening track. "It'll Be Over Soon" is another favourite of mine-great riff.

MF: That's my version of British pop. I used a Hofner. I found out it's called like Club 40 or 50. It's a Les Paul, but it's chambered, like it's hollow and it's got wooden P90s in it. To me everything is the blues. But I did go for the British Invasion pop song on that one.

I like "Dirty Girl" off *Weary and Wired* a lot.

MF: I finally wrote a three-chord song (laughs). That's all I wanted to do.

So, your son Elijah came up with the riff on "1000 Ways"?

MF: He was playing in the background and I heard this riff and I said, 'Do that again.' He's like, 'What, this?' And he played it again. I said, 'What is that?' He's like, 'One of mine.' I said, 'I need that.' I said, 'You're not old enough to be walking around with a riff like that,' (collective laughter).

As your father...

MF: Yeah, as your father, I'm going to take this away from you before you hurt somebody.

Let this be a lesson—you report all riffs to the old man.

MF: That's right. You finish this—you run to me or the police. What I did was, I said, 'Come with me to the studio tomorrow. I wrote another part to it, and he had a couple of lyrics—and the melody and the verses. I'm writing lyrics down in the car on the way to the studio. We get there and the guys show up to track a song with me—we started the night before, but it wasn't happening—I said new songs guys. I told Elijah to grab a guitar and plug into any amp. So we showed them the tune and cut it immediately— fresh off the tree. First take your instincts are always poppin'.

That's the thing about those STAX recordings; they would leave mistakes- if a horn player came in at the wrong time or something, they'd leave it.

MF: Sure, that's where the magic's at-the human-ness. If you got some cats that are that bad and funky you leave the warts because that's the only way you can have the rest of it. If you're being precious about it you're gonna miss out on the whole thing. My whole record was like guerrilla warfare. My engineer and I have worked together enough so he knows what I'm doing, what I like and how I want things. I'd be like, 'Okay let's do the next one'—switch guitars, and change amps—we'd start again. It's like a big barn with open mikes. Here we go…and he was rollin' all the time. It went so easy and so quick. I'm so happy.

Songs like "Running Man Blues"-that was an old Burning Tree song.

MF: Yeah. I thought it was appropriate playing with Doni (Gray-Burning Tree drummer)—it brought the toe up in my boot. I always wanted to have that song. I wrote that song… "Just Take the Money" was an old song. I wrote that toward way back at the end of Burning Tree on a demo. Elijah kept all those demos. He found them and then Burning Tree was his favorite band. It seemed appropriate those old songs found a home. They were just hanging around all the time—getting in the way. We don't get to make records maybe like they did back in the sixties where you're shelling them out every six months.

Although, *Weary and Wired* was recorded and completed, from March to November and hitting the streets in March is quick.

MF: I wish it would have gone a little slower actually because the set up time was thought out too well.

"Smoke Signals" was a Federale song, right?

MF: Yeah, Luther and I wrote that together.

What's he up to these days?

MF: He just makes records. He's got his niche. When I spent time with him in Portland, he lives a simple life and just plays music all the time— records all the time by himself. Lately, I've been getting everything down, so it doesn't—leave. That's why I like having a bunch of different guitars around because when I do pick one up—each of them has their own vibe and story—you play a little different on one than the other. They kinda all got different things to say. I used to be into those four tracks when I was a kid—maybe that's why I understand the process. I got signed off a four track. One of those deals I did in the garage.

What's been the hardest thing to learn through your career?

MF: Besides keeping my eyes open and making sure bitches aren't taking shit from me (laughs)? I would say, settle down and to shut up. Stop running around crazy trying to play all over the place and just sit back— you ain't in no hurry. You know, that STAX stuff just has this groove—it's exclusive. One day…it's like when I saw Steve Cropper play—it was an epiphany…like wow—just driving this shit out the riff. The southern thing is—I don't know if it's the heat (laughs)…

It's the barbecue.

MF: Yeah, the heat, the barbecue—there's just this ass to it-this swing…a nastiness you just want to be a part of. It's slippery. It's solid, but it's all over the place. It's like a Lincoln or a Cadillac. It's gonna get you there, but you're gonna take some wide turns. You'll be comfortable when you get there.

"Currents" is my favorite song from *Weary and Wired*. It seems to fit my personal landscape at the moment. Great tone on that.

MF: Thank you. I was really going for Richard Thompson sort of tone, but what I had available at the time, I came up with that. I wanted a really unique tone for that song.

Is that a new song?

MF: That's a brand new song, a very heartfelt song. People are picking up on that song a lot.

What were the newest songs on *Weary and Wired*?

MF: That one, "Currents". "Dirty Girl".

"Featherweight Dream"?

MF: "Featherweight Dream" was an old one, but I did it a different way. Kinda Allman Brothers in a way—that kind of feel—a bouncing swing. The Willie Dixon tune you can tell mics are open all over the place. You can hear the room. I had a PA system in there singing on some of them. We just tracked them like that because no one wants to wear headphones in the studio—immediately, you're gone from what's happening. Everything was open in a big A-Frame barn, like an old wooden garage. It was just capture it.

What's the tour schedule look like?

MF: It starts trickling in around the fifth of May. We're coming south, but not now. The reason is—I'd go straight over to the East Coast because there's a huge fan base there. Just start there. This European thing is still kinda up in the air. In May, we're gonna stay three or four hundred miles of where I'm living. We'll drive there and come back home. If we go to Europe, when we get back we'll be solid running all over the place.

So you're pushing the record hard, any other peripheral gigs happening?

MF: Well, I gotta finish Ryan's record in a couple days—or a week and a half. Then there's a Spanish band that wants me to go to Portugal to produce them. Then there's talk of me producing Betty Mae from Alabama—her band is the JBs, and I said I wanted to produce the shit out of the JBs! Just give it to me! She lives here. Somebody played the record she has—she's so bad. I sure do hope I get the chance to do that. People that were there said I could probably do her next record—then they told me the JBs were the band, and I said, 'You better let me produce it!' She didn't like her modern R&B record. It's like the country music—like R&B—is so fabricated. It doesn't sound real at all. Everything is overblown and overdone—bigger than life.

How old is the song "Bye Bye Susie"?

MF: It's an old Burning Tree song. I whipped out old ones only because we were jamming. There's that sound again. I can get these songs that have been collecting dirt or forgotten, and the band still knows them. I write way more songs than I can find places to put them.

Pull out some of your country stuff.

MF: I have been getting to pull out the country out with Ryan.

Can you play the pedal steel?

MF: I've never even sat down at one. It's like a B-3 or a semi-truck—you got both knees, feet, and hands goin'.

Well, thanks for doing this interview. Godspeed on the road. I'll stay in touch.

MF: We'll get together when I come south.

Good deal. Enjoy your birthday.

MF: Thanks. Yeah, I'm just gonna sit and do nothing for once.

We'll talk soon.

MF: Okay man. Take it easy James.

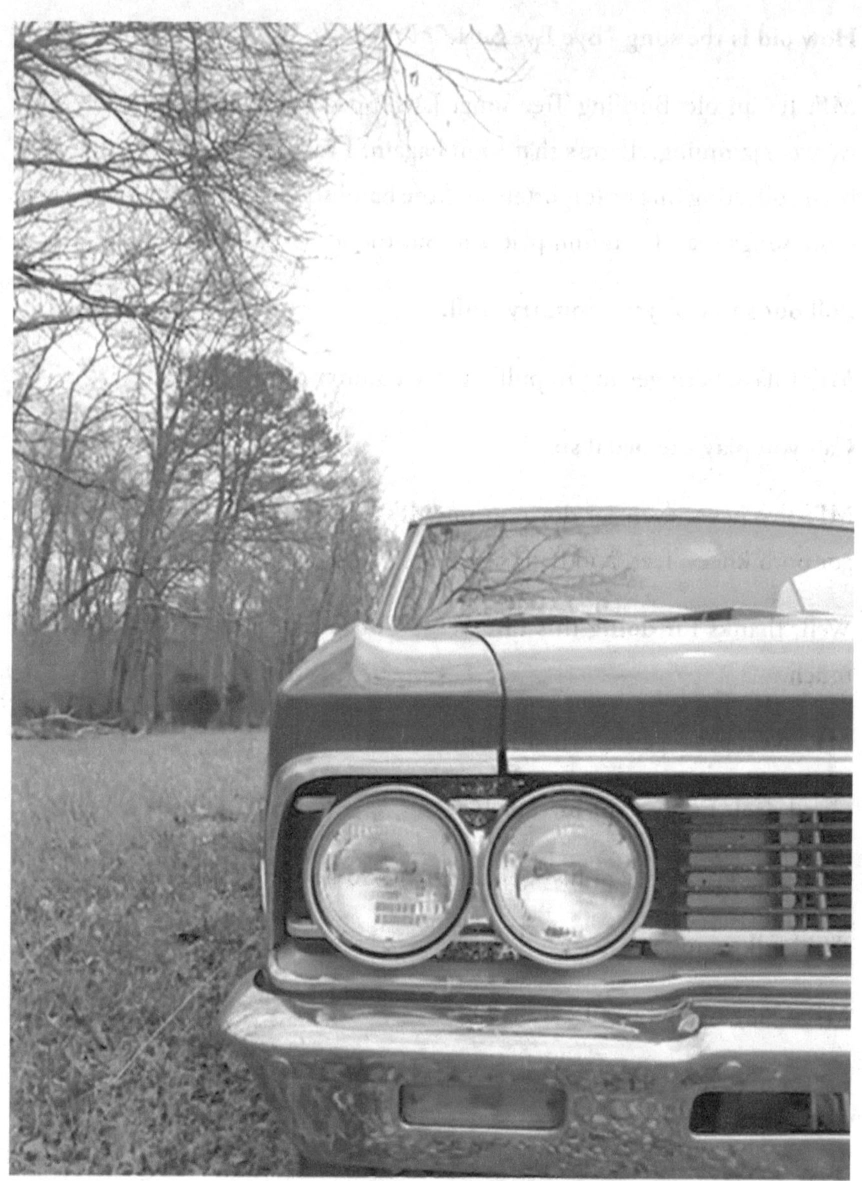

Headlights

Thelonious Monk: *Criss-Cross*

Born October 10, 1917, in Rocky Mount, North Carolina, Thelonious Monk's family soon moved to New York City. Monk worked as a professional musician since his early teens as an organ player for a traveling evangelist.

Monk operated as one of the purveyors of the "Be-bop" jazz movement. After personal struggles and professional tribulations Monk went on to work with jazz legends Miles Davis, John Coltrane, Bud Powell, Billy Smith, "Shadow" Wilson, Lucky Thompson. Coleman Hawkins, Ahmed Abdul-Malik, Art Blakey, Sonny Rollins and many others.

Monk recorded *Criss-Cross* in November of 1962. Serving as his second album on Columbia, *Criss-Cross* ranks as one of Monk's finest releases. "Hackensack" opens the CD by setting a tone with an upbeat sentiment. "Tea For Two" represents Monk's band at a zenith. The title track contains a beat that fits any range or style of music, but Monk possessed his own sound. "Eronel", a quirky ditty, emits a positive sonic influence. Monk's keyboard cascades on "Don't Blame Me" evoke a subterranean mood.

"Crepuscule With Nellie" renders a composition that blurs the line between jazz and blues. Monk's organic musical backgrounds prove his ability to incorporate different American genres into his own style of music. This reissue contains three bonus tracks from these sessions. *Criss-Cross* serves as compelling evidence that Thelonious Monk personifies musical originality.

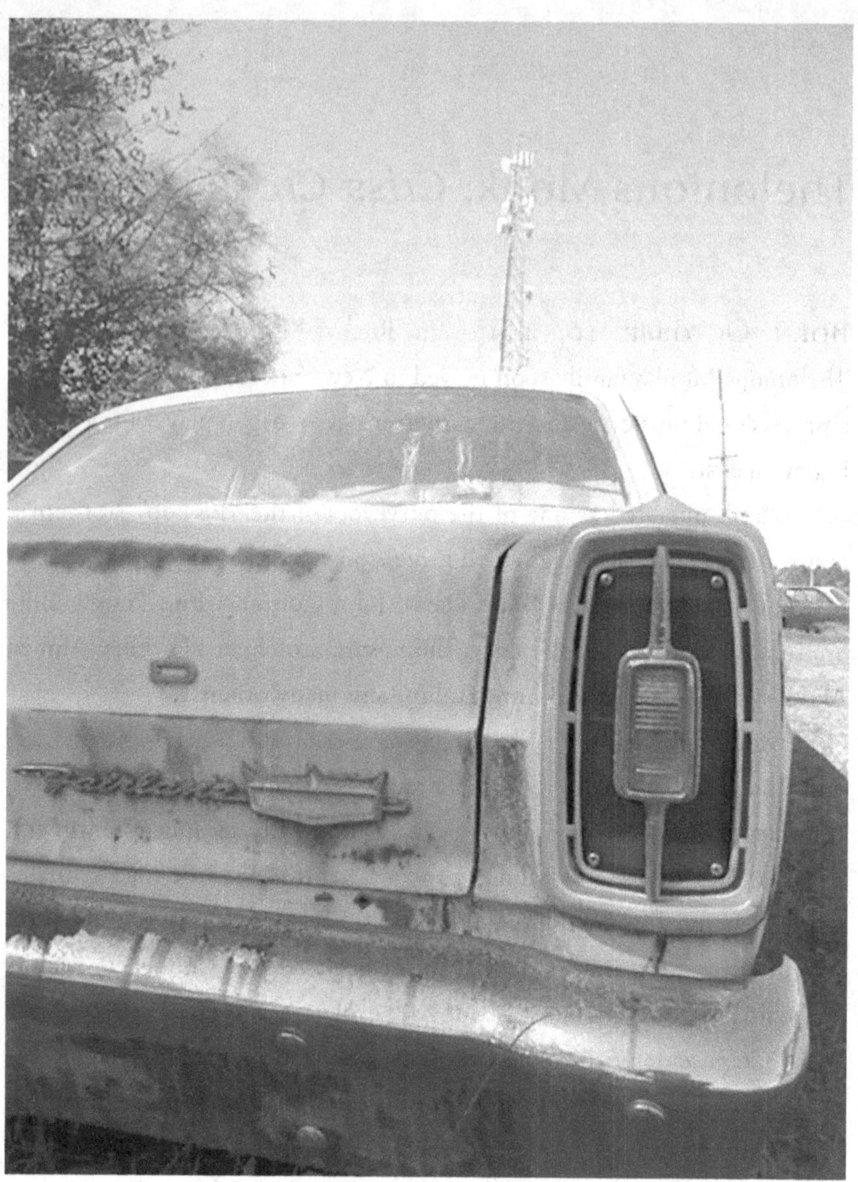

Fairlane

Larry Brown *Big Bad Love*

Mississippi writer Larry Brown wrote ten published books. *Big Bad Love*, his second collection of short stories, ranks as a formidable collection of fiction. Other essential Brown books include *Facing The Music, Dirty Work, Joe, On Fire, Father and Son, Fay, Billy Ray's Farm* and *The Rabbit Factory*.

Big Bad Love contains ten short stories mostly based on love gone wrong. "Falling Out Of Love" tells the story of how a relationship ends over a doomed car ride. "The Apprentice" reveals a story of two lovers—both writers—and how life imitates art when the consequences of publication arise.

These stories take place in bars, run down homes, trucks on dirt roads and lost highways. "Wild Thing" mentions contemporary music groups against the nonfiction locations and the amorous ruin of its characters. The story, "Big Bad Love" begins with the death of a venerable old hound that details the deterioration of old flames and eroded bonds that can never be recaptured.

"Gold Nuggets" takes place in a Mississippi bar and reveals why the North Mississippi Allstars asked Brown to write the liner notes to their first album, *Shake Hands With Shorty*. Bob Dylan informed Jim Dickinson—who told this writer—that he (Dylan) read every word Brown ever published.

"Waiting For The Ladies" weaves a tale of a lonely drinker surviving a day to day grind while waiting to be delivered from his sorrow by a perfect lover. "Sleep" hinges on the delicate balance of a married couple living with one another's idiosyncrasies. Brown evokes vivid images in every sentence.

"Discipline" seems to represent a writer practicing his dialogue because every line in the story is based on a deposition that makes one realize why Hollywood sought to make Brown's novels into film towards the end of his life. "92 Days" represents why a poet like Bob Dylan loved Brown's work. "92 Days" reveals the real loneliness, hardship and dedication required to endure and survive as a writer.

Larry Brown died at the age of 53 in 2004. *Big Bad Love* survives as an essential collection in southern literature.

Johnny Neel: *Mr. Soul*

ON THE FIRST DAY I met Johnny Neel we talked for probably an hour before I said, 'I'll send you something read.' He responded by saying 'I can't read! I'm blind!' It was not my greatest moment, but we became fast friends. I just thought him wearing sunglasses all the time was a musician thing. I'd listened to him for years. I particularly enjoyed his work on the Allman Brothers album *Seven Turns*. I never knew he was blind. In fact, at one point I was going up to Nashville to record some spoken word at his studio, but a snowstorm prevented that session. The following weekend, Johnny had a lot going on—word had it that Marc Ford went AWOL on Blue Floyd because he was rejoining The Black Crowes—which he did. So, after a few events we never got around to recording together. I wrote this article for *Hittin The Note*. Johnny's still out there in all his soulful glory.

You can't teach soul. Johnny Neel ranks as one of the country's most soulful, and versatile, players. Neel's amalgamation of blues, funk, R&B, jazz, gospel, country, and reggae fuse into one indelible personal sound, rendering him a much sought after pro. Although he's a gifted pianist, B-3 organist, and harp player, Neel's best known for his songwriting.

Born June 11, 1954, in Wilmington, Delaware, Neel was the youngest of four siblings. Blind from birth, Neel's handicap influenced his musical inclination. Writing his first song with his father, Neel's aptitude became apparent early. He's more prolific than most keyboard players who can see and read music. Neel cut a single at twelve with his brothers as Johnny Neel and the Shapes of Soul.

Neel revealed his early musical influences: "Motown. Soul music, pretty much back then. There were a lot of black influences down at the blind school. I went to the Maryland School of the Blind in Baltimore. Everyone there either played piano or tuned one.

"Around the Shapes of Soul era the Stevie Wonder *Fingertips* album hit me because we were exactly the same age—12. Since I got older, I leaned more towards Ray Charles tunes. I got stuck on Leon Russell there for a while too. Then I slipped into psychedelic and the rock thing. Then came the jazz—when I heard Oscar Peterson…wow, he fucked me up—I was like holy moly! It was like the fi rst time I heard Weather Report and John Mclaughlin. Then I started doing original stuff…"

In 1983, Neel released two independent albums, *One Hot Night* and *You Should've Been There*. The next year, Neel moved to Nashville where he became a sought after session player and songwriter. Early on Neel earned a publishing deal. "They pay you to write songs for them. You get the song-writer's part, but they get the publishing part. They pay you, say $300 a week—you do demos and they pay for that. If you get a cut you gotta' pay em back. If not, they just write it off or fire you within a couple of years. I stayed with that company five years."

Neel played blues at the Bluebird Café before it became a stuffy song-writers showcase. "People like Stevie Winwood and Dave Mason came through and played with us." It was the Bluebird Café where Dickey Betts saw Neel perform. "I was playing a slide solo on a synthesizer through a twin amp and hired me right there. I got that gig and I worked with him for a while. Back when I first met Dickey he was getting out of the hospital, or rehab, I can't remember, and we played a benefit. Dickey was always very cool to me. We're still pretty tight. Then after a while I quit, and went back doing what I was doing. Then I went back and cut *Pattern Disruptive* with him and that's how Dickey and me got back together. That's a powerful re-cord. I wrote 6 or 7 tunes on there with him. I got Warren into his groove. Me and Kim Morrison introduced Warren to Dickey."

Pattern Disruptive included the Betts/Neel Top 10 AOR hit, "Rock Bottom". Soon Gregg Allman hired Neel to go out on the road with Allman's solo band. "So then I hooked up with Gregg. Danny Toler, him, and me wrote a song on his record. Then I went with the Allman Brothers on the reunion tour."

Neel joined the Allman Brothers Band in 1990. Soon, The Brothers released *Seven Turns*, an album that featured the Betts/Neel composition "Good Clean Fun" which earned the group their highest chart position since "Ramblin' Man".

Neel explained his precarious position in the Allman Brothers, "What was weird to me about 'em was in Dickey's band I was one thing. In Gregg's band, I had horn parts and by the time I got into the Allman Brothers, which was a span of about a year and a half, it was hard for me to settle in. I don't think some of 'em wanted me to be there. I think they just wanted it to be like the original band with just an organ. But, Gregg wanted me to come so they put me in there. I see what they were going after now. I always felt like I was walking on eggshells. Even though they were reunion-ized, they were working through some issues they had. I had to find my own identity. So I had to deal with a whole different concept than what I thought it was. But, it was beautiful because you know it's playing in front of twenty thousand people. It was like riding a big stallion. I loved that and I really enjoyed it. It was one of my dreams to play in a band like that. I played "Statesboro Blues" when I was young. I got crazy and had a good time, and that's what I was supposed to do (laughs). As far as some people know, that's the highlight of my career. Then it changed and I left. I think I might have been a little bit overboard on the jazz and that's why they told me to leave——and I was ready to go. But the *Seven Turns* stuff was great."

For a short period Neel wrote for Huey Lewis' publishing company, Babaloo, along with Bonnie Raitt, Bruce Hornsby, and Delbert McClinton. In 1993, Neel released a solo effort titled *Johnny Neel & The Last Word*. This formidable collection highlighted Neel's songwriting talent. Neel said of that release, "Every time I hear that record I think of Jack Pearson." Pearson provided mighty fine guitar licks on *The Last Word*.

Some of Neel's musical associations over the years include, Carl Perkins, Cyril Lance, David Allen Coe, Joe Diffie, Keith Whitley, Suze

Boggins, Michael McDonald, Smoky Greenwell, Ann Peebles, John Mayall, Gov't Mule, Deep Fried, W.I.N.D, Ricky Ray Rector, Doug Crider, and new country sensation Keith Urban.

In 2000 Neel's label, Breakin' Records, released *Late Night Breakfast*, a great blues infested album. This fine collection includes accomplished musicians such as Shane Theriot (The Neville Brothers), Wayne Jackson (The Memphis Horns), Rick Vito (Fleetwood Mac), and the Charlie Daniels Band drummer Pat McDonald. McDonald recently told this writer: "I do a fair amount of work over at Johnny's studio (Straight Up Sound) and actually that's how I got the CDB gig. Johnny's an amazing player. I love that guy."

Neel played on Gov't Mule's *Life Before Insanity*. During this period Neel performed with Blue Floyd, a fabulous band that included the late, great Allen Woody (Gov't Mule), Matt Abts (Gov't Mule), Marc Ford (Black Crowes), and Berry Oakley (OKB Band). Blue Floyd played blues variations on Pink Floyd's music.

Neel spoke of this great band that was the brainchild of Allen Woody. Neel explained he wasn't the first choice in the band. "They were supposed to use Eddie Harsh from the Black Crowes, but something happened. I stayed out of the politics…and I've stayed out of the politics the older I've gotten. Woody called me up. That was fun, but I didn't know a lot of Pink Floyd music, so it was hard for me to learn it. I was into illicit substances like they were, but I didn't play that stuff—I was doin' it, but I wasn't playin' it. The blues part made it fun for me otherwise, I wouldn't have done it. It was fun. We did some good stuff. And Marc Ford, he's an actual genius. He has the best guitar sound I've ever heard. He's very kind and gracious. Me and him had some good times."

In 2002, X2, an experimental collection of songs—featuring only Neel and Matt Abts—hit the streets. X2 demonstrates Neel's versatile musicianship. "The X2 thing we couldn't get off the ground because people didn't believe we could pull it off," Neel said.

The same year, Neel appeared on Gov't Mule's *The Deep End Vol. 2*. In 2003, The Allman Brothers recent CD, Hittin' The Note, included a

Warren Haynes/Johnny Neel tune "Maydell" that was originally released on Neel's *The Last Word* album.

Last year, Neel released live shows with a smoking band called Grease Factor including old friends Shane Theriot, Jeff Sipe, Derek Jones, and Count M'Butu. Grease Factor's Live CD culled from various 2004 shows, *Off The Cuff*, comes highly recommended.

Also last year, Neel recorded an album he didn't intend to release titled, *Gun Metal Blue*. Neel explained why the album almost didn't see the light of day, "They were just a bunch of songs that were already recorded. It wasn't like I sat down to make an album. These were songs I wrote to pitch around to other songwriters. We decided to get an album together, and I didn't realize how many songs I had in the can. *Gun Metal Blue* is a compilation of songs written in different times, different places over a year or so. I thought it came together pretty good." *Gun Metal Blue* epitomizes the spirit of Johnny Neel.

Recently, Travis Tritt, Montgomery Gentry, and Delbert McClinton recorded Neel's songs. Montgomery Gentry's platinum record *My Town* contains Neel's work. Neel toured with Blue Floyd this spring in the States and at Press Time summer dates are booked. Grease Factor and Deep Fried will play intermittent shows throughout the rest of 2005.

Johnny Neel keeps many irons in the fire. He's a musician's musician operating in the shadow of mega-stardom. When this writer asked Neel what's been the hardest thing to learn in the music business, Neel replied, "It's how you pay attention to what other people tell you what and what not to do. A lot of people try and put you someplace you don't want to be. You always got someone who wants to put you in a box. Then you try it and it doesn't sound right when you shoulda' known that in the first place. Follow your instincts, cause that's all you got in this business."

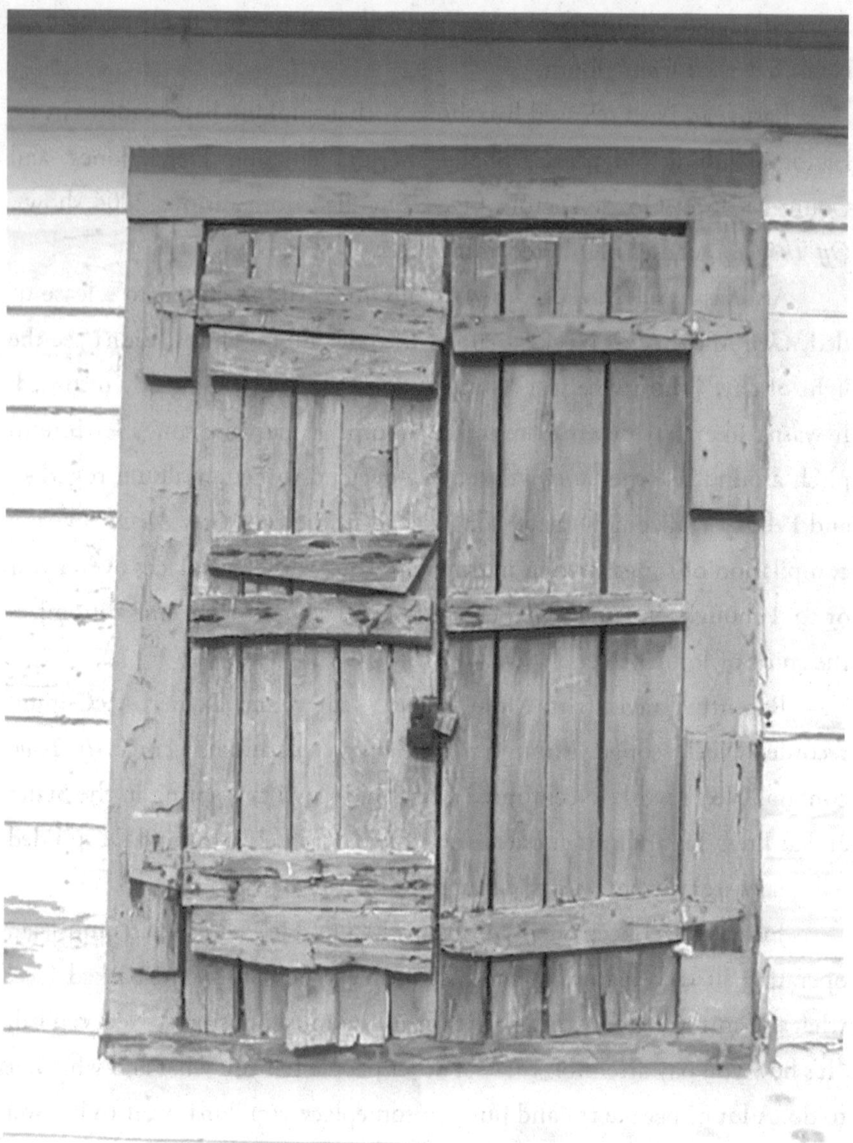

Closed

Neil Young's *Special Deluxe:*
A Memoir of Life & Cars

I JUST RE-READ NEIL Young's 2014 book, *Special Deluxe.* I needed some-thing a bit light and distracting to read from what I'm writing about. Neil's fi rst book, *Waging Heavy Peace* (2012), covered his musical career. His lat-est publication serves as a memoir about cars, and provides a clear insight to how one of the world's premier musicians perceives various current envi-ronmental affairs.

Jimmy McDonough's stellar biography about Young, (*Shakey*) details the musician's fascination with electricity, trains, guitars and cars for busi-ness and personal reasons. Over the years, Young's involvement in Farm Aid, Pono Music, Lincvolt, Lionel Trains, Biodiesel and his latest album— *The Monsanto Years*—attacks the company Monsanto find him addressing eco-issues.

In *Special Deluxe*, Young tells stories about every car he or his family owned. Young illustrated about 50 cars in the book himself. For serious Neil Young fans, *Special Deluxe* provides a nice departure from previous tales of his rock-n-roll grit.

In the book's Preface Young writes: "This is a story about the proud highway of second thoughts. Because I have already written a book about my life. Some events will be familiar to those who have read that book. In this book, I am looking at my relationship with cars over many years."

Yet, Young scatters song lyrics throughout *Special Deluxe.* Most of the lyrics are his own, but others include Roy Orbison, Jerry Lee Lewis, Stephen Stills, Marty Robbins, Jimmy Reed and Curlee Williams. Young keeps it in-teresting. Some of his songs are car related such as "Sedan Delivery", "Long

May You Run", "I Want To Drive My Car", "Eldorado", "Trans Am" and almost every tune from the *Fork In The Road* album. In the book, he reveals probably the only car he ever got repossessed—a 1957 Corvette.

There are too many to list, but a few of Young's favorite vintage rides include a 1948 Buick Hearse named "Mort", a 1934 Bentley Close and a 1959 Lincoln Continental called "Lincvolt". Music serves as in the back-story in *Special Deluxe*. The cars represent different musical eras in Young's life. On page 257, Young writes from a place where his music, cars and personal life intersect:

"In spring of 2012, when Crazy Horse was rehearsing for our first tour in nine years to support our recent album, *Americana*, and our next, *Psychedelic Pill*, the Plymouth Special Deluxe was parked right in front of the stage, ready for any challenge. A new Indian blanket seat, one of the last things designed by Jon McKeig before he retired, was looking beautiful as part of the all-new interior he installed.

"The motor, still humming along, was now started by an improved nine-volt battery system. It had been straining with its original six-volt system. Seemingly reborn, the *Special Deluxe* sprung to life again at the turn of a key. The pain was worn through to rust in some areas, but the body and chrome were still nearly perfect, just as the day I first laid eyes on this beauty."

Special Deluxe compels one to go out for a drive...

Jim Thompson:
After Dark, My Sweet

OKLAHOMA WRITER JIM THOMPSON wrote teeth-rattling novels. He lived his life on the edge, and it emerged in his brutal stories.

By the time he was a teenager, Thompson worked at the Hotel Texas in Ft. Worth. During prohibition he scored customers booze, marijuana and heroin. He possessed a great criminal mind. He worked as an oil field laborer. Louis L'Amour worked under Thompson's direction on the Oklahoma Federal Writers Project, a New Deal program during the great depression.

He later worked as a reporter at the *Los Angeles Mirror*—a tabloid newspaper—until 1949. By 1952, he penned his classic *Killer Inside Me*, which earned him a nomination for the National Book Award. Thompson went on to write over 29 books. His best novels were published in the 1950s.

Stephen King once wrote of Thompson: "The guy was over the top. He was absolutely over the top. Big Jim didn't know the meaning of stop. There are three brave lets inherent in the foregoing: he let himself see everything, he let himself write it down, then he let himself publish it."

After Dark, My Sweet was adapted to film in 1990. The book, published in 1955, revolves around "Kid" Collins—an escaped mental patient. Collins meets the beautiful, but alcoholic widow Fay in the Palm Springs area. Fay soon recruits Collins in an evil kidnapping scheme with her older accomplice "Uncle Bud". Like many of Thompson's novels, the end is not pretty.

Thompson possessed the dark insight into alcoholism and the criminal behavior it leads too, especially if the individual already deals with mental issues. This book finds the reader gritting his teeth over every page.

Thompson learned how to kill the reader. The ending is not defined until the last page.

In the 1960s, Thompson wrote for TV. He worked with filmmaker Sam Peckinpah who adapted Thompson's book, *The Getaway*, to film. Stanley Kubrick commissioned Thompson to assist on films, *The Killing* and *Paths of Glory*. In 1975 Thompson appeared in another film based on one of his books—*Farewell, My Lovely*—with Robert Mitchum.

Thompson stands as testimony that talent does not necessarily constitute a lot of expendable income. At the time of his death at 70 in 1977 all of his novels were out of print. Death for Thompson, like many great artists, proved a good career move. Black Lizard Press began republishing his novels during the 1980s.

After Dark, My Sweet stings like a bloody lip…

Reverend Pearly Brown:
You're Gonna Need That Pure Religion

BORN AUGUST 18, 1915 in Abbeville, Georgia, Reverend Pearly Brown lived his life preaching and singing about the word of God to common folk in the streets. Rev. Brown spoke of his childhood: "I was born blind so I have never seen the world. My mother died when I was quite small and my father had left her. White people raised me, sent me to a school for the blind in Macon. My grandmother taught me slavery songs and spirituals. When I was small I always said when I got to be a big boy, I was gonna get off my people and work for myself. So I learnt how to pick a guitar listening to the radio and records. I been preaching ever since I was fifteen years old. I play mostly in Georgia, Macon, Waycross, Albany, Americus. Two or three times in Florida and Alabama..."

Rev. Brown stands as the first black musician to perform on the Grand Ole Opry. The Reverend often played folk and blues shows, like the Monterey Jazz, Southern Folk, and the Newport Folk Festivals. His career gathered attention in the sixties during the civil rights movement. He hosted radio programs in Macon on WIBB for fifteen minutes every Thursday and in Americus on WDEC for a Sunday morning show.

It was on the streets of Macon, Georgia, where two young guitar players named Duane Allman and Dickey Betts, from a local band called the Allman Brothers, according to Betts would: "get a sackful of quarters and follow him all over just to hear that bottleneck style."

The Macon band, Wet Willie, used a photograph of Rev. Brown for the cover of their *Keep On Smilin'* album in the seventies. Brown always maintained performances in his home state. He often played in Atlanta and

Athens where the University of Georgia students became so fond of the Reverend that they once generated enough money to purchase him some new teeth.

In 1975, Dr. John English, of the University of Georgia recorded a 30 minute documentary on Rev. Brown titled "Mean Old World." In 1981, the Reverend entered a nursing home in Plains, Georgia, where he died in 1986.

The first fifteen songs on *You're Gonna Need That Pure Religion* were recorded by Harry Oster in 1961 at the WIBB Macon studios for an album originally titled *Georgia Street Singer*.

The last five previously unissued songs originated from a radio broadcast hosted by Chris Strachwitz on KPFA in Berkeley, California, on September 24, 1974. At one point Rev. Brown informs radio listeners: "... my grandparents called the guitar, the 'Devil's Box', see and I'm sure the Devil was in the box alright, because I loved myself some music." This new package contains Oster's original 1961 liner notes along with new notes provided by Strachwitz.

These songs serve as testimony to Rev. Brown's gospel message. The opening song, "God Don't Never Change" reminds people no one escapes death, and everyone must reckon with the Creator, sooner or later. Rev. Brown sings "Oh What A Morning", an old African spiritual he learned from his grandmother, a Virginia slave. Rev. Brown remarks on the album: "We need more old time songs. They make us live better to have these old songs come back to our memory."

The title track on this CD forces any humble soul to examine depths and zeniths of their own faith. Rev. Brown covers "Motherless Children" a song Blind Willie McTell (who attended the Georgia Academy for the Blind with Rev. Brown) often played and recorded. Rev. Brown's guitar sound resembles a style between Blind Willie Johnson and the bottleneck tone of Fred McDowell. Brown covers a rendition of McDowell's "You Got To Move" and the traditional, "Keep Your Lamp Trimmed and Burning."

"If I Never See You Anymore", a redemptive song evoking a sad mantra, serves as the most sorrowful tune on the album. Brown's signature song,

"It's A Mean Old World To Try and Live In", contains an unshakable wisdom and remains his best known composition. A few desolate lyrics from the song include:

"You moan night and day your friends will drive you away Don't take everybody to be your friend They'll learn your secrets and turn their back on you. It's a mean old world to try and live in Old death ain't no friend to you. He's calling everybody everyday won't let nobody stay It's a mean old world to try and live in."

Another classic, "The Great Speckled Bird", a beautiful, timeless song with biblical references breathes a spirit of hope. This spiritual collection of songs transcends time by revealing age-old realities of spirit and flesh with unwavering faith. Hearing Rev. Pearly Brown's *You're Gonna Need That Pure Religion* inspires one to remain a little more vigilant in this mean old world.

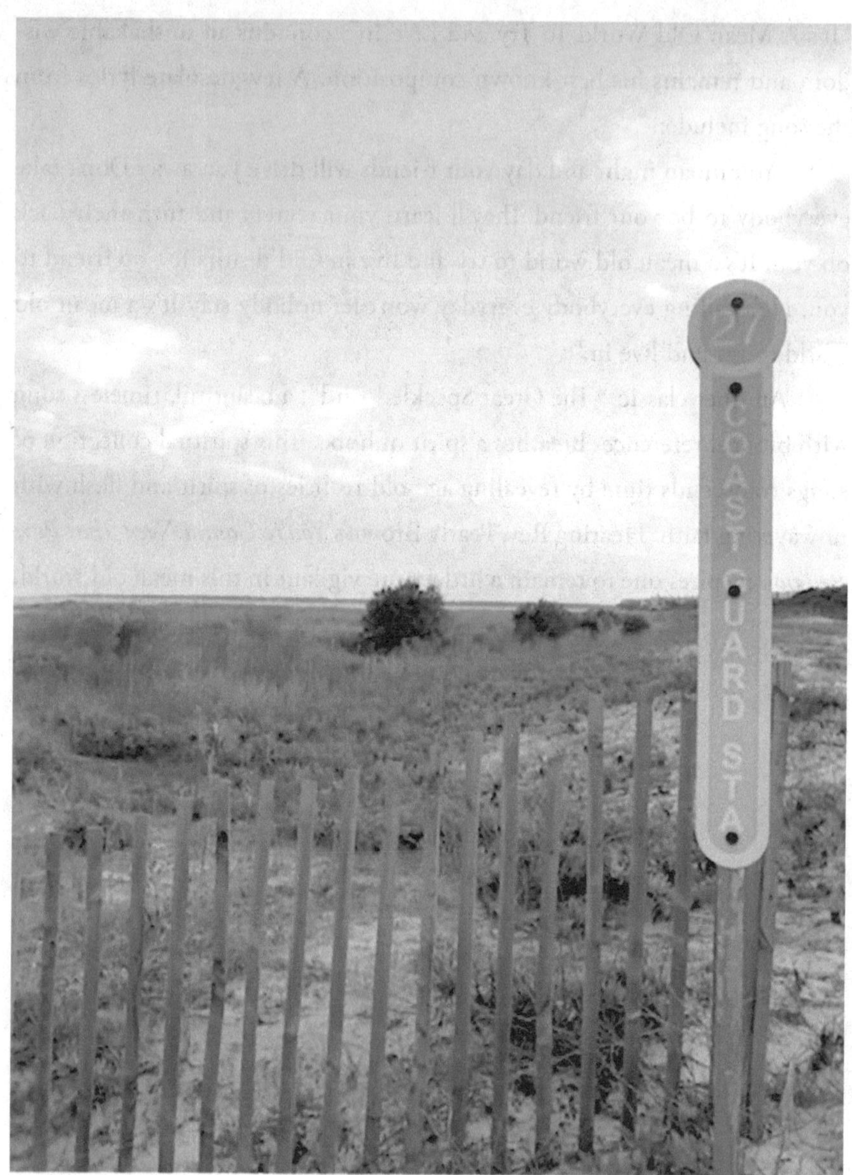

Beachview

Get In Union: Bessie Jones with the Sea Island Singers and Others: Alan Lomax Recordings 1959-1966

ALAN LOMAX ONCE DECLARED the Golden Isles of Georgia home of the American song. *Get In Union: Bessie Jones with the Sea Island Singers and Others*, a 2 CD set, features 26 previously unreleased tracks. This collection truly captures essential roots of American music.

Produced by Grammy-nominated Curator of the Alan Lomax Archive, Nathan Salsburg, spearheaded this collection that includes unheard Sea Island Singers collaborations involving Rev. Gary Davis, Sweet Papa Stovepipe, Mable Hillery and others. These remastered recordings come from Alan Lomax's original tapes.

Bessie Jones exists as one of America's seminal singers. Alan Lomax first visited St. Simons Island, Georgia, in 1935 with folklorist Zora Neale Hurston. Lomax met Bessie Jones there in 1959. Songs from *Get In Union* were recorded between 1959-1966. Lomax recorded the Singers twenty years before for the Library of Congress and he wrote this about the group:

"The Sea Island Singers kept to the speech of their ancestors, and in some places still speak dialects in which many African words and syntactical features survive. Their folk and animal tales show a rich admixture of European and African traits at an early stage of blending. Their funeral customs, their religious ceremonies, indeed, their whole way of life bear the stamp of antebellum days. Yet this is no decadent culture. It has simply grown strong around a conservative base that is part pioneer, part planter gentility, and part African."

In 1959 when Lomax returned to St. Simons Island he noticed the tourist trade creeping in, but Bessie Jones remained alive and singing amid her rustic environs. History lurks in these lands. The Creek Indians occupied this island when the Spanish discovered the Georgia coast in 1540. English General James Oglethorpe infiltrated the Georgia island around 1736 from the British colony in Charleston. Oglethorpe decided St. Simons served as a strategic location to fortify against Spanish forces threatening from Florida. Oglethorpe prevailed—establishing the historical course of this country's culture since English, not Spanish, became the native language.

St. Simons retains a dense history amid traces of today's local hurried activities near oak groves older than the War Between the States. From 1773 to 1778, botanist William Bartram traveled the southeast coastal region. Bartram documented the journey in his timeless book, *Travels of William Bartram*, inspiring poets like Samuel Coleridge and William Wordsworth as well as providing a meticulous document of valuable biological information about the area. English actress, Frances Anne Kemble published her documented stay on St. Simons in *Journal of a Residence on a Georgian Plantation in 1838-1839*.

Upon arriving on St. Simons, the Ebo, an African tribe brought to the island on a slave ship drowned themselves in Dunbar Creek to defy plantation owners. During the Civil War, Union soldiers smashed the organ, burned pews, and broke windows in the second oldest Episcopal Church in the Diocese of Georgia, Christ Church—located at the north end of the island. Old music lingers in the low country...old ghosts...

Slave cabins remain preserved on St. Simons and Cumberland islands along with well documented songs from Lydia Parrish's priceless *Slave Songs of the Georgia Sea Islands*. Lomax steeped himself in the history of the area for years, and he knew the Sea Island Singers were a treasure trove of American heritage. When the slaves were brought to these southern shores... they sang their songs and from these fertile grounds emerged as The Sea Island Singers. The *Get In Union* liner notes provide the deep musical roots Jones possessed:

"A singer and song-bearer of monumental proportions, Mary Elizabeth Smith Jones had been raised in Dawson, GA. in a large and deeply musical family. If someone couldn't sing, they played an instrument. She learned many of her songs from her mother Julia—a dancer, singer and autoharp player—and her step-grandfather Jet Sampson. Sampson, who was born in Africa in 1836 and sold into slavery as a child, taught young Bessie about the slave experience and 'the old ways'. With further formative musical experiences of church, school, and social functions, she was steeped in song."

Bessie Jones picked cotton from Bridgeport, CT., to Brunswick, GA. She also sold moonshine, gambled and sang the blues before she was born again in the Holiness Church. She knew the many faces of the world and understood them with a biblical gravity. During his last trips to the Georgia Sea Islands, Lomax recorded 60 different pieces of music, childhood recollections, ghost stories, interviews, biblical exegesis, healing tips and music from Bessie Jones and the Sea Island Singers.

Bessie Jones explained to Lomax her essential musical education: "I remember a hundred games, I suppose; I would say a hundred because there are so many of them. We had all kinds of plays; we had house plays, we had outdoor plays. Some of the plays have songs, some have just plays—you know, just acts or whatnot.... In my time coming up, the parents they would give quiltings and they would have songs they would sing while they were quilting and we would listen at those songs. And we would have egg crackings and taffy pullings and we would hear all those things—riddles and stories and different things. That's why I'm so loaded.... And then I has a great remembrance of those things, that's another thing about it."

Jones also wrote a book titled *Step It Down*, a study of African-American children's game songs. In 1960, Lomax brought the Singers to Williamsburg, VA. to record. During the Civil Rights era, Lomax exposed the Sea Island Singers to the public at the Newport Folk Festival in 1963, the Poor People's March in 1968 and Jimmy Carter's inauguration in 1977. They also performed college campuses and hip rock & roll spots like the Ash Grove in Los Angeles.

Get In Union deals with matters of the soul. I heard these songs from an old album I recorded to cassette at writer Stanley Booth's Brunswick, Georgia, home in the late 80s. I always felt proud to be one of the few in my generation exposed to this music...and it all took place in my backyard. I grew up on St. Simons Island. I've heard the mysterious stories that linger around the barrier island, and the Sea Island Singers' music always conjures a mysterious, soulful sanctuary for me. *Get In Union* blows like a soothing sea breeze.

The informative book that accompanies this release includes rare Lomax photographs, session notes and handwritten lyrics. In 1965, Lomax connected Bessie Jones and the *Sea Island Singers* to Ed Young and the Southern Fife and Drum Corps and Rev. Gary Davis at the Newport Folk Festival Preview Concert in Central Park.

The musical personnel on the recordings include the Georgia Sea Island Singers: Bessie Jones, Joe Armstrong, George Cohen, Jerome Davis, John Davis, Peter Davis, Jerry Harris, Leola Harris, Viola McQueen, Henry Morrison, Willis Proctor, Ben Ramsey and Emma Lee Ramsey. Hobart Smith sings and plays banjo. Ed Smith blows the fife and Nat Rahmings beats the drum. McKinley Peebles sings and plays guitar.

The session including "Throw Me Overboard" features legendary bluesman Rev. Gary Davis, Peter Davis, Mable Hillery, Bessie Jones and Emma Lee Ramsey. Every song on this collection is a story unto itself, but highlights for this writer include: "No Hiding Place Down Here", "O Death", "Dead And Gone", "This Is A Clean Train", "Beulah Land", "Prodigal Son", "Take Me To The Water", "Drinking That Wine", "One Morning Soon" and "Buzzard Lope".

In 1982, Bessie Jones was awarded a National Heritage Fellowship from the National Endowment for the Arts. She died of leukemia on July 17, 1984 in Brunswick, Georgia. *Get In Union* preserves the legacy of Bessie Jones and the Sea Island Singers in all its timeless grace...

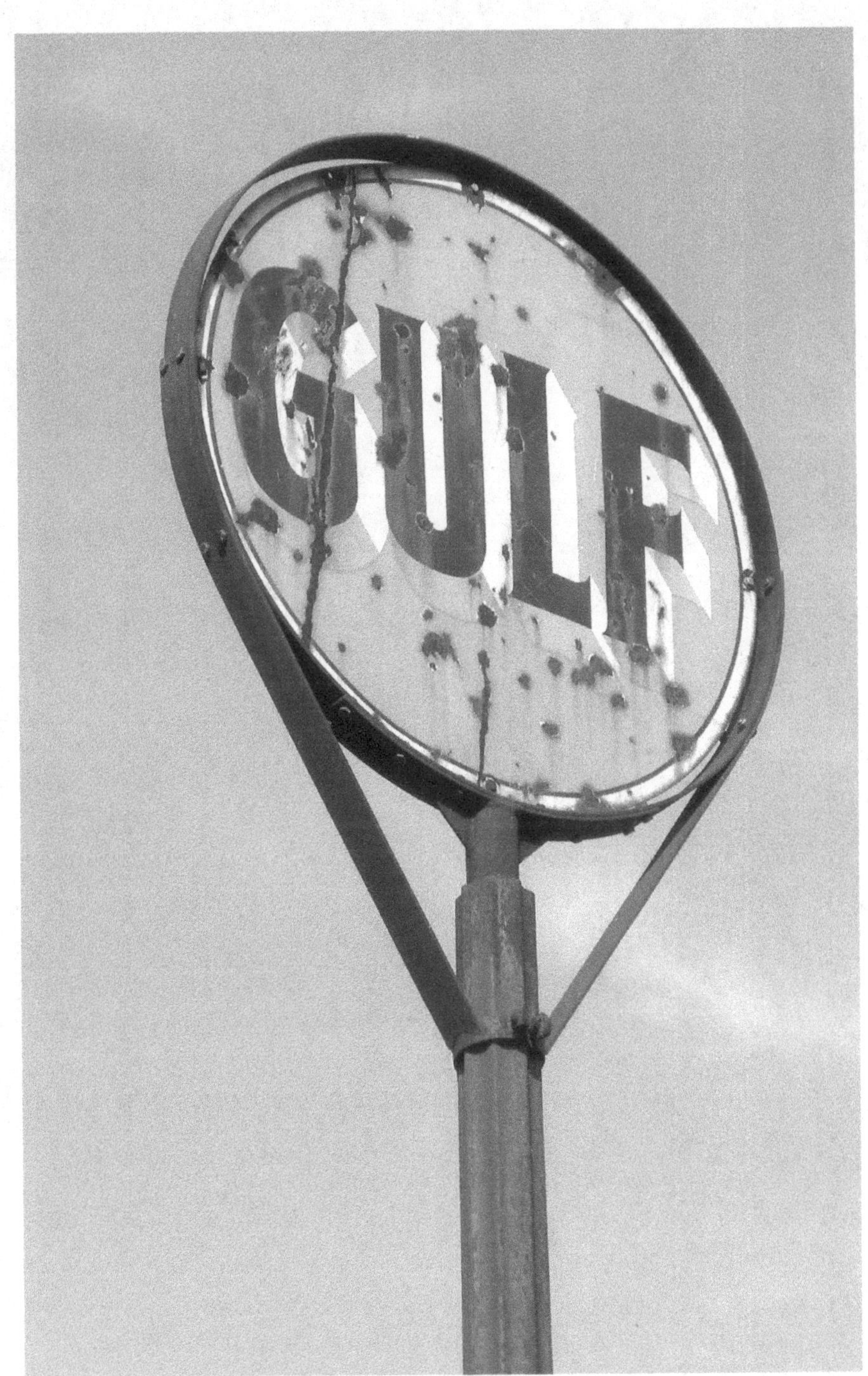

Gulf Sign